T0419358

AMERICAN POLITICAL, ECONOMIC, AND SECURITY ISSUES

VALUE-ADDED TAX (VAT) AND FLAT TAX PROPOSALS

AMERICAN POLITICAL, ECONOMIC, AND SECURITY ISSUES

Additional books in this series can be found on Nova's website
under the Series tab.

Additional E-books in this series can be found on Nova's website
under the E-book tab.

ECONOMIC ISSUES, PROBLEMS AND PERSPECTIVES

Additional books in this series can be found on Nova's website
under the Series tab.

Additional E-books in this series can be found on Nova's website
under the E-book tab.

AMERICAN POLITICAL, ECONOMIC, AND SECURITY ISSUES

VALUE-ADDED TAX (VAT) AND FLAT TAX PROPOSALS

**DAYNA B. ANDREWS
AND
ANGELA M. DAVIS
EDITORS**

Nova Science Publishers, Inc.
New York

Copyright © 2011 by Nova Science Publishers, Inc.

All rights reserved. No part of this book may be reproduced, stored in a retrieval system or transmitted in any form or by any means: electronic, electrostatic, magnetic, tape, mechanical photocopying, recording or otherwise without the written permission of the Publisher.

For permission to use material from this book please contact us:
Telephone 631-231-7269; Fax 631-231-8175
Web Site: http://www.novapublishers.com

NOTICE TO THE READER

The Publisher has taken reasonable care in the preparation of this book, but makes no expressed or implied warranty of any kind and assumes no responsibility for any errors or omissions. No liability is assumed for incidental or consequential damages in connection with or arising out of information contained in this book. The Publisher shall not be liable for any special, consequential, or exemplary damages resulting, in whole or in part, from the readers' use of, or reliance upon, this material. Any parts of this book based on government reports are so indicated and copyright is claimed for those parts to the extent applicable to compilations of such works.

Independent verification should be sought for any data, advice or recommendations contained in this book. In addition, no responsibility is assumed by the publisher for any injury and/or damage to persons or property arising from any methods, products, instructions, ideas or otherwise contained in this publication.

This publication is designed to provide accurate and authoritative information with regard to the subject matter covered herein. It is sold with the clear understanding that the Publisher is not engaged in rendering legal or any other professional services. If legal or any other expert assistance is required, the services of a competent person should be sought. FROM A DECLARATION OF PARTICIPANTS JOINTLY ADOPTED BY A COMMITTEE OF THE AMERICAN BAR ASSOCIATION AND A COMMITTEE OF PUBLISHERS.

Additional color graphics may be available in the e-book version of this book.

Library of Congress Cataloging-in-Publication Data
Value-added tax (VAT) and flat tax proposals / editors, Dayna B. Andrews and Angela M. Davis.
   p. cm.
 Includes index.
 ISBN 978-1-61324-191-2 (hardcover)
 1. Value-added tax--United States. 2. Flat-rate income tax--United States. I. Andrews, Dayna B.
II. Davis, Angela M.
 HJ5715.U6V344 2011
 336.2'7140973--dc22
               2011009089

Published by Nova Science Publishers, Inc. † New York

CONTENTS

Preface		**vii**
Chapter 1	Should the United States Levy a Value-Added Tax for Deficit Reduction? *James M. Bickley*	**1**
Chapter 2	A Value-Added Tax Contrasted with a National Sales Tax *James M. Bickley*	**37**
Chapter 3	Taxable Base of the Value-Added Tax *Maxim Shvedov*	**45**
Chapter 4	Value-Added Taxes: Lessons Learned from Other Countries on Compliance Risks, Administrative Costs, Compliance Burden, and Transition *United States Government Accountability Office*	**51**
Chapter 5	Flat Tax: An Overview of the Hall-Rabushka Proposal *James M. Bickley*	**97**
Chapter 6	The Flat Tax, Value-Added Tax, and National Retail Sales Tax: Overview of the Issues *Jane G. Gravelle*	**123**
Chapter 7	Value-Added Tax: A New U.S. Revenue Source? *James M. Bickley*	**143**
Index		**169**

PREFACE

Long-term fiscal problems, which were exacerbated by the recession that ended in June 2009, resulted in widespread concern about the need to formulate a fiscal solution to the high budget deficits and growing national debt. The levying of a value-added tax (VAT), a broad-based consumption tax, has been discussed as one of many options to assist in resolving U.S. fiscal problems. This book provides an overview and analysis of Value-Added Tax (VAT) and Flat Tax Proposals and their potential policy implications.

Chapter 1- Long-term fiscal problems, which were exacerbated by the recession that ended in June 2009, resulted in widespread concern about the need to formulate a fiscal solution to the high budget deficits and growing national debt. The levying of a value-added tax (VAT), a broad-based consumption tax, has been discussed as one of many options to assist in resolving U.S. fiscal problems. A VAT was not included in the report of the National Commission on Fiscal Responsibility and Reform but was included in the report of the Debt Reduction Task Force of the Bipartisan Policy Center.

Chapter 2- Both a value-added tax (VAT) and a national sales tax (NST) have been proposed by participants in the tax-reform debate as replacement taxes for all or part of the nation's current income tax system. In addition, there is congressional interest in using a consumption tax to finance national health care.

A firm's value added for a product is the increase in the value of that product caused by the application of the firm's factors of production. A VAT on a product would be levied at all stages of production of that product. VATs differ in their tax treatment of purchases of capital (plant and equipment). The type of VAT used by developed countries—termed a consumption VAT—treats a firm's purchases of plant and equipment the same as any other purchase. A firm's net VAT liability is usually calculated by using the credit-invoice method. According to this method, a firm determines its gross tax liability by aggregating VAT shown on its sales invoices. Then the firm computes its net VAT liability by subtracting VAT paid on purchases from other firms from the firm's gross VAT liability. This net tax is remitted to the government. The subtraction method can also be used to calculate the VAT. Under this method, the firm calculates its value added by subtracting its cost of taxed inputs from its taxable sales. Next, the firm determines its VAT liability by multiplying its value added by the VAT rate. A flat tax, based on the proposal formulated by Robert E. Hall and Alvin Rabushka of the Hoover Institution, is a type of modified subtraction method VAT.

Chapter 3- The value-added tax (VAT) is a type of broad-based consumption tax, imposed in about 136 countries around the world. Domestically, it is often mentioned in policy discussions as a potential new or supplemental funding source for such large-scale social programs as Social Security, Medicare, national health insurance, etc. An example of such a proposal is H.R. 15. In addition, the VAT figures prominently in most fundamental tax reform discussions.

The key determinant of the VAT's revenue-raising potential is the size of its taxable base. This report estimates its size under two frequently used "generic" policy options: a broad-based VAT and a VAT with certain frequently mentioned exemptions. Under the assumption of the broad-based VAT, the potential revenue base could be equal to $8.8 trillion in 2008. Exempting certain expenditures, such as food, housing, healthcare, and others is estimated to reduce the taxable base to $5.1 trillion in 2008.

These estimates are likely to overstate the size of the taxable base under either scenario as they assume no behavioral responses and perfect compliance with the law. This report briefly discusses these and other important caveats and their implications for revenue projections and further policy analysis.

Chapter 4- Dissatisfaction with the federal tax system has led to a debate about U.S. tax reform, including proposals for a national consumption tax. One type of proposed consumption tax is a value-added tax (VAT), widely used around the world. A VAT is levied on the difference between a business's sales and its purchases of goods and services. Typically, a business calculates the tax due on its sales, subtracts a credit for taxes paid on its purchases, and remits the difference to the government. While the economic and distributional effects of a U.S. VAT type tax have been studied, GAO was asked to identify the lessons learned from other countries' experiences in administering a VAT. This report describes (1) how VAT design choices, such as exemptions and enforcement mechanisms, have affected compliance, administrative costs, and compliance burden; (2) how countries with federal systems administer a VAT; and (3) how countries that recently transitioned to a VAT implemented the new tax.

GAO selected five countries to study—Australia, Canada, France, New Zealand, and the United Kingdom—that provided a range of VAT designs from relatively simple to more complex with multiple exemptions and tax rates. The study countries also included some with federal systems and some that recently implemented a VAT.

GAO does not make any recommendations in this report.

Chapter 5- The concept of replacing the current U.S. income tax system with a flat rate consumption tax is receiving congressional attention. The term "flat tax" is often associated with a proposal formulated by Robert E. Hall and Alvin Rabushka (H-R), two senior fellows at the Hoover Institution. This report analyzes the idea of replacing the U.S. income tax system with this type of consumption tax. Although the current tax structure is referred to as an income tax, it actually contains elements of both an income and a consumption-based tax. A consumption base is neither inherently superior nor inherently inferior to an income base.

Chapter 6- The current income tax system is criticized for costly complexity and damage to economic efficiency. Reform suggestions have proliferated, including a national retail sales tax, several versions of a value-added tax (VAT), the much-discussed "Flat Tax" on consumption (the "HallRabushka" tax), the "USA" proposal for a direct consumption tax, and revisions of the income tax. The President has indicated that major tax reform will be a priority item in his second term, and his tax reform commission has included a modified flat tax as one of its options.

Chapter 7- Some form of a value-added tax (VAT), a broad-based consumption tax, has been frequently discussed as a full or partial replacement for the U.S. income tax system.

A VAT is imposed at all levels of production on the differences between firms' sales and their purchases from all other firms. For calendar year 2005, a broad-based VAT in the United States would have raised net revenue of approximately $50 billion for each 1% levied. Most other developed nations rely more on broad-based consumption taxes for revenue than does the United States. A VAT is shifted onto consumers; consequently, it is regressive because lower-income households spend a greater proportion of their incomes on consumption than higher-income households. This regression, however, could be reduced or even eliminated by any of three methods: a refundable credit against income tax liability for VAT paid, allocation of some of VAT revenue for increased welfare spending, or selective exclusion of some goods from taxation.

In: Value-Added Tax (VAT) and Flat Tax Proposals
Editors: D. B. Andrews and A. M. Davis

ISBN: 978-1-61324-191-2
© 2011 Nova Science Publishers, Inc.

Chapter 1

SHOULD THE UNITED STATES LEVY A VALUE-ADDED TAX FOR DEFICIT REDUCTION?[*]

James M. Bickley

SUMMARY

Long-term fiscal problems, which were exacerbated by the recession that ended in June 2009, resulted in widespread concern about the need to formulate a fiscal solution to the high budget deficits and growing national debt. The levying of a value-added tax (VAT), a broad-based consumption tax, has been discussed as one of many options to assist in resolving U.S. fiscal problems. A VAT was not included in the report of the National Commission on Fiscal Responsibility and Reform but was included in the report of the Debt Reduction Task Force of the Bipartisan Policy Center.

A VAT is imposed at all levels of production on the differences between firms' sales and their purchases from all other firms. For 2011, a broad-based VAT in the United States would raise net revenue of approximately $55 billion for each 1% levied. Most other developed nations rely more on broad-based consumption taxes for revenue than does the United States. A VAT is shifted onto consumers; consequently, it is regressive because lower-income households spend a greater proportion of their incomes on consumption than higher-income households. This regression, however, could be reduced or even eliminated by any of three methods: a refundable credit against income tax liability for VAT paid, allocation of some of VAT revenue for increased welfare spending, or selective exclusion of some goods from taxation.

From an economic perspective, a major revenue source is better the greater its neutrality—that is, the less the tax alters economic decisions. Conceptually, a VAT on all consumption expenditures, with a single rate that is constant over time, would be relatively neutral compared to other major revenue sources. A VAT would not alter choices among goods, and it would not affect the relative prices of present and future consumption. But a VAT cannot be levied on leisure; consequently, a VAT would affect households' decisions concerning work versus leisure. For a firm, the VAT would not affect decisions concerning method of financing (debt or equity), choice among inputs

---

[*] This is an edited, reformatted and augmented version of Congressional Research Services publication R41602, dated January 21, 2011.

(unless some suppliers are exempt or zero-rated), type of business organization (corporation, partnership, or sole proprietorship), goods to produce, or domestic versus foreign investment.

The imposition of a VAT would cause a one-time increase in this country's price level. But a VAT would not necessarily affect this country's future rate of inflation if the Federal Reserve offset the contractionary effects of a VAT with a more expansionary monetary policy. If the United States continued its policy of flexible exchange rates, then the imposition of a VAT would not significantly affect the U.S. balance-of-trade. There is no conclusive evidence that a VAT would substantially change the rate of national saving more than another type of major tax increase. The administrative costs of a VAT would be significant but relatively low if measured as a percentage of revenue yield. In comparison to other broad-based consumption taxes, VATs have produced relatively good compliance rates. A significant gross receipts threshold for registration could reduce the costs of administration and compliance. Data suggest that 15 to 24 months would be required to implement a VAT. Whether or not a federal VAT would encroach on the primary source of state revenue, the sales tax, is subject to debate. A federal-state VAT could be collected jointly, but a state would lose some of its fiscal discretion.

The prevailing view of tax professionals is that an optimal VAT would have the following characteristics: a broad base, a single rate, the credit-invoice method of collection, the destination principle, and a significant sales threshold for registration.

INTRODUCTION

The value-added tax (VAT) is a broad-based consumption tax. During the 111th Congress, proposals to levy some form of a value-added tax (VAT) were debated. Bills were introduced to replace the U.S. income tax system with a flat tax, a modified VAT.[1] Before the passage of the Patient Protection and Affordable Care Act, a bill was introduced to levy a VAT to finance national health insurance.[2]

Long-term fiscal problems, which were exacerbated by the recession that ended in June 2009, resulted in widespread concern about the need to formulate a fiscal solution to the high budget deficits and growing national debt. The Congressional Budget Office (CBO) published reports with extensive data documenting the severe long-term fiscal problems.[3] Budget documents issued by the Office of Management and Budget (OMB) also quantified the long-term fiscal difficulties. Representatives of some think tanks, international organizations, and academic institutions examined the VAT as part of a possible solution. The mass media also discussed the levying of a VAT for deficit reduction.[4]

On June 11, 2009, Senator Jim DeMint introduced S. 1240, *Roadmap for America's Future Act of 2009*, and on January 27, 2010, Representative Paul D. Ryan introduced H.R. 4529, *Roadmap for America's Future Act of 2010*. These similar bills were designed to be comprehensive plans to address America's long-term economic and fiscal problems. Both bills included a value-added tax as a replacement for the corporate income tax.

On January 25, 2010, the Bipartisan Policy Center established a "Debt Reduction Task Force" led by former Senate Budget Chairman Pete Domenici and former OMB and CBO Director Alice Rivlin. The press release stated that "the Domenici-Rivlin Task Force will develop a comprehensive, balanced, and politically-viable package of spending reductions and revenue increases for expedited consideration by Congress and the Administration."[5]

On February 18, 2010, President Barack Obama issued an executive order establishing the National Commission on Fiscal Responsibility and Reform (the "Commission"). The executive order stated that "no later than December 1, 2010, the Commission shall vote on the approval of a final report." President Obama selected the co-chairs of the Commission: Erskine B. Bowles, former President Bill Clinton's chief of staff; and former U.S. Senator Alan K. Simpson. Alice Rivlin and Representative Paul Ryan were also selected as members of the Commission.

On Tuesday, April 6, 2010, Paul Volcker, economic adviser to President Obama, reportedly said that

> a VAT was not as toxic an idea as it has been, and that both a VAT and some kind of tax on energy need to be on the table. If at the end of the day we need to raise taxes, we should raise taxes.[6]

In reaction to Volcker's comments, three nonbinding resolutions were introduced by Republican members of the House of Representatives that expressed opposition to the imposition of a value-added tax. Furthermore, Senator John McCain introduced S.Amdt. 3724 to H.R. 4851, which expressed the sense of the Senate that the value-added tax (VAT) is "a massive tax increase that will cripple families on fixed income and only further push back America's economic recovery; and the Senate opposes a value-added tax." This amendment passed by a vote of 85 to 13 and is

Section 11 in P.L. 111-157, *Continuing Extension Act of 2010.*

On May 20, 2010, 154 members of the House sent a letter to the National Commission on Fiscal Responsibility and Reform.[7] This letter stated the following:

> ... we urge the Commission to focus on spending reductions, not tax increases. We must avoid the mistake Europe made when it tried to pay for bigger government with new taxes— namely the Value Added Tax (VAT).[8]

On November 10, 2010, the co-chairs of President Obama's Fiscal Commission issued their proposal.[9] On December 1, 2010, the full Fiscal Commission issued its report, which was very similar to the co-chairs' proposal.[10] On December 3, 2010, the members of the Commission cast 11 votes for and 6 votes against the report, which was not enough positive votes to approve the report. Neither report recommended the levying of a value-added tax.

On November 17, 2010, the Bipartisan Policy Center's Debt Reduction Task Force issued its final report titled *Restoring America's Future.* One of the recommendations was the levying of a value-added tax, which it referred to as a "Debt Reduction Sales Tax" or DRST.[11] The DRST would be set at a rate of 3% in 2012 and 6.5% from 2013 onward.[12] Approximately 75% of personal consumption expenditures would be subject to the DRST.[13] The DRST would generate estimated new revenue of $3.048 trillion from 2012-2020, $8.764 trillion from 2012-2030, and $17.333 trillion from 2012-2040.[14]

Arguably, the primary reason for congressional interest in the VAT is its high potential revenue yield.[15] For 2011, the Urban-Brookings Tax Policy Center estimates that a 5% broad-based VAT would yield $277.2 billion ($55.44 billion per 1%).[16] This estimate assumes a 15% noncompliance rate; a 25% revenue offset from lower income and payroll taxes; and a VAT base that excludes education expenditures, rent, housing, and religious and charitable services.[17] This assumed tax base is more comprehensive than the actual VAT base in most developed nations.[18]

Other aspects of a VAT that often raise interest or concern include revenue performance, international comparison of composition of taxes, VAT rates, equity, neutrality, inflation, balanceof-trade, national saving, administrative costs, compliance, VAT registration thresholds, time required for VAT implementation, intergovernmental relations, and size of government.

This report considers the experiences of the 29 nations with VATs in the 30-member Organization for Economic Cooperation and Development (OECD), relevant to the feasibility and operation of a possible U.S. VAT. Currently, the OECD consists of 22 European nations, Turkey, the United States, Canada, Australia, New Zealand, Japan, Mexico, and South Korea. In order to examine different aspects of a VAT, it is important to understand the concept of a value-added tax, the different methods of calculating VATs, exemption, and zero-rating.

CONCEPT OF A VALUE-ADDED TAX

A value-added tax is a broad-based consumption tax, levied at each stage of production, on the value added by each firm at that stage of production. The value added of a firm is the difference between a firm's sales and a firm's purchases of inputs from other firms. In other words, a firm's value added is simply the amount of value a firm contributes to a good or service by applying its factors of production (land, labor, capital, and entrepreneurial ability).[19] Another method of calculating a firm's value added is to total the firm's payments to its factors of production.

Methods of Calculating VAT

There are three alternative methods of calculating VAT: the credit-invoice method, the subtraction method, and the addition method.[20] Under the *credit-invoice method,* a firm would be required to show VAT separately on all sales invoices.[21] Each sale would be marked up by the amount of the VAT. A sales invoice for a seller is a purchase invoice for a buyer. A firm would calculate the VAT to be remitted to the government by a three-step process. First, the firm would aggregate VAT shown on its sales invoices. Second, the firm would aggregate VAT shown on its purchase invoices. Finally, aggregate VAT on purchase invoices would be subtracted from aggregate VAT shown on sales invoices, and the difference remitted to the government.

Under the *subtraction method*, the firm calculates its value added by subtracting its cost of taxed inputs from its sales. Next, the firm determines its VAT liability by multiplying its value added by the VAT rate. Most flat tax proposals are modified subtraction method VATs. Under the *addition method*, the firm calculates its value added by adding all payments for untaxed inputs (e.g., wages and profits). Next, the firm multiplies its value added by the VAT rate to calculate VAT to be remitted to the government.[22]

The credit-invoice method is used by 28 of 29 OECD nations with VATs. Tax economists differ in their classifications of the Japanese VAT. Both the credit-invoice and the subtraction methods have been discussed for the United States. The prevailing view of tax economists is that the credit-invoice method is superior.[23] This method requires registered firms to maintain detailed records that are cross indexed with supporting documentation. A VAT shown on the sales invoice of one firm is the same as the VAT shown on the purchase order of another firm. Hence, the credit-invoice method allows tax auditors to cross check the records of firms. Also, each firm has a vested interest in insuring that the VAT shown on its purchase orders is not understated so the firm can receive full credit against VAT liability for VAT previously paid. Thus, the credit-invoice method would seem to be easier to enforce. Also, the credit-invoice method is probably the only feasible method if there are to be multiple tax rates.

Supporters of the subtraction method maintain that it would have low compliance costs because all necessary data could be obtained from records kept by a firm for other purposes. The subtraction method does not require invoices.[24] Still, a firm would have to make calculations based on these data. For example, deductible expenses would have to be separated from nondeductible expenses, and some data expressed on an accrual basis would have to be converted to a cash flow basis.

The credit-invoice method would have substantial compliance costs because the amount of VAT would have to be shown on every sales invoice (and, conversely, on every purchase invoice). On the plus side, however, the credit-invoice method would yield an additional data base to firms. Some firms might find these additional data useful in decision making. For example, records of purchase invoices and sales invoices may improve some firms' control over their inventories. Compliance costs of the credit-invoice method might be partially offset by the value of the VAT data base to firms, but this value has never been quantified.

The credit-invoice method would have greater administrative costs than the subtraction method because of its requirements for additional data, computations, and record-keeping. Although there are data on the administrative costs of a VAT calculated by the credit-invoice method, empirical data are not available on the subtraction method; consequently, a quantitative comparison of cost currently is not feasible. The subtraction method would not work administratively if many goods are exempt or if multiple tax rates are levied. As will be explained in a subsequent section on the balance of trade, under the destination principle, a VAT using the credit-invoice method is border adjustable, but a standard subtraction method VAT is origin based and thus not border adjustable. Unless specified otherwise, this report will assume that the credit-invoice method is used.

Exemption Versus Zero-Rating

Two alternative special treatments of a product or a business are exemption and zero-rating.

Exemption

A VAT may exempt either a product or a business from taxation.[25] An exempt business would not collect VAT on its sales and would not receive credit for VAT paid on its purchases of inputs. An exempt business would not register with tax authorities, and, consequently, would not be part of the VAT system. Hence, an exempt business would not have the usual VAT compliance costs and would not impose administrative costs on the government (except verification of its exemption, of course). An exempt business's costs, however, include any tax paid on inputs, because it receives no credit for previously paid taxes. A business might be exempt because it only produces an exempt product. Also a business might be exempt because its total sales fall below some threshold. A business that sells both exempt and non-exempt products would be required to allocate its tax payments between the two kinds of sales.

Exemption breaks the VAT chain and, consequently, causes problems. First, if exemption occurs as some intermediate stage, the value added prior to the exempt stage is effectively taxed more than once; that is, cascading of the VAT occurs.[26] Second, the exemption of inputs will induce producers to substitute away from those inputs; that is, input choices are distorted.[27] Third, businesses have an incentive to self-supply rather than purchase an exempt input.[28] Fourth, exemptions may create pressures for additional exemptions.[29] For example, in some countries, the exemption of basic foodstuffs has created pressure for the exemption of agricultural inputs.[30]

Some goods and services are usually exempt because they are difficult to tax.[31] Other products are exempt on equity grounds. Products and services that are usually exempt are in the following categories: free public sector services, education, health, financial services, and real estate.[32] Free public services are usually exempt because "it is hard to tax output that is given away."[33] The standard practice is "to exempt basic education services, and to tax ... more specialist training provided on a commercial basis."[34] Usually basic health services are exempted including professional services of registered doctors and dentists and the supply of prescription drugs.[35] Financial services are usually exempt because "it is difficult to distinguish between the provisions of a service (consumption) and return on investment."[36] "The United Kingdom estimated the exemption of financial services and insurance reduced net VAT revenues collected by approximately 5 percent for 2006."[37]

Many real estate services are self-supplied and have no observable market value.[38] For example, services enjoyed from owner occupation are exempt for VAT. "To avoid distorting the choice between house ownership and renting, the commercial leasing of residential property is commonly also exempt."[39]

Zero-Rating

A business or product could be zero-rated. A zero-rated business would not collect VAT on its sales but would receive credit for VAT paid on its inputs. This is equivalent to the business being charged a zero tax rate. A zero-rated business would be a registered taxpayer and, consequently, would involve the usual compliance and administrative costs. A zero-rated business, however, would receive a refund of any VAT paid on its inputs; therefore, its costs would not include VAT paid at earlier stages. The producer of a zero-rate product would not pay VAT on the inputs used to produce that product nor charge VAT on the sale of that product.

REVENUE YIELD

In estimating a VAT's revenue yield, economists and public officials use the operating assumption that a VAT would be fully shifted to final consumers in the form of higher prices of goods. A VAT (or any other major tax increase) would have a contractionary effect on the economy unless offset by other economic policies. Consequently, a revenue estimate is generally made under the assumption that the Federal Reserve would use an expansionary monetary policy to neutralize the contractionary effects of a VAT. Also, a revenue estimate does not take into account the possible shifts in consumption patterns that might be expected if some items are taxed and others are excluded from taxation.

There are three primary justifications for excluding (zero-rating or exempting) specific items from taxation under a VAT.[40] First, the VAT would be difficult to collect because sellers of some types of goods and services could easily avoid reporting their sales. For example, VAT would be difficult to collect on expenditures for domestic services and expenditures abroad by U.S. residents. Second, some goods are excluded on equity grounds, since these goods claim disproportionately large percentages of the incomes of lower-income families. (Data on spending patterns do not, however, suggest that exclusions can have a very powerful effect on the distribution of a VAT.)[41] Third, some goods may be excluded because they are merit goods, that is "goods the provision of which society (as distinct from the preferences of the individual consumer) wishes to encourage."[42] Some items may be justified for exclusion for more than one reason.

REVENUE PERFORMANCE

Countries' VATs have different exemptions, zero-rated products, thresholds, single rates or multiple rates, levels of compliance, and degrees of administrative efficiency. In order to measure different countries' revenue "efficiency," the OECD developed a tool called the VAT Revenue Ratio (VRR). "The VAT Revenue Ratio" is defined as the ratio between the actual VAT revenue collected and the revenue that would theoretically be raised if VAT was applied at the standard rate to all final consumption.[43] This is shown by the following formula:

VAT Revenue Ratio = (VAT revenue)/([consumption − VAT revenue] x standard VAT rate)[44]

Appendix B shows VAT revenue ratios of the 29 OECD countries with VATs. The VRR is not a precise measure of revenue performance. For example, cascading from exempting a product and levying the VAT on investment goods could raise the VRR to over 1.0.[45] Nevertheless, the VRR is generally considered to be a useful indicator of revenue performance. In 2005, 22 of the 29 OECD had VRR between 0.46 and 0.68. The unweighted average VRR was 0.58. The lowest VRR was 0.33 for Mexico, and the highest VRR was 1.05 for New Zealand. From 1996 through 2005, the VRR rose for 21 countries, was constant for three countries, and declined for five countries.

INTERNATIONAL COMPARISON OF COMPOSITION OF TAXES

One argument frequently made for a U.S. VAT is the relatively heavy reliance on consumption taxes by other developed countries. For 2007, for taxes on general consumption (e.g., VATs and sales taxes), the United States (federal, state, and local governments) had a lower reliance (7.7%) of total tax revenues than any other OECD nation.[46] Also for 2007, the United States' (federal, state, and local governments) general consumption taxes as a percentage of gross domestic product (2.2%) were lower than any other nation in the OECD.[47]

This lower reliance on consumption taxes may result from all other developed nations having a VAT at the national level. A VAT is a requirement for membership in the European Union (EU).[48] Sweden, Norway, Iceland, and Switzerland had retail sales taxes at the national level but eventually switched to a VAT.[49] According to the OECD,

> The spread of Value Added Tax (also called Goods and Services Tax—GST) has been the most important development in taxation over the last half-century. Limited to less than 10 countries in the late 1960s it has now been implemented by about 136 countries; and in these countries (including OECD member countries) it typically accounts for one-fifth of total tax revenue. The recognized capacity of VAT to raise revenue in a neutral and transparent manner drew all OECD member countries (except the United States) to adopt this broad based consumption tax.[50]

Currently, approximately 150 countries have VATs.

Policy insights can be obtained by examining the experiences of other nations; however, just because other nations exhibit a specific tax policy does not necessarily mean that it is appropriate for the United States to adopt this policy. Economic analysis of optimal taxation suggests that those choices depend on issues of efficiency, equity, and administrative and compliance costs, and should be made in the context of the overall tax and spending structure. These considerations may vary from one country to another.

VAT RATES IN OTHER COUNTRIES

As shown in Table C-2, VAT rates vary substantially among the 29 countries with VATs in the OECD and Chile, which will become the 31st member of the OECD. Japan and Canada have the lowest rate of 5%. Iceland has the highest rate of 25.5%, and four nations have a 25% rate. The unweighted average of standard VAT rates has risen from 16.0% in 1976 to 18.0% in 2010. This high average rate is one reason for the robust revenue yield of VATs. Most countries have reduced VAT rates on certain goods and services.

For 2009, Table D-1 lists the standard VAT rate and the year of VAT introduction for 145 countries. Approximately two-thirds of these countries introduced their VATS in 1990 or later.[51] Countries without VATs include the United States, the nations in the Gulf Cooperation Council, and nations in portions of Africa.[52] The Gulf Cooperation Council consists of Bahrain, Kuwait, Oman, Qatar, Saudi Arabia, and the United Arab Emirates.[53] The IMF (International Monetary Fund) has contributed to the global expansion of the VAT through general tax advice and normally requiring a country to implement a VAT in order to receive an IMF loan.[54]

EQUITY

A major topic concerning any proposed tax or tax change is the distribution or equity of the tax among households. There are two types of equity: vertical and horizontal. Vertical equity concerns the tax treatment of households with different abilities-to-pay. Horizontal equity concerns the degree to which households with the same ability-to-pay are taxed equally. Both vertical and horizontal equity may be affected by the measure of ability-to-pay and the tax period.

Ability-to-Pay

The most common measure of ability-to-pay is income.[55] Proponents of income as a measure of ability-to-pay argue that saving yields utility by providing households with greater economic security. Federal data are more readily available on different measures of income than different levels of consumption. For example, the federal government reports levels of disposable income, which equals consumption plus saving. Thus, tax economists can more easily calculate tax incidence if income instead of consumption is the measure of ability-to-pay.

Some arguments for the consumption tax base suggest that personal consumption is the best measure of ability-to-pay because consumption is the actual taking of scarce resources from the economic system. Some economists argue that consumption may be a better proxy for permanent income than is current income (see discussion below).

Time Period

Tax incidence usually is measured by using a one-year period. Data on consumption and income are readily available in one-year increments and the concept of a one-year period is easily understood. But many economists believe tax incidence is more accurately determined by measuring consumption and income over a household's lifetime. Lifetime income and consumption are affected by the life cycle concept and transitional components of income. According to this life cycle concept, a household makes current consumption decisions based on its expected future flow of income, averaging its consumption over its lifetime.

For example, a common life cycle is low income in the household's early years, high income in the household's middle years, and low income in the household's retirement years. A young household may save a small percentage of its income in order to acquire consumer durables. In its middle years, this household may save a high percentage of its income while its income is highest. Finally, during its retirement years, this household may save a small percentage of its income in order to maintain its consumption level. Thus, annual consumption tends to be more stable than annual income over the household's life cycle.

Although many economists prefer the concept of lifetime income, federal data are not collected on a lifetime basis. Consequently, economists have developed life-cycle models in an attempt to measure equity, but the distributional results from these models are subject to widespread debate.

Vertical Equity[56]

If disposable income over a one-year period is the measure of ability-to-pay, then a VAT would be viewed as extremely regressive; that is, the percentage of disposable income paid in VAT would decrease rapidly as disposable income increases. In most discussions of tax policy, both a one-year period and annual disposable income (or some other annual income measure) are used; consequently, the VAT is viewed as being extremely regressive. For example, CBO calculated the annual incidence of a 3.5% broad-based VAT for 1992. CBO found that all families would have paid 2.2% of their income in VAT. The burden on family income was 4.8% on the lowest quintile, 3.2% on the second quintile, 2.8% on the middle quintile, 2.3% on the fourth quintile, and 1.5% on the highest quintile.[57]

If disposable income over a lifetime is the measure of ability-to-pay, a VAT would be mildly regressive. For lower- and middle-income households, it appears that nearly all savings are eventually consumed.[58] Thus, it may be that for the vast majority of households, lifetime consumption and lifetime income are approximately equal. High-income households tend to have net savings over their lifetimes; consequently, they would pay a lower proportion of their disposable incomes in VAT than would lower-income groups. But these highly stylized life-cycle models are controversial.[59]

If consumption is used as a measure of ability-to-pay, a single-rate VAT with a broad base would be approximately proportional regardless of the time period. In other words, the percentage of consumption paid in VAT by households would be approximately constant as the level of household consumption rises.

Another equity issue concerns the burden of a VAT on different age groups. If older individuals on the average consume more out of savings than younger individuals, then a VAT would fall more heavily on the old than the young. Most of the elderly are covered by Social Security, which is indexed for changes in the cost-of-living. Thus most of the elderly poor would be largely protected from a rise in the price level due to the levying of a VAT.

Policy Options to Alleviate Regressivity

Some supporters of progressive taxation oppose the VAT primarily because they believe that it is regressive. No mechanism is likely to introduce progressivity at higher income levels. But critics are especially concerned about the absolute burden of a VAT on low-income households. The degree of regressivity on lower-income households, however, can be reduced by government policy. Three often-mentioned policies are exclusions and multiple rates, income tax credits, and earmarking of some revenues for increased social spending (including indexed transfer payments).

Exclusions and Multiple Rates

The incidence of the VAT depends on its tax base; therefore, the regressivity of the VAT can be reduced or eliminated by excluding (zero-rating or exempting) those goods that account for a disproportionately high percentage of the incomes of lower-income households. The exclusion of many necessities on equity grounds from retail sales taxes has been politically popular at the state level. All members of the European Union (EU) exclude some goods from VAT on equity grounds. Also, most EU nations have multiple tax rates on equity grounds. Reduced rates are applied to necessities and premium rates are levied on luxuries.

Despite the existing policies in the EU, most tax economists oppose exclusions and multiple rates to reduce regressivity for three reasons. First, the administrative costs, compliance costs, and neutrality costs are substantial.[60] If a VAT is to raise a given amount of revenue, then revenue lost from excluding goods must be offset by higher VAT rates. These higher rates increase the distortion in relative prices, and consequently, reduce the neutrality of the tax system. Second, the possible reduction in regressivity from exclusion and multiple rates is declining because consumption patterns for different income levels are becoming more similar.[61] Third, for a one-year time period, the reduction in regressivity is limited, particularly for low-income households. Money saved for exclusions is largely offset by higher tax rates (needed for revenue neutrality) on taxed goods.[62]

Tax Credits

The federal government could allow either a flat tax credit or a credit that diminishes as income rises, in order to overcome the regressivity of a VAT. This credit method could be operated in two ways. First, an individual could apply the credit against his federal income tax liability, thus lowering his liability on a dollar-for-dollar basis. If the tax credit exceeded the individual's tax liability, he could apply for a refund of the excess credit. A taxpayer already due a tax refund could increase the size of his refund by the amount of the tax credit. A household not subject to income taxation could apply for a tax refund equal to the credit. An income tax credit that declines as income increases could reduce regressivity more sharply than a flat income tax credit.

Second, a stand-alone credit system could be established which would not require an eligible household to file an income tax return in order to obtain a refund for VAT paid. An eligible household would have to submit a simple form in order to receive a refund. A stand-alone credit system may be more effective than the income tax credit in encouraging low-income households to file for a refund, but administrative and compliance costs would be higher.

But a federal credit system would incur some administrative costs, which would increase the total administrative costs of a VAT. Furthermore, households incur implicit taxes if their credits are phased out (or income tested transfers reduced).

At the federal level, studies have concluded that the refundable earned-income tax credit (EITC) has had "a significant positive impact on participation in the labor force."[63] But compliance with EITC provisions has been an ongoing issue.[64]

Earmarking of VAT Revenues

A third option to reduce or eliminate regressivity is to earmark some of the revenue from a VAT to finance an increase in income tested transfers. Henry J. Aaron estimated that an increase in benefits of approximately $5 billion for a VAT yielding $100 billion could fully protect low-income families from paying the VAT.[65]

> For example, a 10 percent increase in food stamp entitlements would approximately offset the effect on households eligible for the full food stamp allotment of a VAT that raised $100 billion in revenue. This estimate is based on the fact that $100 billion will be

approximately three percent of consumption in 1989 and that food is estimated to absorb about 30 percent of the budget in estimates of poverty thresholds.[66]

Many households with low taxable incomes do not currently receive transfers and would not be protected by Aaron's proposal.

Before the passage of the *Patient Protection and Affordable Care Act*, Leonard E. Burman proposed that a VAT be levied with the revenue dedicated to paying for a new universal health insurance voucher. "The health care voucher would offset the inherent regressivity of a VAT, since the voucher would be worth more than the VAT tax paid by most households."[67]

Horizontal Equity

If disposable income is the measure of ability-to-pay, the horizontal equity of a VAT would depend on the time period. For a one-year period, a VAT would be very inequitable because households with the same level of disposable income would have widely differing levels of consumption and, consequently, payments of VAT.

For a lifetime period, the VAT would have a high degree of horizontal equity. For low- and middle-income households, almost all income is consumed over these households' lifetimes; consequently, households with the same lifetime incomes would have the same levels of consumption and the same VAT payments.[68] Over their lifetimes, high-income households with equal incomes differ in their levels of consumption and, consequently, VAT payments. For example, assume that two households have $10 million in lifetime income, but the first household spends $4.5 million on consumption and the second household spends $9 million on consumption. The second household would pay twice as much in VAT as the first household. Thus, for a lifetime period, the VAT is not horizontally equitable for high-income households.

NEUTRALITY

In public finance, the more *neutral* is a tax, the less the tax affects private economic decisions and, consequently, the more efficient is the operation of the economy. Conceptually, a VAT on all consumption expenditures, with a single rate that is constant over time, would be relatively neutral compared to other major revenue sources.

For households, two out of three major decisions would not be altered by this hypothetical VAT. First, this VAT would not alter choices among goods because all would be taxed at the same rate. Thus, *relative* prices would not change. In contrast, other taxes, such as excise taxes, which change relative prices, would distort household consumer choices by encouraging the substitution of untaxed goods for taxed goods. But a hypothetical income tax on all income would be neutral in this respect.

Second, a VAT does not affect the relative prices of present and future consumption. In contrast, the individual income tax affects the relative prices of present and future consumption because the income tax is levied on income which is saved, and then the returns on saving are taxed.

A household's work-leisure decision, however, would be affected by a VAT or any other tax on either consumption or income.[69] Since leisure would not be taxed, any tax increase would fall on the returns to work.

A VAT would have conflicting effects on the number of hours worked by each household. A household would have an incentive to substitute leisure for work because of the relative rise in the value of leisure to work (substitution effect). Conversely, a household would have an incentive to increase its hours worked in an attempt to maintain its current living standards (income effect). Thus, a VAT could decrease, increase, or not change a household's hours worked.

For a firm, the VAT would not affect decisions concerning method of financing (debt or equity), choice among inputs (unless some suppliers are exempt or zero-rated), type of business organization (corporation, partnership, or sole proprietorship), goods to produce, or domestic versus foreign investment. Other types of taxes may affect one or more of these types of decisions.

But a VAT cannot be levied on all consumer goods; consequently, prices of taxed goods will rise relative to untaxed goods. Furthermore, most nations with VATs have more than one rate. Multiple VAT rates alter relative prices of taxed goods. Finally, VAT rates in most nations have tended to rise over time. Despite these deviations from a pure form of VAT, a broad-based VAT is relatively neutral compared to most other taxes. This neutrality is greater if the tax rate is relatively low. But the relative neutrality of a VAT compared to an increase in the personal income tax is uncertain.[70]

INFLATION

If the Federal Reserve implemented an expansionary monetary policy to offset the contractionary effects of a VAT then there would be a one-time increase in the price level. For example, an expansionary monetary policy to accommodate a 5% VAT on 60% of consumer outlays might directly cause an estimated one-time increase in consumer prices of approximately 3%. There would also be some secondary price effects. Some goods would rise in price because their factors of production, especially labor, are linked to price indexes. Yet, if the Federal Reserve disregarded these secondary price increases in formulating monetary policy, these secondary price increases would tend to be offset by price reductions in other sectors of the economy.

An examination of VATs in the OECD has found only an initial effect of a VAT on the price level. But it is difficult to empirically isolate the effect of a VAT from other possible causes of a change in the price level.

It has been suggested that the federal government exclude the VAT from price indexes. Hence, existing indexing would not have an inflationary effect.[71] But such an approach might prove unpopular and it might be contested in court.

In summary, the proper monetary accommodation for a VAT would probably cause a one-time increase in the price level but not affect the subsequent rate of inflation (i.e., cause continual increases in the general price level).

BALANCE-OF-TRADE

Currently, all nations with VATs zero-rate exports and impose their VATs on imports. This procedure for taxing trade flows is referred to as the *destination principle* because a commodity is taxed at the location of consumption rather than production. An alternative would be to apply the *origin principle* that would levy a tax at the location of production. Thus, under the origin principle, nations would levy their VATs on exports but not imports. All leading experts on the VAT recommend that nations adopting a VAT use the destination principle, which would be consistent with existing practices of other countries.

The destination principle creates a level playing field because imported commodities rise in price by the percentage of the VAT, but exported commodities do not increase in price. For a particular nation, the VAT rate on domestically produced and imported products would be the same. The VAT rate on a particular good would still vary among nations.

A simple example demonstrates this concept of a level playing field. Assume nation A has a 10% VAT and nation B has a 20% VAT. Exports from nation A to nation B would not be taxed by nation A. But nation B would levy a 20% VAT on imports from nation A. Thus, consumers in nation B would pay a 20% VAT regardless of whether their purchased goods were domestically produced or imported. Furthermore, exports from nation B to nation A would not be taxed by nation B. Nation A would levy a 10% VAT on imports. Hence, consumers in nation A would pay a 10% VAT on both domestically produced and imported commodities.

In 1962, the rules applicable to taxation were included in the General Agreement on Tariffs and Trade (GATT). Under these GATT rules, indirect taxes were rebatable on exports but direct taxes were not rebatable. Taxes which are not shifted but borne by the economic entity on which they are levied are classified as direct taxes. From 1962 through 1972, a fixed exchange rate system prevailed and the United States ran deficits in its balance-of-payments. U.S. officials complained that the GATT rules favored nations with VATs because their exports were zero-rated. In contrast, corporate income taxes were not rebated on exports.

In early 1973, the United States and its major trading partners formally shifted to a flexible exchange rate system. Under this system, the supply and demand for different currencies determine their relative value. If a country has a deficit in its balance-of-trade, this deficit must be financed by a net importation of foreign capital. But net capital inflows cannot continue indefinitely. Thus, over time, this country's currency will tend to decline in value relative to the currencies of other nations. Consequently, this country's balance-of-trade deficit will eventually decline as its exports rise and imports fall. Hence, economic theory indicated that a VAT offers no advantage over other major taxes in reducing a deficit in the balance-of-trade. Thus, U.S. officials ended their complaints about the effects of GATT tax rules on international trade.

Since early 1973 there have been periods when exchange rates have been "managed" by mutual agreement among governments. Central banks have coordinated purchases and sales of different currencies in order to stabilize their relative values to promote international economic stability.

Even if there were a fixed exchange rate, a U.S. VAT would have slight impact on the balance-oftrade because the proposed VAT rate of 5% or less is a low tax rate. During the last 25 years the value of the dollar has fallen relative to an index of major currencies, yet a serious U.S. balanceof-trade deficit persists. In summary, a U.S. VAT offers no major advantage over other major tax increases in reducing the U.S. balance-of-trade deficit.

Any large U.S. tax increase, which reduces the federal deficit, could reduce the U.S. balance-oftrade deficit. The U.S. Treasury would reduce its borrowing on financial markets, interest rates would decline, and foreign capital would flow out of the United States. This capital outflow would reduce the demand for dollars relative to other currencies. This decline in the value of the dollar would raise exports, reduce imports, and, consequently, reduce the U.S. balance-oftrade deficit.

As indicated previously, under the destination principle, a VAT using the credit-invoice method is border adjustable. Exports are zero-rated and imports are taxed. A standard subtraction method VAT is origin based and thus is not border adjustable.

> Border adjusting a subtraction-method VAT may elicit a challenge under WTO [World Trade Organization] rules. Under those rules (as originally developed under the General Agreements on Tariffs and Trade ("GATT"), a border tax adjustment applied to a "direct" tax is a prohibited trade subsidy. In contrast, WTO rules allow countries to border-adjust "indirect taxes." Further, WTO rules require that imported products be accorded treatment no less favorable than like products of national origin. Lastly, WTO rules require that border adjustments for indirect taxes not exceed the tax levied on similar products sold in the domestic market. A subtraction-method VAT might be challenged as a direct tax under WTO rules.[72]

NATIONAL SAVING

National saving consists of government saving, business saving, and personal saving.[73] A VAT or any other tax that reduces the budget deficit would be expected to reduce government dissaving, and, consequently, raise national saving.

A second issue concerns the effect on the personal savings rate of levying a VAT compared to increasing income taxes. A VAT would tax savings when they are spent on consumption, allowing savings to compound at a pre-tax rate. But an income tax is levied on all income at the time it is earned, regardless of whether the income is consumed or saved. The income tax is also levied on the earnings from income saved. Consequently, some proponents of the VAT have argued that choosing a VAT, rather than an income tax, to raise revenue would increase the return from saving and, consequently, raise the savings rate.

The rate of return on savings, however, has never been shown to have a significant effect on the savings rate because of two conflicting effects. First, each dollar saved today results in the possibility of a higher amount of consumption in the future. This relative increase in the return from saving causes a household to want to substitute saving for consumption out of current income (substitution effect).

But a higher rate of return on savings raises a household's income; consequently, the household has to save less to accumulate some target amount of savings in the future (income effect). Thus, this income effect encourages households to have higher current consumption and lower current saving.

A CRS study compared the long-run effects on the capital stock and consumption of a $60 billion VAT and a $60 billion increase in individual income taxes. This study's results suggest that selecting a VAT instead of an increase in individual income taxes would raise the capital stock by less than 2% and consumption by only a quarter to a third of a percent after 50 years.[74]

An empirical study by the Congressional Budget Office analyzed the economic effects of replacing a quarter of the current income tax with a 6% VAT on all consumption. CBO estimated that this tax substitution would, in the long-run, increase the saving rate by 0.5%, raise the capital stock by 7.9%, increase output by 1.5%, and raise consumption by 1.2%.[75] These CBO findings of only slight economic effects in the long-run are consistent with the estimates of the CRS study.

ADMINISTRATIVE COSTS

The value-added tax would require the expansion of the Internal Revenue Service. But the high revenue yield from a VAT could cause administrative costs to be low measured as a percentage of revenue yield. The administrative expense per dollar of VAT collected would vary with the degree of complexity of the VAT, the amount of revenue raised, the national attitude towards tax compliance, and the level of the small business exemption.

For tax year 1995, the Government Accountability Office (GAO) estimated the cost of administering a U.S. VAT at $1.221 billion if the VAT had a single rate, a broad base, and an exemption for businesses with gross receipts of less than $100,000.[76] For tax year 1995, Professor Sijbren Cnossen estimated that the overall administrative cost of a hypothetical single rate U.S. VAT at $1 billion.[77] He assumed that "the administration of the VAT would be fully integrated with the administration of the federal income taxes."[78]

In 2008, GAO examined the administrative costs of a VAT. GAO stated that "according to European Commission officials, VATS in Europe cost between 0.5 percent and 1 percent of VAT revenue collected to administer."[79]

COMPLIANCE

Although considerable research has been conducted over the past 15 years on income tax compliance, research on VAT compliance has been limited.[80] For tax year 1995, Professor Sijbren Cnossen estimates the compliance costs of a single rate U.S. VAT would equal approximately $5 billion.[81] He emphasizes that compliance costs "can be reduced by broadening the base of the VAT, imposing a single rate, and increasing the threshold for registration."[82] Agha and Haughton summarized estimates of VAT evasion for five European countries.[83] These five countries and their percentage of revenue lost through evasion were Belgium (8%), France (3%), Italy (40%), Netherlands (6%), and United Kingdom (2%-4%).[84] In comparison to other broad-based consumption taxes such as the retail sales tax, a VAT has produced relatively good compliance for four reasons.

First, a VAT collected using the credit-invoice method offers the opportunity to cross-check returns and invoices. For example, VAT shown on a sales invoice of a wholesaler will appear on the purchase invoice of a retailer. A tax auditor can examine both invoices to cross-check the accuracy of the tax returns of both the wholesaler and the retailer.

Second, each firm has an incentive not to allow suppliers to understate VAT on their sales invoices. A firm is able to credit VAT paid on inputs against VAT collected on sales; consequently, a firm's net VAT liability will increase if VAT shown on its purchase invoices was understated by suppliers.

Third, tax auditors can compare information about a VAT with information about business income taxation, which will increase compliance with both types of taxes. For example, the sales revenue figure reported on business income tax forms may be checked for consistency with gross VAT collected as shown on VAT forms. Also, a check of cash receipts during a VAT audit may identify the under reporting of sales. Firms may attempt not only to evade the VAT but also to evade the business income tax.[85]

Fourth, some firms legally required to remit VAT may not register. But these firms receive no credit for VAT paid on inputs. Hence, these firms are only partially able to evade the VAT because of the compliance with the VAT by suppliers.

Although compliance with a VAT is higher than other broad-based consumption taxes, the level of noncompliance is significant. As previously discussed, some firms legally required to remit VAT may not register.

Furthermore, firms may evade VAT by altering or omitting information as indicated in the following 10 major types of evasion. First, a registered firm may not record resales of goods purchased from unregistered suppliers. Second, a seller of both exempt and taxable goods may divert purchased inputs on which VAT is claimed against taxed sales to help produce and sell exempt goods. Third, a firm may claim credit for purchases that are not creditable. For example, a firm's owner may claim credit for VAT paid on an automobile but then use it for nonbusiness purposes. Fourth, a firm may illegally import goods, charge VAT on their sale, but not report this VAT. Fifth, a firm may simply under-report sales, which is the most common type of evasion. Retailers are the most frequent users of this type of evasion. Sixth, a firm may collect VAT on sales and then disappear. This type of evasion is particularly common to small firms in the construction industry. Seventh, in those nations with multiple rates, a firm may illegally reclassify goods into categories with lower tax rates. Eighth, the owners of some small firms, particularly retailers, may consume part of their firms' production but not record their consumption. Ninth, a firm may submit completely false export claims in order to obtain illegal VAT refunds. And tenth, two firms may barter goods in order to evade the VAT.[86]

VAT REGISTRATION THRESHOLDS

"Experience has taught, sometimes harshly, that a critical decision in designing a VAT is the threshold level of firm size above which registration for the tax is compulsory."[87] The threshold level is important in reducing administrative and compliance costs. "Most countries, but not all, allow those below the VAT threshold to register voluntarily."[88] Thus a small business with gross receipts below the threshold could decide whether or not to register and collect the VAT or to be exempt. "Despite significant variation, a useful rule of thumb is that the largest 10 percent of all firms commonly account for 90 percent or more of all turnover."[89] Many nations adopting VATs have set threshold level below that recommended by the Fiscal Affairs Department of the International Monetary Fund.[90] Tax authorities must consider the tradeoff between lower administrative and compliance costs versus reduced revenue and costs of distortions due to differential treatment.[91]

Time Required for VAT Implementation

Since a U.S. VAT would be a new tax, the time to implement a VAT is important. In a 2008 study, GAO examined the time to implement VATs in three nations with relatively new VATs and preexisting consumption tax administrative structures.

> The amount of time tax administrations in Australia, Canada, and New Zealand had to implement a VAT ranged from 15 to 24 months due to the varying circumstances leading up to initial implementation in each of these countries. Australia and its states and territories reached agreement on a VAT in April 1999, 15 months prior to the effective implementation date of July 1, 2000. In Canada, much of the planning and early efforts to prepare for VAT implementation occurred before legislation was actually passed. According to one Canadian official involved in implementation, planning began nearly 2 years in advance, but Canadian tax authorities had only 2 weeks between final passage of legislation and implementation. However, because of delays in education activities, implementation was delayed an additional 6 months.[92]

An IMF official formulated a "chronological schedule of work to be done to introduce a VAT in about eighteen months."[93] This schedule lists actions required of tax officials on a month by month basis.

INTERGOVERNMENTAL RELATIONS

For the United States, a federal VAT raises two primary intergovernmental issues: the federal encroachment of the state sales tax, and the joint collection of a VAT.[94]

Encroachment on a State Tax Source

It has been claimed that broad-based consumption taxation has traditionally been a state source of revenue while income taxation has been a federal revenue source; consequently, a federal VAT would encroach on a primary source of tax revenue for the states.[95]

Most states, however, adopted their individual income taxes before they adopted their general sales taxes. Thirty-nine states levy both individual income taxes and general sales taxes. Twenty-three of these states adopted their individual income taxes in an earlier year then they adopted their general sales taxes. Three states adopted both taxes in the same year. Thirteen states adopted their general sales taxes in an earlier year than they adopted their individual income taxes.[96]

No constitutional restriction prevents the federal government from levying a VAT. Precedents exist for the federal government to levy a new tax that many states already levy. For example, the federal government levied the personal income tax after many states had already imposed this tax. Also, both the federal government and the states impose many of the same excise taxes.

The federal government relies primarily on income taxes, but taxation of income by states has risen steadily over the years.[97] For 2009, 34.4% of state tax collections consisted of individual income taxes and 5.6% consisted of corporation income taxes.[98] Thus, total state taxes on income accounted for 40.0% of all state taxes collected. In comparison, for 2009, general sales taxes accounted for 31.9% of state taxes collected.[99] Hence, it can be argued that the states have encroached on the primary source of revenue of the federal government.

States could continue to levy their retail sales taxes while the federal government levies a VAT. In Canada, the federal government levies a VAT, and the provinces continue to collect their retail sales taxes.

Joint Collection

States could piggy-back on a federal VAT. To do this, states would have to replace their retail sales taxes with a VAT and adopt the federal tax base. Because a federal VAT would probably have a broader base than any state sales tax, more revenue would be yielded for each 1% levied. Also, the VAT would eliminate duplication of administrative effort, permit the taxation of interstate mail order sales, permit the taxation on Internet sales, and lower total compliance costs of firms.

But, states may decline the opportunity for joint collection because of their desire to maintain greater fiscal independence from the federal government. In 1972, federal legislation permitted states to adopt the federal individual income tax base and have the federal government collect its state income tax, without cost to the states.[100] No state delegated collection of its income tax to the federal government. The law was repealed in 1990.[101]

In a 2008 VAT study, GAO found that "Canada's experience demonstrates that, while multiple consumption tax arrangements in a federal system are possible, such arrangements create additional administrative costs and compliance burden for governments and businesses."[102]

SIZE OF GOVERNMENT

In the public policy debate over a VAT, on of the more divisive issues concerns the size of the public sector.[103] There is widespread debate among economists and public policy expert concerning the variables that determine the size of government. These variables include urbanization, the growth of income, the age distribution of the population, technological change, relative costs of public services, social philosophy, rates of voter turnout, perceived need for defense spending, tax structure, and the size of a nation.[104]

There is an hypothesis that a VAT is a "money machine" because the higher revenue yield per 1% levied could allow the government to finance a growing public sector by periodically raising the VAT rate. It can be argued that the VAT is a partially "hidden" tax because consumers pay a small amount of VAT with each purchase and are not fully cognizant of the aggregate VAT paid for a year. Furthermore, the tax authorities have the option of prohibiting the VAT from being shown on retail sales slips.

Most experts generally agree that these concerns lack merit. After all, the tax rate for any tax can be increased at the margin. And, there is no proof that taxpayers are any less cognizant of a tax paid in small amounts than in one lump sum. (Although, even if taxes are visible, it does not mean that they are superior in inducing voters to make the "right" choices, unless the benefits of taxes are similarly visible.)

Some empirical studies have found that tax increases lead to increased spending, but other empirical studies have found that public demands for a larger public sector lead to tax increases. The President's [Bush] Advisory Panel on Federal Tax Reform found:

> ... sophisticated statistical studies that control for other factors that may affect the relationship between the size of government and the presence of a VAT yield mixed results. The evidence neither conclusively proves, nor conclusively disproves, the view that supplemental VATs facilitate the growth of government.[105]

APPENDIX A. CREDIT-INVOICE, SUBTRACTION, AND ADDITION METHODS

This appendix provides numerical examples of the two methods of calculating a VAT: credit-invoice and subtraction methods. The tax rate for a VAT may be *price inclusive* (included in the sales price) or *price exclusive* (added to the sales price). Most developed nations levy their VAT rates on a price exclusive basis.

Table A-1. Credit-Invoice Method
(Price-exclusive VAT rate assumed at 10%)

Stage of Production	Sales	VAT	VAT on Purchases	Net VAT
Raw Materials	$100 x 10%	$10	$0	$10
1st processor	$120 x 10%	$12	($10)	$2
Distributor	$140 x 10%	$14	($12)	$2
Retailer	$180 x 10%	$18	($14)	$4
Total				$18

Source: Annette Nellen, "How the VAT works," *Consumption Tax Information*, pp. 6, available at http://www.cob.sjsu.edu/nellen_a/ConsumptionTax.html, visited January 18, 2011. The author is Professor, Department of Accounting and Finance, San Jose State University.

Note: There would be no need to separately state the VAT on the invoice because the customer would not be entitled to a credit for the VAT paid.

Table A-2. Subtraction Method
(Price-exclusive VAT rate assumed at 10%)

Stage of Production	Sales	Less Purchases	Calculation	VAT
Raw Materials	$100	$10	$100 x 10%	$10
1st processor	$120	$12	$20 x 10%	$2
Distributor	$140	$14	$20 x 10%	$2
Retailer	$180	$18	$40 x 10%	$4
Total				$18

Source: Annette Nellen, "How the VAT works," *Consumption Tax Information*, pp. 6,7, available at http://www.cob.sjsu.edu/nellen_a/ConsumptionTax.html, visited Jan. 18, 2011. The author is Professor, Department of Accounting and Finance, San Jose State University.

Note: Taxpayer's records will likely show purchases including the VAT. Thus, an alternative calculation would be to use the tax-inclusive rate of 9.0909%, rather than the tax-exclusive rate of 10% (rate applied to sales amount exclusive of the VAT):

Raw materials: ($110 - $0) x 9.0909% = $10 1st processor: ($132 - $110) x 9.0909% = $2 Distributor: ($154 - $132) x 9.0909% = $2 Retailer: ($198 - $154) x 9.0909% = $4

APPENDIX B. VAT REVENUE RATIOS IN OECD

Table B-1. OECD VAT Revenue Ratios, 1996-2000

Country	Standard VAT Rate (2005)	1996	2000	2005	Difference 1996-2005
Australia[a]	10.0		0.47	0.57	0.10
Austria	20.0	0.58	0.60	0.60	0.02
Belgium	21.0	0.47	0.51	0.50	0.03
Canada[b]	7.0	0.48	0.52	0.52	0.04
Czech Republic	19.0	0.44	0.44	0.59	0.15
Denmark	25.0	0.58	0.60	0.62	0.04
Finland	22.0	0.54	0.61	0.61	0.06
France	19.6	0.51	0.50	0.51	0.00
Germany	16.0	0.60	0.60	0.54	−0.06
Greece	18.0	0.42	0.48	0.46	0.04
Hungary	25.0	0.43	0.53	0.49	0.05
Iceland	24.5	0.54	0.58	0.62	0.08
Ireland	21.0	0.53	0.64	0.68	0.15
Italy	20.0	0.40	0.45	0.41	0.00
Japan	5.0	0.72	0.70	0.72	0.00
Korea	10.0	0.62	0.65	0.71	0.10
Luxembourg	15.0	0.57	0.68	0.81	0.24

Table B-1. (Continued).

Country	Standard VAT Rate (2005)	1996	2000	2005	Difference 1996-2005
Mexico	15.0	0.26	0.31	0.33	0.07
Netherlands	19.0	0.57	0.60	0.61	0.04
New Zealand	12.5	1.00	1.00	1.05	0.04
Norway	25.0	0.60	0.67	0.58	−0.03
Poland	22.0	0.41	0.42	0.48	0.07
Portugal	19.0	0.57	0.62	0.48	−0.10
Slovak Republic[c]	19.0		0.46	0.53	0.07
Spain	16.0	0.45	0.53	0.56	0.11
Sweden	25.0	0.50	0.52		0.05
Switzerland	7.6	0.70	0.78	0.55	0.05
Turkey	18.0	0.55	0.59		-0.02
United Kingdom	17.5	0.50	0.50	0.76	-0.02
Unweighted average	17.7	0.54	0.57	0.53	0.04

Source: OECD, Consumption Tax Trends 2008: VAT/GST and Excise Rates, Trends and Administrative Issues, Paris, 2008, p. 69.

Notes: VAT Revenue Ratio= (VAT revenue)/([consumption - revenue] x Standard VAT rate)

a For Australia the differential VRR is calculated on the period 2000-2005 since GST was introduced in 2000.

b Calculation for Canada is for federal VAT only.

c For Slovak Republic, the differential VRR is calculated on the period 2000-20005 since data is not available for 1996.

APPENDIX C. GENERAL CONSUMPTION TAXES IN OECD COUNTRIES

Table C-1. Data on General Consumption Taxes in OECD (All levels of government)

Country	Total Tax Revenue as a % of GDPa at Market Prices (2007)	General Consumption Taxes as a % of GDP (2007)	General Consumption Taxes as a % of Total Tax Revenues (2007)
Australia	30.8%	4.0%	13.0%
Austria	42.3	7.7	18.3
Belgium	43.9	7.1	16.3
Canada	33.3	4.5	13.6
Czech Republic	37.4	6.6	17.6
Denmark	48.7	10.4	21.4

Should the United States Levy a Value-Added Tax for Deficit Reduction? 23

Country	Total Tax Revenue as a % of GDPa at Market Prices (2007)	General Consumption Taxes as a % of GDP (2007)	General Consumption Taxes as a % of Total Tax Revenues (2007)
Finland	43.0	8.4	19.5
France	43.5	7.4	17.0
Germany	36.2	7.0	19.4
Greece	32.0	7.5	23.4
Hungary	39.5	10.3	26.0
Iceland	40.9	10.6	25.9
Ireland	30.8	7.4	24.1
Italy	43.5	6.2	14.2
Japan	28.3	2.5	8.8
Korea	26.5	4.2	15.8
Luxembourg	36.5	5.7	15.7
Mexico	18.0	3.7	20.4
Netherlands	37.5	7.4	19.8
New Zealand	35.7	8.4	23.5
Norway	43.6	8.3	19.1
Poland	34.9	8.2	23.5
Portugal	36.4	8.8	24.1
Slovak Republic	29.4	6.7	22.9
Spain	37.2	6.0	16.2
Sweden	48.3	9.3	19.3
Switzerland	28.9	3.8	13.1
Turkey	23.7	5.1	21.3
United Kingdom	36.1	6.6	18.2
United States	28.3	2.2	7.7

Source: Adapted by CRS from OECD, *Revenue Statistics 1965-2008*, Paris, 2009.

a. GDP is an abbreviation for gross domestic product, which is a measure of total domestic output of goods and services.

Table C-2. VAT/GST Rates in OECD Member Countries

Country	Implementeda Year Imple-mented	1976	1980	1984	1988	1990	1992	1994	1996	1998	2000	2002	2004	2006	2007	2008	2009	2010	Reduced Ratesb	Specific Rates in Specific Regions
Australia	2000	-	-	-	-	-	-	-	-	-	10.0	10.0	10.0	10.0	10.0	10.0	10.0	10.0	0.0	-
Austriac	1973	18.0	18.0	20.0	20.0	20.0	20.0	20.0	20.0	20.0	20.0	20.0	20.0	20.0	20.0	20.0	20.0	20.0	10.0/12.0	19.0
Belgium	1971	18.0	16.0	19.0	19.0	19.0	19.5	20.5	21.0	21.0	21.0	21.0	21.0	21.0	21.0	21.0	21.0	21.0	0.0/6.0/12.0	-
Canadad	1991	-	-	-	-	-	7.0	7.0	7.0	7.0	7.0	7.0	7.0	7.0	6.0	5.0	5.0	5.0	0.0	13.00
Chilee	1975	20.0	20.0	20.0	20.0	16.0	18.0	18.0	18.0	18.0	18.0	18.0	19.0	19.0	19.0	19.0	19.0	19.0	-	-
Czech Republic	1993	-	-	-	-	-	-	23.0	22.0	22.0	22.0	22.0	22.0	19.0	19.0	19.0	19.0	20.0	10.0	-
Denmark	1967	15.0	22.0	22.0	22.0	22.0	25.0	25.0	25.0	25.0	25.0	25.0	25.0	25.0	25.0	25.0	25.0	25.0	0	-
Finland	1994	-	-	-	-	-	-	22.0	22.0	22.0	22.0	22.0	22.0	22.0	22.0	22.0	22.0	22.0	0.0/8.0/13.0	-
Francef	1968	20.0	17.6	18.6	18.6	18.6	18.6	18.6	20.6	20.6	20.6	19.6	19.6	19.6	19.6	19.6	19.6	19.6	2.1/5.5	See note
Germany	1968	11.0	13.0	14.0	14.0	14.0	14.0	15.0	15.0	16.0	16.0	16.0	16.0	16.0	19.0	19.0	19.0	19.0	7	-
Greeceg	1987	-	-	-	16.0	18.0	18.0	18.0	18.0	18.0	18.0	18.0	18.0	19.0	19.0	19.0	19.0	19.0	4.5/9.0	3.0/6.0/13.0
Hungary	1988	-	-	-	25.0	25.0	25.0	25.0	25.0	25.0	25.0	25.0	25.0	20.0	20.0	20.0	20.0	25.0	18.0/5.0	-
Iceland	1989	-	-	-	-	22.0	22.0	24.5	24.5	24.5	24.5	24.5	24.5	24.5	24.5	24.5	24.5	25.5	0.0/7.0	-
Ireland	1972	20.0	25.0	23.0	25.0	23.0	21.0	21.0	21.0	21.0	21.0	21.0	21.0	21.0	21.0	21.0	21.5	21.0	0.0/4.8/13.5	-
Italy	1973	12.0	15.0	18.0	19.0	19.0	19.0	19.0	19.0	20.0	20.0	20.0	20.0	20.0	20.0	20.0	20.0	20.0	0.0/4.0/10.0	-
Japan	1989	-	-	-	-	3.0	3.0	3.0	3.0	5.0	5.0	5.0	5.0	5.0	5.0	5.0	5.0	5.0	-	-
Korea	1977	-	10.0	10.0	10.0	10.0	10.0	10.0	10.0	10.0	10.0	10.0	10.0	10.0	10.0	10.0	10.0	10.0	0	-
Luxembourg	1970	10.0	10.0	12.0	12.0	12.0	15.0	15.0	15.0	15.0	15.0	15.0	15.0	15.0	15.0	15.0	15.0	15.0	3.0/6.0/12.0	-

Country	Implemented[a]																						Reduced Rates[b]	Specific Rates in Specific Regions
	Year Imple- mented	1976	1980	1984	1988	1990	1992	1994	1996	1998	2000	2002	2004	2006	2007	2008	2009	2010						
Mexico[h]	1980	-	10.0	15.0	15.0	15.0	10.0	10.0	15.0	15.0	15.0	15.0	15.0	15.0	15.0	15.0	15.0	16.0					0.0	11
Nether-lands	1969	18.0	18.0	19.0	20.0	18.5	17.5	17.5	17.5	17.5	17.5	19.0	19.0	19.0	19.0	19.0	19.0	19.0					6.0	-
New Zealand	1986	-	-	-	10.0	12.5	12.5	12.5	12.5	12.5	12.5	12.5	12.5	12.5	12.5	12.5	12.5	12.5					0	-
Norway	1970	20.0	20.0	20.0	20.0	20.0	20.0	22.0	23.0	23.0	23.0	24.0	24.0	25.0	25.0	25.0	25.0	25.0					0.0/8.0/14.0	-
Poland	1993	-	-	-	-	-	-	22.0	22.0	22.0	22.0	22.0	22.0	22.0	22.0	22.0	22.0	22.0					0.0/7.0	-
Portugal[i]	1986	-	-	-	17.0	17.0	16.0	16.0	17.0	17.0	17.0	17.0	19.0	21.0	21.0	21.0	20.0	20.0					5.0/12.0	4.0/8.0/14.0
Slovak Republic	1993	-	-	-	-	-	-	25.0	23.0	23.0	23.0	23.0	19.0	19.0	19.0	19.0	19.0	19.0					10	-
Spain[j]	1986	-	-	-	12.0	12.0	13.0	16.0	16.0	16.0	16.0	16.0	16.0	16.0	16.0	16.0	16.0	16.0					4.0/7.0	See note
Sweden	1969	17.65	23.46	23.46	23.46	23.5	25.0	25.0	25.0	25.0	25.0	25.0	25.0	25.0	25.0	25.0	25.0	25.0					0.0/6.0/12.0	-
Switzerland	1995	-	-	-	-	-	-	6.5	6.5	6.5	7.5	7.6	7.6	7.6	7.6	7.6	7.6	7.6					0.0/2.4/3.6	-
Turkey	1985	-	-	-	10.0	10.0	10.0	15.0	15.0	15.0	17.0	18.0	18.0	18.0	18.0	18.0	18.0	18.0					1.0/8.0	-
United Kingdom	1973	8.0	15.0	15.0	15.0	15.0	17.5	17.5	17.5	17.5	17.5	17.5	17.5	17.5	17.5	17.5	15.0	17.5					0.0/5.0	-
Unweighted Average		16.0	16.9	17.9	17.3	16.7	16.5	17.6	17.8	17.9	17.8	17.9	17.8	17.7	17.8	17.7	17.6	18.0						

Source: OECD from national delegates, January 2010.

a In order to summarize these data, all years are not included.

b A number of countries apply a domestic zero-rate (or an exemption with right to deduct input tax) on certain goods and services. This is shown as 0.0% in this table. This does not include zero-rated exports.

c A standard rate of 19% applies in Jungholz and Mittelberg.

d The provinces of Newfoundland and Labrador, New Brunswick, and Nova Scotia have harmonized their provincial sales taxes with the federal Goods and Services Tax and levy a rate of GST/HST of 13.0% . The provinces of Ontario and British Columbia have proposed to harmonize their provincial sales taxes with the federal Goods and Services Tax effective July 1, 2010, the proposed rates of GST/HST for the provinces is 13.0% and 12.0%, respectively. Other Canadian provinces, with the exception of Alberta, apply a provincial tax to certain goods and services. These provincial taxes apply in addition to GST.

e In June 1988, the VAT rate was decreased from 20.0% to 16.0%; In July 1990, the VAT rate was increased from 16.0% to 18.0%; In October 2003, the VAT rate was increased from 18.0% to 19.0%.

d Rates of 0.9%; 2.1%; 8.0%; 13.0% apply in Corsica; rates of 1.05%; 1.75%; 2.1%; 8.5% apply to overseas departments (DOM). There is no VAT in French Guyana.

g Rates of 3.0%; 6.0% and 13.0% apply in the regions Lesbos, Chios, Samos, Dodecanese, Cyclades, Thassos, Northern Sporades, Samothrace and Skiros.

h A VAT rate of 10.0% applies in the border regions (the border zone is usually up to 20 kilometers south of the U.S.- Mexico border).

i The standard VAT rate in the Islands of Azores and Madeira is 14.0%; reduced VAT rates in these areas are 4.0% and 8.0%.

j Rates of 2.0%; 5.0%; 9.0%; 13.0% apply in the Canary Islands. The standard VAT rate will be increased from 16.0% to 18.0% and the reduced rate from 7.0% to 8.0% on 1st July 2010.

Table C-3. Annual Turnover Concessions for VAT/GST Registration and Collection 2010

| | Registration/Collection Threshold[sa] | | | | | | | |
| | General Threshold | | | Reduced Threshold for Suppliers of Services Only | | Special Threshold for Non-Profit and Charitable Sector | | | |
Country	National Currency		USD	National Currency	USD	National Currency	USD	Registration/ Collection Allowed Prior to Exceeding Threshold[b]	Minimum Registration Period[c]
Australia	AUD	75,000	51,197			150,000	102,393	Yes	1 year
Austriad	EUR	30,000	33,783					Yes	5 years
Belgiumd	EUR	5,580	6,119					Yes	None
Canada	CAD	30,000	25,172			50,000	41,953	Yes	1 year
Chile	CLP	none							
Czech Republice	CZR	1,000,000	68,389					Yes	1 year
Denmarkf	DKK	50,000	5,923					Yes	None
Finland	EUR	8,500	8,803					Yes	None
Franceg	EUR	80,000	87,265	32,000	34,906			Yes	2 years
Germany	EUR	17,500	20,473					Yes	5 years
Greece	EUR	10,000	13,519	5,000	6,760			Yes	5 years

| Country | Registration/Collection Threshold[a] | | | | | | | Registration/ Collection Allowed Prior to Exceeding Threshold[b] | Minimum Registration Period[c] |
| | | General Threshold | | Reduced Threshold for Suppliers of Services Only | | Special Threshold for Non-Profit and Charitable Sector | | | |
	National Currency	National Currency	USD	National Currency	USD	National Currency	USD		
Hungary	HUF	5,000,000	36,914					Yes	2 years
Iceland	ISK	500,000	3,733					Yes	2 years
Ireland	EUR	75,000	80,071	37,500	40,036			Yes	None
Italy[h]	EUR	30,000	35,302					Yes	None
Japan[i]	JPY	10,000,000	86,969					Yes	2 years
Korea	KRW	none							
Luxembourg	EUR	10,000	10,800					Yes	5 years
Mexico	MXN	none							
Netherlands[j]	EUR	1,345	1,548					No	None
New Zealand	NZD	60,000	37,891					Yes	None
Norway	NOK	50,000	5,755			140,000	16,114	Yes	2 years
Poland	PLN	100,000	50,702					Yes	1 year
Portugal[k]	EUR	10,000	14,962					Yes	None
Slovak Republic	EUR	49,790	90,311					Yes	1 year
Spain	EUR	none							
Sweden	SEK	none							
Switzerland	CHF	100,000	61,450			150,000	92,175	Yes	1 year
Turkey	TRY	none							

Table C-3. (Continued).

Country	Registration/Collection Threshold[sa]						Registration/ Collection Allowed Prior to Exceeding Threshold[b]	Minimum Registration Period[c]
	General Threshold			Reduced Threshold for Suppliers of Services Only		Special Threshold for Non-Profit and Charitable Sector		
	National Currency	USD		National Currency	USD	National Currency	USD		
United Kingdom	GBP	68,000	102,808					Yes	None

Source: OECD, data from national delegates, January 1, 2010. Notes:

a Registration/collection thresholds identified in this chart are general concessions that relieve suppliers from the requirement to register and/or to collect for VAT/GST until such time as they exceed the threshold. Except where specifically identified, registration thresholds also relieve suppliers from the requirement to charge and collect VAT/GST on supplies made within a particular jurisdiction. Relief from registration and collection may be available to specific industries or types of traders (for example non resident suppliers) under more detailed rules, or a specific industry or type of trader may be subject to more stringent registration and collection requirements.

b "Yes" means a supplier is allowed to voluntarily register and collect VAT/GST where their total annual turnover is less than the registration threshold.

c Minimum registration/collection periods apply to general concessions. Specific industries, types of traders, or vendors that voluntarily register/collect may be subject to different requirements.

d In these countries, a collection threshold applies. All taxpayers are required to register for VAT/GST, but will not be required to charge and collect VAT/GST until they exceed the collection threshold.

e The registration threshold does not apply to fixed establishments in the Czech Republic of non-resident businesses.

f A higher threshold of DKK 170 000 (EUR 22 840) applies to the blind, and a threshold of DKK 300 000 (EUR 40 300) applies to the first sale of works of art by their creator or his successors in title. For the purposes of the latter exemption, the threshold of DKK 300 000 must not have been exceeded in the current or preceding year."

g Specific thresholds apply for certain activities. EUR 41 700 for lawyers, writers and artists; EUR 32 000 for providers of services other than hotel accommodations and restaurants.

h "Self-employed that have an income lower than EUR 30,000 can choose the Lower Taxpayer Regime (regime dei contribuenti minimi). It involves IRAP (Regional tax on productive activities), VAT exemption and a 20% tax rate in place of the ordinary PIT."

i Businesses (companies and individuals) are not required to register and account for Consumption Tax (VAT) during the first two years of establishment (except for companies whose capital is of JPY 10 000 000 or more. In this case they should be registered for Consumption Tax from the beginning). After this two year period, whether businesses should be registered as a taxable person is determined every year based on their annual taxable turnover for the accounting period/tax year two years before the current accounting period/tax year. If that turnover has exceeded JPY 10 000 000, the business should be registered. Businesses can opt for a voluntary registration for Consumption Tax, even if their turnover is below the threshold. In that case, the businesses have to remain registered for two years.

j The amount of EUR 1 345 is based on the special scheme for small businesses. It is not a threshold based on turnover but on net annual VAT due. If the net annual VAT due (VAT on outputs minus VAT on inputs) is EUR 1 345 or less, the taxpayer gets a full VAT rebate and no VAT is due to the Tax Authorities. In this case, the taxpayer has no obligation to file VAT returns. However, businesses under the small business scheme must still register as VAT taxpayers. In that sense, there is no threshold for registration for VAT purposes. If the net annual VAT due is more than EUR 1 345 but less than EUR 1 883, the taxpayer gets a partial VAT rebate. In this case, the taxpayer must file a VAT return.

k The collection threshold does not apply to commercial legal entities; for small retailers that fulfill some specific conditions the collection threshold is EUR 12 500.

APPENDIX D. VAT RATES BY COUNTRY

Table D-1. Standard VAT Rates by Country
(Tax-exclusive rate in percentage for 2009)

Country	Year VAT Introduced	(Goods/Services 2009)
Albania	1996	20%
Algeria	1992	17
Antigua and Barbuda	2007	15
Argentina	1975	21
Armenia	1992	20
Australia	2000	10
Austria	1973	20
Azerbaijan	1992	18
Bangladesh	1991	15
Barbados	1997	15
Belarus	1992	18
Belgium	1971	21
Benin	1991	18
Bolivia	1973	13
Bosnia and Herzegovina	2006	17
Botswana	2002	10
Brazil	1967	19
Bulgaria	1994	20
Burkina Faso	1993	18
Cambodia	1999	10
Cameroon	1999	19.25
Canada	1991	5
Cape Verde	2004	15
Central African Republic	2001	19
Chad	2000	18
Chile	1975	19
China	1994	17
Colombia	1975	16
Congo	1997	18
Cook Islands	1997	10
Costa Rica	1975	13
Cote d'Ivoire	1960	18
Croatia	1998	22
Cyprus	1992	15
Czech Republic	1993	19
Denmark	1967	25
Djibouti	2009	7
Dominica	2006	15
Dominican Republic	1983	16
Ecuador	1970	12
Egypt	1991	10
El Salvador	1992	13
Equatorial Guinea	2004	15

Country	Year VAT Introduced	(Goods/Services 2009)
Estonia	1992	18
Ethiopia	2003	15
Fiji	1992	12.50
Finland	1994	22
France	1968	19.60
French Polynesia	1998	16/10
Gabon	1995	18
Georgia	1992	18
Germany	1968	19
Ghana	1998	12.50
Greece	1987	19
Grenada	2010	10
Guatemala	1983	12
Guinea	1996	18
Guinea-Bissau	2001	15
Guyana	2007	16
Haiti	1982	10
Honduras	1976	12
Hungary	1988	20
Iceland	1990	24.50
India	2005	12.50
Indonesia	1985	10
Ireland	1972	21.50
Israel	1976	15.50
Italy	1973	20
Jamaica	1991	16.50
Japan	1989	5
Kazakhstan	1992	12
Kenya	1990	16
Kosovo	2001	15
Kyrgyzstan	1992	12
Laos	2009	10
Latvia	1992	21
Lebanon	2002	10
Lesotho	2003	14
Liberia	2009	7
Lithuania	1992	19
Luxembourg	1970	15
Macedonia	2000	18
Madagascar	1994	20
Malawi	1989	16.50
Mali	1991	18
Malta	1995	18
Mauritania	1995	14
Mauritius	1998	15
Mexico	1980	15
Moldova	1992	20
Mongolia	1998	10
Montenegro	2003	17

Table D-1. (Continued).

Country	Year VAT Introduced	(Goods/Services 2009)
Morocco	1986	20
Mozambique	1999	17
Namibia	2000	15
Nepal	1997	13
Netherlands	1969	19
New Zealand	1986	12.50
Nicaragua	1975	15
Niger	1986	18
Nigeria	1994	5
Norway	1970	25
Pakistan	1990	16
Panama	1977	5
Papua New Guinea	1999	10
Paraguay	1993	10
Peru	1973	19
Philippines	1988	12
Poland	1993	22
Portugal	1986	20
Romania	1993	19
Russia	1992	18
Rwanda	2001	18
Senegal	1980	18
Serbia	2005	18
Singapore	1994	7
Slovak Republic	1993	19
Slovenia	1999	20
South Africa	1991	14
South Korea	1977	10
Spain	1986	16
Sri Lanka	1998	12
Sudan	2000	15
Suriname	1999	10/8%
Sweden	1969	25
Switzerland	1995	7.60
Tajikistan	1992	20
Tanzania	1998	20
Thailand	1992	7
Togo	1995	18
Tonga	2005	15
Trinidad and Tobago	1990	15
Tunisia	1988	18
Turkey	1985	18
Turkmenistan	1992	15
Uganda	1996	18
Ukraine	1992	20
United Kingdom	1973	15
Uruguay	1968	22

Country	Year VAT Introduced	(Goods/Services 2009)
Uzbekistan	1992	20
Vanuatu	1998	13
Venezuela	1993	9
Vietnam	1999	10
Zambia	1995	16
Zimbabwe	2004	15

Source: Leah Durner, Bobby Bui, and Jon Sedon, "Why VAT Around the Globe?," *Tax Notes*, November 23, 2009, pp. 5-7. The authors compiled data for this table from a variety of sources.

End Notes

[1] The combined individual and business taxes proposed by the typical flat tax can be viewed as a modified value-added tax (VAT). The individual wage tax would be imposed on wages (and salaries) and pension receipts. Part or all of an individual's wage and pension income would be tax-free, depending on marital status and number of dependents. The business tax would be a modified subtraction-method VAT with wages (and salaries) and pension contributions subtracted from the VAT base, in contrast to the usual VAT practice. For a comprehensive analysis of the flat tax, see CRS Report 98-529, *Flat Tax: An Overview of the Hall-Rabushka Proposal*, by James M. Bickley.

[2] On January 6, 2009, Representative John D. Dingell introduced H.R. 15, *National Health Insurance Act*, which would have levied a VAT to finance national health insurance.

[3] For example, see U.S. Congressional Budget Office, *The Long-Term Budget Outlook*, June 2010, 74 p.

[4] For example, see Lori Montgomery, "Once Considered Unthinkable, U.S. Sales Tax Gets Fresh Look," *The Washington Post*, May 27, 2009, p. A15, and George F. Will, "Higher Taxes, Anyone?," Sunday Opinion, *The Washington Post*, July 12, 2009, p. A15, and more recently, Seth McLaughlin, "VAT Back as Proposal to Solve Revenue Ills," *Washington Times*, vol. 28, no 238, pp. A1, A9..

[5] Bipartisan Policy Center, "Bipartisan Policy Center Launches Debt Reduction Task Force," Press Release, January 25, 2010, p. 1.

[6] "Volcker on the VAT," *The Wall Street Journal*, WSJ.com, April 8, 2010, p. 1.

[7] Congressional letter to co-chairs of National Commission on Fiscal Responsibility and Reform, May 20, 2010, 12 p.

[8] Ibid., p. 1.

[9] National Commission on Fiscal Responsibility and Reform, *Co-Chairs' Proposal*, November 2010, 50 p.

[10] National Commission on Fiscal Responsibility and Reform, *The Moment of Truth*, December 2010, 64 p.

[11] Bipartisan Policy Center's Debt Reduction Task Force, *Restoring America's Future*, November 17, 2010, pp 40-43.

[12] Ibid., p. 41.

[13] Ibid., p. 42.

[14] Ibid., p. 32.

[15] The revenue for a VAT would vary depending on the tax base. For a discussion of this issue, see CRS Report RS22720, *Taxable Base of the Value-Added Tax*, by James M. Bickley.

[16] Urban-Brooking Tax Policy Center, "5 Percent Broad Based Value Added Tax (VAT) Impact on Tax Revenue ($ billions), 2010-19," November 12, 2009, p. 1.

[17] Ibid.

[18] For further information , see CRS Report RS22720, *Taxable Base of the Value-Added Tax*, by James M. Bickley.

[19] These factors of production have specific meanings to an economist. Labor consists of all employees hired by the firm. Land consists of all natural resources including raw land, water, and mineral wealth. Capital is anything used in the production process that has been made by man. The entrepreneur is the decision maker who operates the firm.

[20] Numerical examples of the credit-invoice method and the subtraction method of calculating VAT are shown in Appendix A.

[21] An exception is the final retail stage where policymakers have the option of including or excluding the VAT from the retail sales slip.

[22] No developed national uses the addition method; consequently, if receives no further discussion in this report.

[23] For a comparison of the credit-invoice method and the subtraction method as a partial replacement VAT, see Itai Grinberg, "Where Credit is Due: Advantages of the Credit-Invoice Method for a Partial Replacement VAT, presented at the American Tax Policy Institute Conference, Washington, D.C., February 18, 2009, 41 p..

[24] Ibid, p. 9.

[25] For a current examination of exemptions, see Walter Hellerstein and Harley Duncan, "VAT Exemptions: Principles and Practice," *Tax Notes*, August 30, 2010, pp. 989-999.

[26] Liam Ebrill, Michael Keen, Jean-Paul Bodin, and Victoria Summers, *The Modern VAT*, International Monetary Fund, Washington, D.C., 2001, p. 85.

[27] Ibid., p. 86.

[28] Ibid., pp. 86-87.

[29] Ibid., p. 89.

[30] Ibid.

[31] Ibid.

[32] Ibid., pp. 91-99.

[33] Ibid., p. 92

[34] Ibid., p. 93.

[35] Ibid., p. 94.

[36] U.S. Government Accountability Office, *Value-Added Taxes: Lessons Learned from Other Countries on Compliance Risks, Administrative Costs, Compliance Burden, and Transition*, Report no. GAO-08-566, pp. 23-24.

[37] Ibid., p. 24.

[38] Ebrill, et al., p. 98.

[39] Ibid.

[40] This classification of justifications for exclusion from VAT taxation was derived from the following source: Alan A. Tait, *Value-Added Tax: International Practice and Problems* (Washington, International Monetary Fund, 1988), p. 56.

[41] U.S. Congressional Budget Office, *Effects of Adopting a Value-Added Tax* (Washington, U.S. Govt. Print. Off., Feb. 1992), pp. 22-26.

[42] Richard A. Musgrave and Peggy B. Musgrave, *Public Finance in Theory and Practice*. 4th ed. (New York: McGraw-Hill, 1984), p. 78.

[43] OECD, *Consumption Tax Trends 2008: VAT/GST and Excise Rates, Trends and Administrative Issues*, (Paris: OECD Publishing, 2008), p. 67.

[44] Ibid.

[45] Ibid.

[46] OECD, *Revenue Statistics: 1965-2008* (Paris: OECD Publishing, 2009), p. 89. For data by country, see Table C-1 in Appendix C.

[47] Ibid. For data by country, see Table C-1 in Appendix C.

[48] Sijbren Cnossen, "VAT and RST: A Comparison," *Canadian Tax Journal*, vol. 35, no. 3, May/June 1987, p. 583.

[49] Cnossen, *VAT and RST: A Comparison*, p. 585 and OECD, *Consumption Tax Trends* (OECD, March 2005), p. 11.

[50] OECD, *International VAT/GST Guidelines* (OECD, February 2006), p. 1.

[51] Leah Durner, Bobby Bui, and Jon Sedon, "Why VAT Around the Globe?," *Tax Notes*, November 23, 2009, p. 929.

[52] Ibid.

[53] Ibid.

[54] Ibid., p. 930.

[55] For an overview of the incidence of the VAT using income as a measure of ability-to-pay, see U.S. Congressional Budget Office, *Effects of Adopting a Value-Added Tax* (Washington: February 1992), pp. 31-47.

[56] For a comprehensive analysis of the vertical equity of a VAT, see Erik Caspersen and Gilbert Metcalf, "Is a Value-Added Tax Progressive? Annual Versus Lifetime Incidence Measures," *National Tax Journal*, vol. 47, no. 4, December 1994, pp. 731-746; and U.S. Congressional Budget Office, *Effects of Adopting a Value-Added Tax*, pp. 31-47.

[57] U.S. Congressional Budget Office, *Effects of Adopting a Value-Added Tax*, p. 35.

[58] Franco Modigliani, a Nobel Laureate in economics, estimated that at least 80% of all savings by households are eventually spent on consumption. See Franco Modigliani, "The Role of Intergenerational Transfer and Life Cycle Saving in the Accumulation of Wealth," *Journal of Economic Perspectives*, vol. 2, no. 2, spring 1988, pp. 15-23.

[59] For examples of life-cycle models, see Don Fullerton and Diane Lim Rogers, "Lifetime Effects of Fundamental Tax Reform," in *Economic Effects of Fundamental Tax Reform*, Henry J. Aaron and William G. Gale, eds. (Washington: Brookings Institution Press, 1996), pp 321-352; and David Altig, Alan J. Auerbach, Laurence J. Kotlikoff, Kent A. Smetters, and Jan Walliser, "Stimulating Fundamental Tax Reform in the United States," *The American Economic Review*, vol. 91, no. 3, June 2001, pp. 574-595.

[60] For an examination of increased administrative and compliance costs resulting from exclusions and multiple rates, see Liam Ebrill, et al., pp.78-79.

[61] Tait, p. 218.

[62] Edith Brashares, Janet Furman Speyrer, and George N. Carlson, "Distributional Aspects of a Federal Value-Added Tax," *National Tax Journal*, vol. 41, no. 2, June 1988, p. 165.

[63] CRS Report RL31768, *The Earned Income Tax Credit (EITC): An Overview*, by Christine Scott, pp. 14-15.

[64] Ibid., pp 16-17.

[65] Henry J. Aaron, "The Political Economy of a Value-Added Tax in the United States," *Tax Notes*, vol. 38, no. 10, March 7, 1988, p. 1,113.

[66] Ibid.

[67] Leonard E. Burman, "A Blue print for Tax Reform and Health Reform," Urban Institute, p. 1. Available at http://www.urban.org, visited January 6, 2011.

[68] Henry J. Aaron, "The Value-Added Tax: Sorting Through the Practical and Political Problems," *The Brookings Review*, summer 1988, p. 13.

[69] In economics, leisure is any time spent not working.

[70] See U.S. Congressional Budget Office, *Effects of Adopting a Value-Added Tax*, pp. 56-60; and Jane G. Gravelle, "Income, Consumption, and Wage Taxation in a Life-Cycle Model: Separating Efficiency from Redistribution," *American Economic Review*, vol. 81, no. 4, September 1991, pp. 985-995.

[71] Aaron, "The Political Economy of a Value-Added Tax in the United States," p. 1,113.

[72] Ibid., p. 32.

[73] For an analysis of the U.S. savings rate, see CRS Report RS21480, *Saving Rates in the United States: Calculation and Comparison*, by Craig K. Elwell. For an analysis of saving Incentives, see CRS Report RL 33482, *Saving Incentives: What May Work, What May Not*, by Thomas L. Hungerford.

[74] CRS Report 88-697 S, *Economic Effects of a Value-Added Tax on Capital Formation*, by Jane G. Gravelle, p. 2. (Archived report available on request).

[75] CBO, *Effects of Adopting a Value-Added Tax*, pp. 52-53.

[76] U.S. General Accounting Office, *Value-Added Tax: Administrative Costs Vary with Complexity and Number of Businesses*, Washington, May 1993, p. 63.

[77] Sijbren Cnossen, "Administrative and Compliance Costs of the VAT: A Review of the Evidence," *Tax Notes*, vol. 62, no. 12, June 20, 1994, p. 1,610.

[78] Ibid.

[79] U.S. Government Accountability Office, *Value-Added Taxes: Lessons Learned from Other Countries on Compliance Risks, Administrative Costs, Compliance Burden, and Transition*. pp. 15-16.

[80] For a current examination of VAT compliance from the approach of behavior economics, see Paul Webley, Caroline Adams, and Henk Elffers, "Value Added Tax Compliance," in *Behavioral Public Finance*, eds. Edward J. McCaffery and Joel Slemrod (New York: Russell Sage Foundation, 2006), pp. 175-205.

[81] Sijbren Cnossen, "Administrative and Compliance Costs of the VAT: A Review of the Evidence," p. 1,609.

[82] Ibid., p. 1,615.

[83] Ali Agha and Jonathan Haughton, "Designing VAT Systems: Some Efficiency Considerations," *Review of Economics and Statistics*, vol. 78, no. 2, May 1996, pp. 304-305.

[84] Ibid., p. 305.

[85] Organization of Economic Co-Operation and Development, *Taxing Consumption*, pp. 199-200.

[86] For a detailed discussion of these 10 types of evasion, see Tait, pp. 308-314.

[87] Ebrill, et al., p. 113.

[88] Ibid., p. 116.

[89] Ibid., p. 117.

[90] Ibid., p. 113.

[91] Table C-3 has data on annual turnover concessions for VAT registration and collection, which includes registration thresholds.

[92] U.S. Government Accountability Office, *Value-Added Taxes: Lessons Learned from Other Countries on Compliance Risks, Administrative Costs, Compliance Burden, and Transition*, p. 41.

[93] Tait, pp. 409-416.

[94] For an overview of state tax officials' concerns related to the enactment of a broad-based federal consumption tax, see U.S. General Accounting Office, *State Tax Officials Have Concerns About a Federal Consumption Tax*, Washington, March 1990, 77 p.

[95] For an examination of this issue, see Robert P. Strauss, "Administrative and Revenue Implications of Federal Consumption Taxes for the State and Local Sector," *State Tax Notes*, vol. 16, March 15, 1999, pp. 831-868.

[96] For data on the dates of adoption of major state taxes by state, see Tax Foundation, *Facts and Figures on Government Finance*, Washington: Tax Foundation, 2010.

[97] For historical data on state tax collection by source, see Tax Foundation, *Facts & Figures on Government Finance*, Washington: Tax Foundation, 2010. Historical data on federal receipts by source is available from the following source: Office of Management and Budget, *Budget of the U.S. Government, Historical Tables, Fiscal Year 2011* (Washington: GPO, 2010), pp. 30-35.

[98] Tax Policy Center, "State Tax Collection Shares by Type, 1999-2009," July 14, 2010, p. 1.. [99] Ibid.

[100] The Federal-State Tax Collection Act was enacted as Title II of the legislation that created the federal revenue sharing program. U.S. Congress, Joint Committee on Internal Revenue Taxation. *State and Local Fiscal Assistance Act and the Federal-State Tax Collection Act of 1972, H.R. 14370, 92d Congress, Public Law 92-512*, JCS-1-73, Feb. 12, 1973, Washington, GPO, 1973, pp. 51-72.

[101] Provisions of the Federal-State Tax Collection Act of 1972 (subchapter 64(E), sec. 6361 through 6365 of the Internal Revenue Code) were repealed by the Omnibus Budget Reconciliation Act of 1990, P.L. 101-508, sec. 11801(a)(45).

[102] U.S. General Accountability Office, *Value-Added Taxes: Lessons Learned from Other Countries on Compliance Risks, Administrative Costs, Compliance Burden, and Transition*, p. 5.

[103] The optimal size of government is a value judgment. A larger public sector is neither inherently better nor worse than the existing size of the public sector. For a comprehensive examination of this issue, see Joseph E. Stiglitz, *Economics of the Public Sector*, 3rd edition (New York: W. W. Norton & Company, 2000), pp. 3-22.

[104] For a discussion of variables that may affect the size of Government, see Richard A. Musgrave and Peggy B Musgrave, *Public Finance in Theory and Practice*, 4th ed. (New York: McGraw-Hill, 1984), pp.146-153.

[105] President's Advisory Panel on Federal Tax Reform, *Simple, Fair, & Pro-Growth: Proposals to Fix America's Tax System* (Washington: U.S. Department of the Treasury, November 1, 2005), p. 203.

In: Value-Added Tax (VAT) and Flat Tax Proposals
Editors: D. B. Andrews and A. M. Davis

ISBN: 978-1-61324-191-2
© 2011 Nova Science Publishers, Inc.

Chapter 2

A VALUE-ADDED TAX CONTRASTED WITH A NATIONAL SALES TAX[*]

James M. Bickley

SUMMARY

Both a value-added tax (VAT) and a national sales tax (NST) have been proposed by participants in the tax-reform debate as replacement taxes for all or part of the nation's current income tax system. In addition, there is congressional interest in using a consumption tax to finance national health care.

A firm's value added for a product is the increase in the value of that product caused by the application of the firm's factors of production. A VAT on a product would be levied at all stages of production of that product. VATs differ in their tax treatment of purchases of capital (plant and equipment). The type of VAT used by developed countries—termed a consumption VAT—treats a firm's purchases of plant and equipment the same as any other purchase. A firm's net VAT liability is usually calculated by using the credit-invoice method. According to this method, a firm determines its gross tax liability by aggregating VAT shown on its sales invoices. Then the firm computes its net VAT liability by subtracting VAT paid on purchases from other firms from the firm's gross VAT liability. This net tax is remitted to the government. The subtraction method can also be used to calculate the VAT. Under this method, the firm calculates its value added by subtracting its cost of taxed inputs from its taxable sales. Next, the firm determines its VAT liability by multiplying its value added by the VAT rate. A flat tax, based on the proposal formulated by Robert E. Hall and Alvin Rabushka of the Hoover Institution, is a type of modified subtraction method VAT.

In contrast to a VAT, an NST would be a federal consumption tax collected only at the retail level by vendors. an NST would equal a set percentage of the retail price of taxable goods and services. Retail vendors would collect the NST and remit tax revenue to the federal government. Both a VAT and an NST are frequently assumed to be ultimately paid by consumers. For calendar year 2007, CRS estimated a VAT or NST would have raised net revenue of between $46 and $86 billion for each 1% levied if used as a replacement tax. Alternatively, if the VAT or NST would have been used as an

---

[*] This is an edited, reformatted and augmented version of Congressional Research Services publication RL33438, dated March 19, 2010.

additional revenue source, than those revenue estimates would be reduced by 25% because of partially offsetting declines in income tax revenues.

The operating differences between a consumption VAT and an NST have important policy implications. On the one hand, the administrative cost of a VAT would exceed that of an NST because a VAT would require more information to be reported and audited. Also, an opportunity exists for an NST to be collected jointly with state sales taxes, but a federal VAT offers no readily available joint collection possibilities. A VAT would require more time to implement than an NST because a VAT is more complicated, covers more firms, and is a new tax method. On the other hand, a consumption VAT with the credit method more easily excludes inputs from double taxation than does an NST. A consumption VAT would be easier to enforce than an NST. It is in the self-interest of a firm to have accurate purchase invoices so that it can obtain full credit for prior VAT paid. Tax authorities can double check the accuracy of the VAT remitted by any firm because data are collected from producers at all levels of production. For a given year, a VAT could have a broader base than an NST because a VAT is easier to enforce. A VAT may be less visible to consumers than an NST. A VAT is levied at all stages of production, and policymakers have the option of not requiring the amount of VAT to be shown on retail sales receipts. As of March 19, 2010, the following bills concerning an NST or VAT have been introduced in the 111th Congress: H.R. 15, H.R. 25, S. 296, S. 741, H.R. 1040, S. 963, S. 932, H.R. 4529, and S. 1240.

This report will be updated as issues develop or new legislation is introduced.

INTRODUCTION

In Congress, both a value-added tax (VAT) and a national sales tax (NST) have been proposed by Members in the tax-reform debate as replacement taxes for part or all of the nation's current income tax system.[1] In addition, there is congressional interest in using a consumption tax to finance national health care. Both the VAT and the NST are taxes on the consumption of goods and services and are conceptually similar.[2] Yet, these taxes also have significant differences. This report discusses some of the potential policy implications associated with these differences.[3]

CONCEPT OF A VALUE-ADDED TAX

The value added of a firm is the difference between a firm's sales and a firm's purchases from all other firms.[4] In other words, a firm's value added is simply the amount of value that a firm contributes to a good or service by applying its factors of production (land, labor, capital, and entrepreneurial ability). A value-added tax is a tax, levied at each stage of production, on each firm's value added.

Types of VATs

There are three types of VATs; they differ in their tax treatment of purchases of capital inputs (plant and equipment). The consumption-type VAT treats capital purchases the same way as the purchase of any other input (the equivalent to "expensing" under an income tax).

The other two types of VATs are the income VAT and the gross product VAT. Under the income VAT, the VAT paid on the purchases of capital inputs is amortized (credited against the firm's VAT liability) over the expected lives of the capital inputs. Under the gross product VAT, no deduction for the VAT on purchases of capital inputs is allowed against the firm's VAT liability. The consumption VAT is the only type of VAT that is used in developed nations and has been proposed for the United States; consequently, the consumption VAT is contrasted with the NST in this report.

Methods of Calculating VAT

There are three alternative methods of calculating VAT: the credit method, the subtraction method, and the addition method.[5] Under the *credit-invoice method,* a firm would be required to show VAT separately on all sales invoices.[6] Each sale would be marked up by the amount of the VAT. A sales invoice for a seller is a purchase invoice for a buyer. A firm would calculate the VAT to be remitted to the government by a three-step process. First, the firm would aggregate VAT shown on its sales invoices. Second, the firm would aggregate VAT shown on its purchase invoices. Finally, aggregate VAT on purchase invoices would be subtracted from aggregate VAT shown on sales invoices, and the difference remitted to the government. The credit-invoice method is calculated on a transactions basis.

Under the *subtraction method*, the firm calculates its value added by subtracting its cost of taxed inputs from its taxable sales. Next, the firm determines its VAT liability by multiplying its value added by the VAT rate. Most flat tax proposals are modified subtraction method VATs. Under the *addition method*, the firm calculates its value added by adding all payments for untaxed inputs (e.g., wages and profits). Next, the firm multiplies its value added by the VAT rate to calculate VAT to be remitted to the government.

The credit-invoice method is used by 28 of 29 nations in the Organization for Economic Cooperation and Development (OECD) with VATs.[7] Tax economists differ in their classifications of the Japanese VAT. Both the credit-invoice and the subtraction methods have been discussed for the United States. The prevailing view of economists is that the credit-invoice method is superior. This method requires registered firms to maintain detailed records that are cross indexed with supporting documentation. A VAT shown on the sales invoice of one firm is the same as the VAT shown on the purchase order of another firm. Hence, the credit-invoice method allows tax auditors to cross check the records of firms. Also, each firm has a vested interest in insuring that the VAT shown on its purchase orders is not understated in order for that firm to receive full credit against VAT liability for VAT previously paid. Thus, the credit-invoice method would seem to be easier to enforce. Also, the credit-invoice method is probably the only feasible method if there are to be multiple tax rates.

A flat tax, based on the proposal formulated by Robert E. Hall and Alvin Rabushka of the Hoover Institution, is a type of modified subtraction method VAT. Their proposal would have two components: a wage tax and a cash-flow tax on businesses. (A wage tax is a tax only on salaries and wages; a cash-flow tax is generally a tax on gross receipts minus all outlays.) It is essentially a modified VAT, with wages and pensions subtracted from the VAT base and taxed at the individual level. Under a standard VAT, a firm would not subtract its wage and pension contributions when calculating its tax base. Under this proposal, some wage income would not be included in the tax base because of exemptions. Under a standard VAT, all wage income would be included in the tax base.

A NATIONAL SALES TAX

A national sales tax (NST) would be a federal consumption tax collected only at the retail level by vendors. The NST would equal a set percentage of the retail price of taxable goods and services. Retail vendors would collect the NST and remit tax revenue to the federal government. A buyer of intermediate products (that is, inputs used to produce goods and services) would register and receive an exemption certificate. This buyer would present the exemption certificate to the seller and thus would be exempt from paying the retail sales tax.

The retail price of a good or service equals the sum of value added at all stages of production. Consequently, a value-added tax and a national sales tax with the same tax rate and tax base would yield the same amount of revenue. The operating assumption of policymakers and economists is that both taxes are fully shifted forward onto consumers; that is, the price to the consumer increases by the (full) amount of the tax. For calendar year 2007, based on CRS estimates of VAT tax bases, a VAT or NST would have raised net revenue of between $46 and $86 billion for each 1% levied if used as a replacement tax.[8] If the VAT or NST would have been used as an additional revenue source, than these revenue estimates would be reduced by 25% because of partially offsetting declines in revenue from taxes on income.[9]

POLICY IMPLICATIONS

The operating differences between a VAT and an NST have many important policy implications in eight areas: administrative cost, joint tax collections, avoiding double taxation of intermediate goods and services, enforcement, broadness of tax base, time required to implement, visibility, and experiences of other nations.

Administrative Costs

Under a VAT, all firms would have to report tax information and collect taxes. Under an NST, firms without retail sales would not report or collect taxes. But the substantial majority of all firms would collect the NST since they have some retail sales. Under a VAT with a credit-invoice method of collection, each firm must keep invoices on all sales and purchases from other firms, and these invoices would be subject to audit by tax authorities. Hence, the value-added tax would require more information to be reported and audited than a national sales tax, and, consequently, a VAT would likely be more expensive to administer than an NST.[10]

Joint Tax Collection

Since 45 states and the District of Columbia have general sales taxes, an opportunity exists for an NST to be collected jointly with state sales taxes.[11] A federal VAT could not be jointly collected with state sales taxes. States could convert their sales taxes to a VAT with the federal tax base, but this is unlikely since it would require that the states establish entirely new tax systems. Consequently, no administrative costs saving would be expected from a VAT; therefore, the collection costs of a VAT can be expected to be higher than an NST.[12]

Avoiding Double Taxation of Intermediate Goods and Services

Double taxation occurs if an input is taxed at the time of purchase and then a tax is levied on the same input again when it becomes part of the output of the firm. A consumption VAT, with the credit-invoice method of tax computation, easily excludes inputs from taxation. The exclusion of inputs from an NST would be more difficult. Usually, firms buying inputs would have to provide sellers with exemption certificates before making their purchases. At the state level, procedures to exempt input purchases from state retail sales taxes have worked imperfectly. It is therefore reasonable to expect that excluding inputs from taxation would be more difficult with an NST than with a VAT.

Enforcement

With a VAT, a firm would have a financial interest in ensuring that amounts of VAT paid on input purchases are accurately reported on its purchase invoices since the firm could receive credits against its VAT liability. In addition, the VAT would provide the tax authorities with an opportunity to cross-check the amount of VAT collected because data are gathered from producers at different stages of production. Nonetheless, some enforcement problems do exist with a VAT. For example, firms at different stages of production could collude to falsify invoices. But the NST lacks both the self-enforcing procedure and the cross-checking opportunity of the VAT. Hence, better compliance is expected from a VAT than with an NST.[13]

Broadness of Tax Base

Because of the potential for better enforcement of a VAT, it may be possible to levy a VAT on more goods and services than an NST. This view is supported by the fact that VATs of European nations, on the average, are levied on more goods and services than most state sales taxes in the United States.[14] For a given revenue yield, tax economists prefer a broad tax base because the tax rate, needed to raise a given amount of revenue, is lower. Lower tax rates reduce economic distortions and thus raise economic efficiency. Thus, if a VAT has a broader base then an NST, then it would be more efficient because a lower tax rate would be needed to raise a given amount of revenue.

Time Required to Implement

A VAT would take more time to implement than an NST because a VAT is more complicated and would cover more firms than an NST. Also, business executives are not familiar with this form of taxation, hence, the U.S. government would face the need to conduct an educational campaign.

The Government Accountability Office (GAO) analyzed VATs in five developed nations: Canada, New Zealand, Australia, France, and the United Kingdom. GAO found that Australia, Canada, and New Zealand, all with relatively new VATs, took between 15 and 24 months to implement their VATs, even though they had preexisting consumption tax administrative structures.[15] Another estimate reports a similar time table. Alan A. Tait, former Deputy Director of the Fiscal Affairs Department of the International Monetary Fund, wrote a "chronological schedule of work to be done to introduce a VAT in about eighteen months."[16]

Visibility

The value-added tax may be less visible to consumers than a national sales tax. Policymakers and economists assume that 100% of both the VAT and the NST are passed onto consumers. But the perceptions of many consumers may be different about a VAT. Many consumers may believe that a VAT tax would at least partially fall on firms because the VAT is collected at each stage of production. Since the NST is levied only at the retail level, consumers may more readily believe that they would pay the entire tax. Furthermore, policymakers have the option as to whether the amount of a VAT should be stated on retail sales receipts.[17] New Zealand gives each retailer the option of whether or not to explicitly state the amount of VAT on its retail sales receipts.[18] The amount of an NST would be explicitly stated on sales receipts.

The lower visibility of the VAT relative to the NST may be either desirable or undesirable depending on one's political ideology. It can be argued that taxes should be visible so that the costs of taxation may be compared with the benefits of government spending. Conversely, it can be argued that people generally do not like the idea of paying taxes; consequently, in this view, to finance public sector responsibilities, it is better to have taxes seem as painless as possible.

Experiences of Other Nations

Currently, all developed nations except the United States have a VAT at the national level. A VAT is a requirement for membership in the European Union (EU).[19] Sweden, Norway, Iceland, and Switzerland had retail sales taxes at the national level but eventually switched to VATs.[20] According to the Organization for Economic Co-Operation and Development (OECD)

> The spread of Value Added Tax (also called Goods and Services Tax—GST) has been the most important development in taxation over the last half-century. Limited to less than 10 countries in the late 1960s it has now been implemented by about 136

A Value-Added Tax Contrasted with a National Sales Tax 43

countries; and in these countries (including OECD member countries) it typically accounts for one-fifth of total tax revenue. The recognized capacity of VAT to raise revenue in a neutral and transparent manner drew all OECD member countries (except the United States) to adopt this broad based consumption tax.[21]

Policy insights can be obtained by examining the experiences of other nations, however, just because other nations exhibit a specific tax policy does not necessarily mean that it is appropriate for the United States to adopt this policy.

LEGISLATION IN THE 111TH CONGRESS

As of March 19, 2010, nine bills have been introduced in the 111th Congress concerning the value-added tax or the retail sales tax.[22] Representative John Linder's proposal (H.R. 25) and Senator Saxby Chambliss's proposal (S. 296, a companion bill to H.R. 25) would replace our current income-based tax system and estate/gift taxes with a national retail sales tax.. Senator Arlen Specter's proposal (S. 741) and Senator Richard C. Shelby's proposal (S. 932) would replace individual and corporate income taxes and estate and gift taxes with a flat tax based on the Hall-Rabushka concept.[23] Representative Paul D. Ryan's proposal (H.R. 4529) and Senator Jim DeMint's proposal (S. 1240) are comprehensive plans to address America's long-term economic and fiscal issues. Both proposals include the replacement of the current corporate income tax with a subtraction-method VAT referred to as a Business Consumption Tax. In addition, in the 111th Congress, Representative John Dingell introduced H.R. 15, which would levy a VAT to finance national health insurance.

End Notes

[1] For an overview of proposals for tax reform, see CRS Report R40414, *Tax Reform: An Overview of Proposals in the 111th Congress*, by James M. Bickley.

[2] In Nov. 2005, The President's Advisory Panel on Federal Tax Reform [established by President Bush] issued its final report that included analyses of both an NST and a VAT.

[3] A classic article on this topic is: Sijbren Cnossen, "VAT and RST: A Comparison," *The Canadian Tax Journal*, v. 35, no. 3, May/June 1987, pp. 559-615.

[4] For a comprehensive analysis of the concept of a U.S. value-added tax, see CRS Report RL33619, *Value-Added Tax: A New U.S. Revenue Source?*, by James M. Bickley.

[5] For a comprehensive explanation and analysis of methods to calculate VAT, see *Value-Added Tax: Methods of Calculation*, by James M. Bickley, a CRS general distribution memorandum available from the author.

[6] An exception is the final retail stage where policymakers have the option of including or excluding the VAT from the retail sales slip.

[7] The OECD is an intergovernmental economic organization in which the 30 economically developed countries discuss, develop, and analyze economic and social policy and share expertise. The OECD members are 22 European nations, Turkey, the United States, Canada, Mexico, Australia, New Zealand, South Korea, and Japan. The United States is the only member without a VAT. For an examination of the OECD, see CRS Report RS21128, *The Organization for Economic Cooperation and Development*, by James K. Jackson.

[8] CRS Report RS22720, *Taxable Base of the Value-Added Tax*, by Maxim Shvedov.

[9] U.S. Congressional Budget Office, "The Role of the 25 Percent Revenue Offset in Estimating the Budgetary Effects of Legislation," *Economic and Budget Issue Brief*, Jan. 13, 2009.

[10] For an examination of the administrative costs of a VAT, see Sijbren Cnossen, "Administrative and Compliance Costs of the VAT: A Review of the Evidence," *Tax Notes*, vol. 62, no. 12, June 20, 1994, pp. 1,609-1,626.

[11] For a list of states with retail sales taxes and corresponding tax rates, see Tax Foundation, "2009 Facts & Figures: How Does Your State Compare?," available at http://www.taxfoundation.org/files/.

[12] The authors of a study of the Canadian VAT (goods and services tax) concluded that "the introduction of a federal VAT in the U.S. would not create any great technical problems for either the states or business." See Richard M. Bird, Jack M. Mintz, and Thomas A. Wilson, "Coordination Federal and Provincial Sales Taxes: Lessons from the Canadian Experience," *National Tax Journal*, vol. 49, no. 4, Dec. 2006, pp. 889-903.

[13] Cnossen, *VAT and RST: A Comparison*, pp. 609-611.

[14] Cnossen, *VAT and RST: A Comparison*, pp. 593-595.

[15] U.S. Government Accountability Office, *Value-Added Taxes: Lessons Learned from Other Countries on Compliance Risks, Administrative Costs, Compliance Burden, and Transition*, GAO-08-566, Apr. 2008, p. 5.

[16] Alan A. Tait, *Value-Added Tax: International Practice and Problems* (Washington, International Monetary Fund, 1988), pp. 409-416.

[17] Ibid., p. 357.

[18] Ibid.

[19] Cnossen, *VAT and RST: A Comparison*, p. 583.

[20] Cnossen, *VAT and RST: A Comparison*, p. 585 and OECD, *Consumption Tax Trends* (OECD, March 2005), p. 11.

[21] OECD, *International VAT/GST Guidelines* (OECD, Feb. 2006), p. 1. Available at http://www.oecd.org.

[22] For the most current information about pending legislation including copies of bills, please consult the Legislative Information System (LIS) at http://www.congress.gov.

[23] For an analysis of the Hall-Rabushka concept, see CRS Report 98-529, *Flat Tax: An Overview of the Hall-Rabushka Proposal*, by James M. Bickley.

In: Value-Added Tax (VAT) and Flat Tax Proposals
Editors: D. B. Andrews and A. M. Davis

ISBN: 978-1-61324-191-2
© 2011 Nova Science Publishers, Inc.

Chapter 3

TAXABLE BASE OF THE VALUE-ADDED TAX[*]

Maxim Shvedov

SUMMARY

The value-added tax (VAT) is a type of broad-based consumption tax, imposed in about 136 countries around the world. Domestically, it is often mentioned in policy discussions as a potential new or supplemental funding source for such large-scale social programs as Social Security, Medicare, national health insurance, etc. An example of such a proposal is H.R. 15. In addition, the VAT figures prominently in most fundamental tax reform discussions.

The key determinant of the VAT's revenue-raising potential is the size of its taxable base. This report estimates its size under two frequently used "generic" policy options: a broad-based VAT and a VAT with certain frequently mentioned exemptions. Under the assumption of the broad-based VAT, the potential revenue base could be equal to $8.8 trillion in 2008. Exempting certain expenditures, such as food, housing, healthcare, and others is estimated to reduce the taxable base to $5.1 trillion in 2008.

These estimates are likely to overstate the size of the taxable base under either scenario as they assume no behavioral responses and perfect compliance with the law. This report briefly discusses these and other important caveats and their implications for revenue projections and further policy analysis.

INTRODUCTION

Avalue-added tax (VAT) is a type of broad-based consumption tax, even though it is levied on a firm's value added at all stages of the production chain. The value added by a firm is the difference between the total value of the firm's sales and its purchases from all suppliers.

---

[*] This is an edited, reformatted and augmented version of Congressional Research Services publication RS22720, dated October 6, 2009.

About 136 countries around the world impose some form of the VAT.[1] There are several administratively different forms of the VAT, but the so called "credit method" is the most widely used. While different in form, all methods are economically equivalent to each other, but may vary in terms of simplicity, administrative costs, and compliance rates.

In the United States, the VAT is often mentioned in policy discussions as a potential new funding source for such large-scale social programs as Social Security, Medicare, national health insurance, etc. For example, Representative John Dingell introduced H.R. 15, which proposes levying a 5% VAT on most goods and services to pay for a national health care system. In addition, the VAT figures prominently in most fundamental tax reform discussions. This report estimates the size of the VAT's taxable base—the key factor determining the tax's revenue-raising potential—under two frequently considered, "generic" policy options.

OPTION 1. "GENERIC" BROAD-BASED VALUE-ADDED TAX

Conceptually, the VAT is a type of a consumption tax imposed on sales of goods and services, even though it is collected at all stages of the production chain. Thus, the VAT taxable base can be estimated as the value of all consumption spending taking place in the economy. Table 1 presents calculations of the broad-based consumption tax base.[2]

The size of the taxable base is estimated at $8.8 trillion ($8,772.5 billion) in 2008, using Bureau of Economic Analysis (BEA) data.[3] The largest contributor to the base, at $10.1 trillion ($10,129.9 billion), is "personal consumption expenditures" (PCE). Private real estate investments in owner-occupied structures add an estimated $318.0 billion of additional expenditures potentially subject to the VAT.

The deductions from the base include the imputed rental value of owner-occupied housing and farm dwellings ($1,186.8 billion and $24.9 billion, respectively). These are the amounts homeowners would have had to pay if they had rented an identical property from somebody else. It is easier to understand this concept by considering a homeowner in a dual capacity: an owner of the property and a tenant at the same property. The tenant-homeowner consumes housing services provided by himself or herself. BEA includes this value in PCE, because from an economic standpoint this transaction is no different from a regular "explicit" housing rental. No actual monetary exchange occurs in this case, however, and therefore, unlike a regular "explicit" housing rental, these hypothetical transactions would be non-taxable.

State sales taxes ($443.9 billion) are also deducted from the base, because presumably a VAT would be imposed on the price net of state sales taxes. PCE data report the amounts consumers pay including the state sales taxes. The estimate also accounts for "Net foreign travel"—a relatively small in size item, equal to the difference between expenditures in the United States by nonresidents and foreign travel spending by U.S. residents.

Table 1. Taxable Base for Broad-based VAT, 2008

Description	2008 (billions of dollars)
The sum of:	
Personal consumption expenditures (PCE)	10,129.9
Residential private fixed investment in owner-occupied structures	318.0
Owner-occupied nonfarm dwellings—space rent	-1,186.8
Rental value of farm dwellings	-24.9
Net foreign travel	-19.8
Sales taxes	-443.9
Taxable base of the broad-based VAT	8,772.5

Sources: Bureau of Economic Analysis data and CRS calculations.
Note: Totals may not add due to rounding.

This estimate has an important limitation: it does not incorporate the likely taxable base reduction triggered by changes in taxpayers' behavior. For example, taxpayers may choose to reduce or somehow rearrange their consumption, so that the value of transactions subject to the VAT would be smaller. This behavior, called tax avoidance, while legal, would reduce the size of the taxable base. Some other taxpayers may evade the VAT illegally. The reduction would likely be more pronounced if the VAT rate were higher. It would also depend on the comprehensiveness of the taxable base and other specifics of the law.

To make the estimate more realistic, it would be necessary to account for taxpayers' non-compliance and tax avoidance. In the absence of a specific proposal and historic data on the VAT in the United States, however, making reliable quantitative predictions about the magnitude of the taxable base reduction is problematic. International experiences range widely and therefore cannot serve as a proxy.

On the other hand, it would be reasonable to expect the size of the taxable base to grow with time roughly in proportion to nominal economic growth. The estimates in this report do not incorporate such growth. The rate of economic growth itself might also depend on the VAT's taxable base and rate, as well as on the eventual use of the collected revenues.

OPTION 2. VALUE-ADDED TAX WITH CERTAIN EXEMPTIONS

Another policy option would be a VAT with a narrower taxable base, which exempts, for example, food, medical care, housing, higher education, and religious and welfare activities.[4] In selecting the set of potential exemptions, CRS attempted to choose the most frequently proposed ones. Of course, any specific proposal does not have to incorporate all of them or might include some additional ones. For example, H.R. 15 sets forth exemptions for food, housing, medical care, exports, interest, governmental entities, and certain tax-exempt organizations.

Table 2 shows the estimated taxable base of this policy option. Given these exemptions, the VAT taxable base would be $5.1 trillion ($5,095.0 billion) in 2008, or about 58% of the above-estimated broad base.

Similar to the estimates of the previous section, non-compliance and tax avoidance would reduce the taxable base in this case as well. In addition, as exemptions add complexity to the tax system, the reduction in revenue might be somewhat more pronounced compared to the broad-based VAT.

In addition, the categories in Table 2 are quite broad. Depending on the implementation, exemptions from the VAT under the actual law might encompass less than the whole segment of the economy. For example, the housing exemption might apply only to owner-occupied housing, but not to the housing rental payments. If so, the VAT taxable base would be larger than this estimate indicates. On the other hand, if some additional categories, such as the financial sector, were excluded from the base, it would be smaller.

Table 2. The VAT Taxable Base After Certain Exemptions, 2008

Description	Taxable base, 2008 (billions of dollars)
Broad-based VAT taxable base	8,772.5
Exemptions:	
Food excluding alcoholic beverages	1,194.6
Health care	1,554.2
Housing (included in the broad base)	649.3
Higher education	135.0
Social services and religious activities	144.4
Total exemptions	3,677.5
Total after all exemptions	5,095.0

Note: Totals may not add due to rounding.
Sources: BEA data and CRS calculations.

REVENUE PROJECTION USING THESE ESTIMATES

Revenues from VAT would equal, as a first approximation, the VAT rate multiplied by the taxable base. There are, however, a number of issues that make revenue projection more complicated.

First, this simple calculation works reasonably well only for low VAT rates. As the rate gets higher, the discrepancy between this simple projection and the real revenue yield would likely grow due to various feedback effects. [5] In a more sophisticated analysis, the level of the VAT rate affects the size of the taxable base through economic agents' behavioral responses. Economic theory suggests that there would be some kind of a revenue-reducing response to imposition of the VAT, but its magnitude is highly speculative. Beyond the rate per se, it would depend to a great extent on specifics of the VAT's implementation.

Second, the estimates presented above are based on a single year of observation, 2008, and thus depend on the specific economic situation that year. For example, to the extent housing values were first above and then below their long-term trends in the last decade, the magnitude of all estimates involving housing would be above or below the trend, too.

Third, any revenue calculations should take into account the reduction in corporate income or other taxes that would likely occur after the imposition of the VAT. For example, the VAT would become an additional new cost of doing business for companies, which might reduce their profits. This, in turn, would reduce the corporate income tax revenues of the federal government. Thus the net revenue gain from imposing the VAT would be smaller due to this feedback effect.

Fourth, any revenue projections should also account for any transitional or cash-flow issues, which may be significant. There would also be some administrative costs involved.

Finally, estimates of the VAT taxable base size might serve as a starting point for calculating the taxable bases of other consumption taxes, such as a national retail sales tax. It is important to remember, however, that behavioral responses and other issues discussed in this section may be even more pronounced with national sales tax or other consumption taxes. Any analysis overlooking such feedback effects may yield a misleading picture of the revenue-raising potential of a tax.[6]

End Notes

[1] Organization for Economic Co-operation and Development, *International VAT/GST Guidelines* (OECD, Feb. 2006), p. 1, visited on Sept. 21, 2008, at http://www.oecd.org/dataoecd/16/36/36177871.pdf.

[2] The methodology follows, with modifications, Congressional Budget Office, *Reducing the Deficit: Spending and Revenue Options,* March 1997, p. 391.

[3] U.S. Department of Commerce, BEA, Table 3.3, *State and Local Government Current Receipts and Expenditures*, revised Aug. 27, 2009; and Tables 2.4.5, *Personal Consumption Expenditures by Type of Product*, and 5.4.5, *Private Fixed Investment in Structures by Type*, both revised Aug. 20, 2009, from http://www.bea.gov. BEA periodically revises its estimates after their initial publication, which frequently results in changes in the reported amounts, typically relatively small in magnitude.

[4] For examples of similar, but not identical, estimates see Congressional Budget Office, *Reducing the Deficit: Spending and Revenue Options,* March 1997, p. 391, or William G. Gale and C. Eugene Steuerle, "Tax Policy Solution," in Alice M. Rivlin and Isabel Sawhill, eds., *Restoring Fiscal Sanity—2005* (Washington: Brookings Institution Press, 2005), p. 113.

[5] Feedback effects reflect the fact that not only does the VAT taxable base depend on broad economic variables, such as consumption expenditures, but also broad economic variables in turn depend on the VAT and its parameters. For example, as a result of imposing the VAT, consumers might reduce their consumption expenditures. Feedback effects are present whenever a bi-directional causal relationship exists between any pair of variables.

[6] For an overview of the issues, please see CRS Report RL32603, *The Flat Tax, Value-Added Tax, and National Retail Sales Tax: Overview of the Issues*, by Jane G. Gravelle.

In: Value-Added Tax (VAT) and Flat Tax Proposals ISBN: 978-1-61324-191-2
Editors: D. B. Andrews and A. M. Davis © 2011 Nova Science Publishers, Inc.

Chapter 4

VALUE-ADDED TAXES: LESSONS LEARNED FROM OTHER COUNTRIES ON COMPLIANCE RISKS, ADMINISTRATIVE COSTS, COMPLIANCE BURDEN, AND TRANSITION[*]

United States Government Accountability Office

WHY GAO DID THIS STUDY

Dissatisfaction with the federal tax system has led to a debate about U.S. tax reform, including proposals for a national consumption tax. One type of proposed consumption tax is a value-added tax (VAT), widely used around the world. A VAT is levied on the difference between a business's sales and its purchases of goods and services. Typically, a business calculates the tax due on its sales, subtracts a credit for taxes paid on its purchases, and remits the difference to the government. While the economic and distributional effects of a U.S. VAT type tax have been studied, GAO was asked to identify the lessons learned from other countries' experiences in administering a VAT. This report describes (1) how VAT design choices, such as exemptions and enforcement mechanisms, have affected compliance, administrative costs, and compliance burden; (2) how countries with federal systems administer a VAT; and (3) how countries that recently transitioned to a VAT implemented the new tax.

GAO selected five countries to study—Australia, Canada, France, New Zealand, and the United Kingdom—that provided a range of VAT designs from relatively simple to more complex with multiple exemptions and tax rates. The study countries also included some with federal systems and some that recently implemented a VAT.

GAO does not make any recommendations in this report.

---

[*] This is an edited, reformatted and augmented version of United States Government Accountability Office's publication GAO-08-566, dated April 2008.

WHAT GAO FOUND

Like other tax systems, even a simple VAT—one that exempts few goods or services—has compliance risks and, largely as a consequence, generates administrative costs and compliance burden. For example, all of the study countries reported that they devoted significant enforcement resources to addressing compliance. Businesses whose taxable purchases exceed their taxable sales are entitled to a refund under a VAT, which makes VATs vulnerable to fraudsters creating phony invoices in order to falsely claim refunds. Also, similar to other taxes, adding complexity through exemptions of some goods or services and reduced tax rates generally decreases revenue and increases compliance risks because of the incentive to misclassify purchases and sales. Such complexity also increases the record-keeping burden on businesses and increases the government resources devoted to enforcement.

Canada's experience administering a national VAT along with a variety of provincial VATs and sales taxes demonstrates that multiple arrangements in a federal system are feasible, but increase administrative costs and compliance challenges for both the governments and businesses. Businesses, particularly retailers, in provinces with a sales tax face greater compliance burdens than those in other provinces because they are subject to dual reporting, filing, and remittance requirements.

Australia, Canada, and New Zealand, all with relatively new VATs, built on preexisting consumption tax administrative structures to implement the new tax. Nevertheless, they devoted considerable resources to educate, assist, and register businesses and implementation took from 15 to 24 months. Both Australia and Canada provided monetary assistance to qualifying small businesses to help meet new bookkeeping and reporting requirements. Despite their efforts, Australia and Canada had some difficulty getting businesses to register for the VAT by the implementation date.

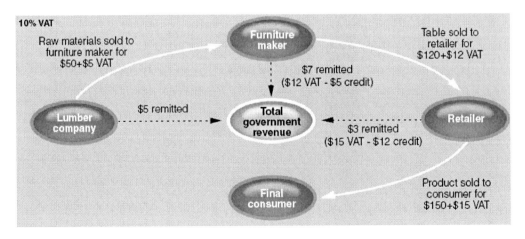

How a VAT Works.

Source: GAO.

April 4, 2008
The Honorable Jim McCrery
Ranking Member
Committee on Ways and Means
House of Representatives

The Honorable Jim Ramstad
Ranking Member
Subcommittee on Oversight
Committee on Ways and Means
House of Representatives

Concerns about our current income tax system have fueled a debate about fundamental tax reform in the United States. The debate is partly about whether to reform the current income tax, for example by broadening its base and lowering rates, or to switch to some form of a consumption tax. The concerns about our tax system include its economic inefficiency, unfairness, and complexity. In addition, issues have been raised about whether its design provides fertile ground for noncompliance, with an estimated annual gross tax gap of approximately $345 billion for tax year 2001, or 17 percent of federal revenue that year.

In recent years, a variety of tax reforms have been proposed for the United States. Some proposals involve switching to a consumption tax or combining a consumption tax with an income tax. One consumption tax that some have proposed is a value-added tax (VAT). Others have proposed consumption taxes with features similar to a VAT. For example the Department of the Treasury (Treasury) recently outlined a VAT-like tax, called a business activity tax, in a report that discussed alternatives to reform U.S. business taxation.[1]

A VAT is applied to the difference between a business's sales of goods and services and its purchases of goods and services (excluding wages), therefore taxing the value added by each business. Unlike retail sales taxes (RST), VATs are collected at all stages of production and distribution.

VATs have grown in popularity over the past five decades. Today, the United States is the only member of the Organization for Economic Cooperation and Development (OECD) without a VAT.[2] On average, VATs raise over 18 percent of government revenue in OECD countries that have a VAT. Worldwide, by one estimate, more than 130 countries have a VAT.

A VAT is a broad-based consumption tax. As such, it avoids some of the complications of an income tax, such as the need to define and compute depreciation and capital gains. Because VAT is remitted by businesses, it also avoids issues related to collecting taxes from individuals.

As a consumption tax, a VAT has different economic and distributional impacts than an income tax. Treasury, the Congressional Budget Office, and others have studied those impacts.[3] In addition, we reported in 1993 on the estimated cost that the Internal Revenue Service (IRS) and other federal agencies could be expected to incur if a simple VAT were added as a federal revenue source in the United States.[4] However, less has been reported in the United States on how other countries have designed their VATs, including tax rates, exemptions, filing requirements, and enforcement mechanisms, and how those design choices have affected businesses and tax administrators.[5]

You requested that we report on the important lessons learned from selected other countries' experiences administering a VAT. Our specific objectives were to describe for the selected countries (1) how VAT design choices have affected compliance, administrative costs, and compliance burden; (2) how countries with federal systems administer a VAT in conjunction with subnational consumption tax systems; and (3) how countries that recently transitioned to a VAT implemented the new tax.

We selected five countries—Australia, Canada, France, New Zealand, and the United Kingdom—to study based on several criteria, including the complexity of VAT design, the age of the VAT system, and whether the country had a federal system.[6] We used expert recommendations to help ensure a range of VAT designs in our five study countries. For all of the countries we studied, we performed an in-depth literature review, including government documents, OECD studies, and academic papers. We collected and analyzed data on the countries and their VAT systems, including VAT revenue trends, administrative and compliance activities and costs, and the size and distribution of economic activity within the study countries. To provide assurance that the data used in our report were sufficiently reliable, we used data from commonly used and cited sources of statistical data, such as the OECD, and from publicly available reports from international government agencies. We also discussed these data with OECD officials, government agency officials, and noted VAT experts in several professional services and research organizations. We interviewed knowledgeable government officials from the study countries, including officials from their tax administration agencies and the national audit institutions. We also interviewed VAT experts, including academic and private-sector tax experts and researchers at the OECD and the International Monetary Fund. In addition, we interviewed members of a number of professional services organizations that represent and serve businesses subject to VAT requirements. We provided the national audit institutions and the tax administration agencies of our study countries a copy of our report to verify data and specific factual and legal statements about the VAT in those countries. We made technical corrections to our report based on these reviews. A more detailed discussion of our methodology is in appendix I.

We do not make any recommendations in this report. We conducted this performance audit from December 2006 through April 2008 in accordance with generally accepted government auditing standards. Those standards require that we plan and perform the audit to obtain sufficient, appropriate evidence to provide a reasonable basis for our findings and conclusions based on our audit objectives. We believe that the evidence obtained provides a reasonable basis for our findings and conclusions based on our audit objectives.

RESULTS IN BRIEF

The experiences of our five study countries show that all VAT designs have compliance risks that generate considerable administrative costs and compliance burden and that, similar to the U.S. tax system, adding complexity to the tax's design increases these risks, costs, and burdens. While our study countries had VATs of varied designs and complexity, they all devoted significant enforcement resources to addressing compliance that would be found in even a simple VAT—one with a broad base that exempts few goods or services. These risks include refund fraud and missing trader fraud. VATs are vulnerable to refund fraud because businesses with taxable sales less than taxable purchases are entitled to refunds. All of our study countries were concerned about illegitimate businesses or fraudsters submitting fraudulent refund claims based on false paperwork that result in the theft of funds from the government. Missing traders set up businesses for the sole purpose of collecting VAT on sales and then disappear with the proceeds. Because of such compliance risks, even simple VATs require enforcement activities, such as audits, and record-keeping by businesses that create administrative costs for the government and compliance burden for businesses. Of course, compliance risks and the associated administrative costs and compliance burdens are not peculiar to VATs. While the specifics may vary, other types of taxes also carry compliance risks.

Some available data indicate a VAT may be less expensive to administer than an income tax. The tax administration agency in the United Kingdom measured administrative costs for the VAT to be 0.55 percent of revenue collected compared to 1.27 percent for income tax. Officials at the New Zealand Inland Revenue Department also told us that administering their VAT was easier than administering some of their other taxes. Adding complexity through exemptions, exclusions, and reduced rates, which can exist in other tax systems, generally decreases revenues and increases compliance risks, administrative costs, and compliance burden. All of our study countries do not fully include certain goods and services, such as food, health care, commercial property, and sales of religious and cultural services in the tax base for social, political, or administrative reasons. Two of our study countries, France and the United Kingdom, collected less than half of the revenue potentially collectible, due in part to preferential treatment of certain sectors and noncompliance. Adding complexity also increases the risk of noncompliance because of the incentive to avoid tax by misclassifying goods or services as exempt or excluded. For example, in Australia and Canada, where certain food items are not taxed, businesses need to accurately categorize their sales as taxable or nontaxable.

Canada's experience demonstrates that, while multiple consumption tax arrangements in a federal system are possible, such arrangements create additional administrative costs and compliance burden for governments and businesses. Canada is the only one of our study countries with multiple consumption tax systems across the provinces that include:

- separate federal and provincial VATs administered by a province (Québec),
- joint federal and provincial VATs administered by the federal government,
- separate federal VAT and provincial RSTs administered separately, and
- a federal VAT only.

Tax system complexity and compliance burden in Canada vary among provinces depending on the level of coordination between the provinces and the federal VAT. Businesses in provinces where the provincial and federal VATs tax the same goods and services and are administered by the federal government have less compliance burden since they only have to comply with one set of requirements.

Australia, Canada, and New Zealand, the study countries that most recently implemented a VAT, all built on preexisting administrative structures. All had national consumption taxes that were paid by businesses. Despite the preexisting structure, implementation of the new tax in these countries involved multiple agencies, the development of new policies and processes, and the hiring of additional staff. The countries took 15 to 24 months to implement the VAT with a great deal of time and effort devoted to education activities. For example, Australian officials said a key part of their education and outreach strategy was to target key players in various industry sectors, such as local chambers of commerce. Both Canada and Australia also provided direct monetary assistance to qualifying small businesses to defray the costs of acquiring the necessary supplies needed to meet new bookkeeping and reporting requirements. Despite significant efforts to encourage businesses to submit materials early for VAT registration, both Australia and Canada still had difficulty getting businesses to register prior to the VAT implementation date. In both countries, this resulted in significant spikes in registration and education-related workload just prior to implementation. In Canada, for example, only 500,000 or 31 percent of the 1.6 million total registrants had voluntarily registered 3 months prior to VAT implementation.

BACKGROUND

VATs are taxes levied on the difference between a business's sales of goods and services to consumers or other businesses and its purchases of goods and services. Thus, businesses pay tax on the value they add to the goods and services they purchase from other businesses. All types of businesses, not just retail businesses, are subject to the tax, and sales to both consumers and other businesses are taxable.

VAT liability is typically calculated in industrialized countries using the credit-invoice method.[7] Businesses apply the VAT rate to their sales but claim a credit for VAT paid on purchases of inputs from other businesses (shown on purchase invoices). The difference between the VAT collected on sales and the credit for VAT paid on input purchases is remitted to the government.

Figure 1 illustrates a VAT with a 10 percent rate. A lumber company cuts and mills trees and has sales of $50 to a furniture maker. Assuming no input purchases from other businesses to keep the illustration simple, the company adds the tax to the price of the goods sold and remits $5 in tax to the government. The purchase invoice received by the furniture maker would list $50 in purchases plus $5 in VAT paid.

If the furniture maker has sales of $120 to a retail store, $12 of VAT would be added to the sales price but the furniture maker could subtract a credit for the $5 VAT paid on purchases and remit $7 to the government. The retailer would receive an invoice showing purchases of $120 and $12 of VAT.

Similarly, if the retailer then has sales of $150, $15 of VAT would be added but the retailer could subtract a credit for the $12 paid on purchases and remit $3 to the government.

In total, the government would receive VAT equal to 10 percent of the final sales price to consumers. Thus, a 10 percent VAT is equivalent to a 10 percent RST in terms of revenue. Figure 2 illustrates a RST. Under both taxes, the final consumer ultimately bears the economic burden of the tax ($15).

A major distinction between these two types of consumption taxes is the number of businesses responsible for collecting and remitting tax. A VAT widens the number of businesses collecting and remitting the tax. However, unlike a RST, businesses do not have to verify the status of the customer as either a business or a final consumer.

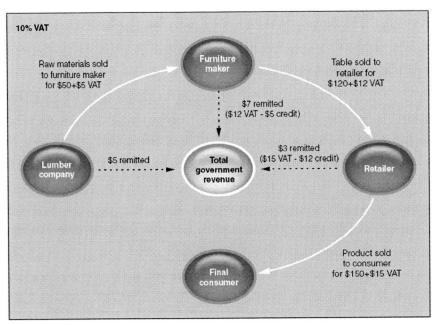

Source: GAO.

Figure 1. Example of How a VAT Works.

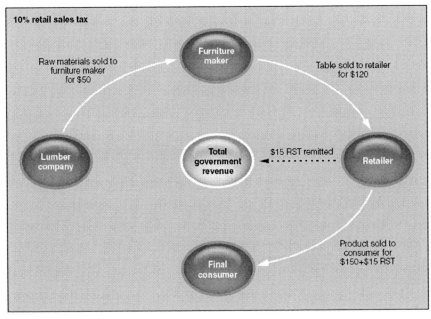

Source: GAO.

Figure 2. Example of How a RST Works.

Consumption taxes can be administered in a number of different ways—as the previous examples of a VAT and RST demonstrate—but are intended to tax expenditures on goods and services rather than total income.[8] The part of a final consumer's income that is saved is not subject to current taxation under a consumption tax.

Spread of VAT Around the World

A VAT was developed and first introduced in France in 1954.[9] According to an estimate by the OECD, a VAT is now imposed in approximately 136 countries, including every OECD country except the United States. Every OECD country that imposes a VAT also has income taxes.

VATs provide a significant amount of revenue. For example, in 2003, VAT revenues accounted for approximately 18 percent of total tax revenues collected in OECD countries with a VAT. As figure 3 shows, 2005 tax revenues from a VAT range from just over 10 percent in Canada to more than 23 percent in New Zealand. However, personal and corporate income taxes account for a larger percentage of total revenues than a VAT in all of the study countries.

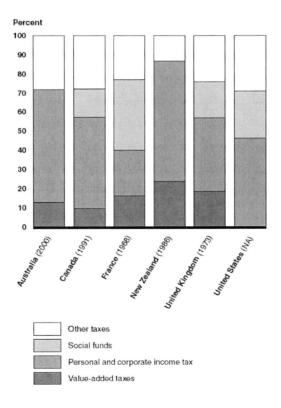

Source: OECD.
Note: The "other taxes" category is comprised of various federal, state, and local government taxes that vary in nature and relevant magnitude from country to country. For example, in the case of the United States, this includes excise taxes, property taxes, use taxes, and state and local sales taxes.

Figure 3. Revenues by Tax Type in Selected OECD Countries (2005) and Year of VAT Introduction.

The Current U.S. Tax System

The current federal tax system in the United States consists primarily of five types of taxes: (1) personal income taxes; (2) corporate income taxes; (3) social insurance taxes (employee and employer contributions for Social Security, Medicare, and unemployment compensation); (4) estate and gift taxes; and (5) other taxes such as excise taxes on selected goods and services including fuel, tobacco, alcohol, and firearms. At the state and local levels, the important taxes are income, retail sales, and Estimates of the total burden placed on businesses to comply with these taxes are uncertain because neither the government nor businesses maintain regular accounts of these costs and many important elements of the costs are difficult to measure because, among other things, federal tax requirements often overlap with recordkeeping and reporting that businesses do for other purposes. However, based on a review of studies by others, we reported that individual and corporate compliance costs are approximately 1 percent of gross domestic product (GDP) when using the lowest available and incomplete estimates. Other studies estimate the costs to be as high as 1.5 percent of GDP.[10]

IRS estimates the gross tax gap—the difference between what taxpayers actually paid and what they should have paid on a timely basis—to be $345 billion for tax year 2001. IRS also estimates that it will collect $55 billion, leaving a net tax gap of $290 billion.

IRS's budget for fiscal year 2008 is $10.9 billion. In administering the tax laws, IRS's two main functions are to provide (1) service to individual and business taxpayers—including responding to telephone queries and providing Web services, and (2) enforcement activities—including examinations and collections. Major examination efforts include computerized matching of third-party information with tax returns as well as audits.

Criteria for Evaluating Tax Systems

In a 2005 report, we describe the criteria typically used for evaluating tax systems as (1) equity; (2) economic efficiency; and (3) simplicity, transparency, and administrability. [11] A tax system is generally considered better than alternatives that raise the same amount of revenue if it is more equitable, more economically efficient, simpler for taxpayers to comply with, and easier and less costly to administer. Designing a tax system that is superior on each of these criteria is difficult because the criteria frequently conflict with one another and trade-offs often must be made. For example, a tax system that provides credits to low-income individuals may be judged by some to be more equitable than a system without this feature. However, if including credits makes it necessary for more individuals to calculate their income and file tax returns, the tax system could become more complex, thus decreasing its transparency to taxpayers and increasing the costs of administration. As noted earlier, in this report we focus on the third of the above criteria.

LIKE OTHER TAXES, VATS HAVE COMPLIANCE RISKS, ADMINISTRATIVE COSTS, AND COMPLIANCE BURDEN THAT INCREASE WITH THE COMPLEXITY OF THE DESIGN

VAT design choices include whether to exempt specific goods and services such as real estate and health care and specific entities such as small businesses, nonprofits, and governments from tax. Such design choices generally result in decreased tax revenue and increased compliance risks.

A Conceptually Simple VAT Design Has Compliance Risks and Generates Significant Administrative Costs and Compliance Burden

Our study countries' experiences with noncompliance suggest that even a conceptually simple VAT would have compliance risks and would generate significant administrative costs and compliance burden. A conceptually simple VAT would have a single rate that applies to all goods and services and is outlined in table 1.[12]

Table 1. Elements of a Conceptually Simple VAT System

Element	Definition
Single tax rate	One rate applies to the tax base.
Broad, nonexclusionary tax base	All goods and services are subject to the VAT, including financial transactions and real estate.
All business, government, and nonprofit entities are taxed	All entities are subject to paying VAT on purchases and required to charge VAT on qualifying sales of goods and services.
Destination principle	Goods and services are subject to taxation in the jurisdiction in which they are consumed. Therefore, importsare subject to VAT in the importing country, and exports are excluded from the domestic tax base.
Credit-invoice mechanism	Tax calculations are based on valid invoices and sales receipts for each transaction by subtracting the taxes paidon all input purchases from taxes collected on all output sales.

Source: GAO analysis.

Compliance Risks

All of the countries we studied faced compliance risks that are associated with the elements of a conceptually simple VAT. Compliance risks for a VAT can stem from either underpayment of taxes owed on sales, or overstating taxes paid on purchases.[13] Table 2 shows major types of VAT compliance risks for a conceptually simple VAT. Although the countries we studied had VATs that varied in complexity and consequently faced a range of additional compliance risks, they all reported that addressing risks outlined in table 2 is an important part of their overall compliance efforts.

Value-Added Taxes   61

Table 2. Major Types of Compliance Risks in a Conceptually Simple VAT System

Compliance risks			
Undercollection of tax due on sales		Overclaiming of tax paid on inputs	
Missing trader fraud	A business is created for purposes of collecting VAT on sales and disappears without remitting VAT to the government.	Fraudulent refunds	A business or fraudster submits false returns requesting VAT refundsfrom the government.
Failed businesses	A business fails or goes bankrupt before remitting VAT collected to the government.	Misclassifying purchases	A business falsely claims input tax credits by misclassifying personal consumption expenses as business expenses.
Underreporting cash transactions	A business either charges a lower, VAT-free price for cash transactions or underreports cash sales and retains VAT collected.	Fictitious or altered invoices	A business creates or alters invoices to inflate the amount of input tax credits they can claim.
Import fraud	A business or individual imports items for personal consumption and under values them for VAT purposes.	Export fraud	A business creates fraudulent export invoices for goods that are not exported to claiminput tax credits.

Source: GAO analysis.

The VAT compliance risks in table 2 are shared to varying extents with an income tax or RST. For example, underreporting cash transactions is a compliance issue for the income tax and RST in the United States. Similarly, failed businesses can be a problem if income tax payroll withholdings or RST collected on sales are used to finance business operations rather than being remitted to the government before the business fails.

A VAT's reliance on credits and refunds makes the tax more susceptible than an income tax or RST to the compliance risks of fraudulent refund claims. Fraudulent refund claims could exist under a conceptually simple VAT and are a particular concern for all of our study countries. Businesses in the position of paying more VAT on purchases than they receive through sales are entitled to a refund. Businesses in a legitimate refund position tend to be start-up companies or exporters, neither of whom may have taxable sales. All of our study countries were concerned that illegitimate businesses or fraudsters submitting fraudulent refund claims could result in theft of funds from the treasury through false paperwork. Because of the significance of this threat, our study countries reported that auditing refund claims is an important enforcement activity.

Missing trader fraud would be another problem under a conceptually simple VAT and was another common compliance issue for our study countries. Missing trader fraud is a challenge in a VAT because fraudsters may set up a business for the sole purpose of collecting VAT on sales and then disappear with the proceeds. When a missing trader walks away with the proceeds, the buyer still has an input tax invoice showing VAT paid and is entitled to an input credit. In some countries, imports are particularly susceptible to missing trader fraud, which is discussed in more detail in appendix V in the context of challenges of carousel fraud in the European Union.[14]

VATs avoid some of the compliance risks of other tax systems. For example, under a RST, sellers must determine whether the buyer is a taxable consumer or has a valid exemption certificate. Improper or fraudulent use of these certificates reduces RST revenue.

62   United States Government Accountability Office

Under an income tax, businesses must comply with complex depreciation rules, which can result in misclassification of assets and tax calculation errors.

Administrative Costs

The drivers of administrative costs in many tax systems include the number of taxpayers (businesses, individuals, or both) subject to the tax, how often they file returns, and the percentage of taxpayers audited. In the case of a VAT, administration requires the government to process tax returns and provide certain services to businesses. Even a simple VAT warrants education and assistance services, in part, to address compliance risks. Tax administrators also need to spend significant resources on audit and enforcement activities. We estimated in a 1993 report that over 70 percent of annual administrative costs for a VAT would be compliancerelated.[15]

Additionally, even in the case of a conceptually simple VAT, a mechanism is needed to assess VAT on imports as they enter the country. In the case of New Zealand, 62 percent of total customs revenue in 2006-2007 was expected to come from VAT on imports. In all of our study countries, the agency responsible for monitoring trade border activity was also responsible for collecting VAT on imports. With the exception of the United Kingdom, this agency was not part of the tax administration agency.

Some data indicate that a VAT may be less expensive to administer than an income tax. HM Revenue & Customs (HMRC) in the United Kingdom estimated in 2006 that collection costs for the VAT were approximately 0.55 percent of revenue collected, compared to 1.27 percent for income tax collection costs. According to European Commission officials, VATs in Europe cost between 0.5 percent and 1 percent of VAT revenue collected to administer. In addition, officials at the New Zealand Inland Revenue Department (IRD) told us that administering their VAT has been easier than administering some of their other taxes, including their income tax. For example, only 3 percent of VAT returns are submitted to IRD with errors that require IRD intervention, compared to approximately 25 percent for income tax returns.

Compliance Burden

Under a VAT, as with other taxes, compliance burden is mostly driven by record-keeping requirements, filing frequency requirements, and time and resources to deal with audits. Three studies conducted between 1986 and 1992, the most comparable studies we identified, estimated that compliance burden as a percentage of annual sales by size of business in Canada, New Zealand, and the United Kingdom ranged from approximately 2 percent for businesses with less than $50,000 in sales to as low as 0.04 percent for businesses with over $1,000,000 in sales. The 'fixed cost' nature of many compliance costs associated with a VAT and ensuing economies of scale—whereby average costs fall as business size increases— means that smaller businesses often face a proportionally higher burden than larger businesses in complying with the VAT. Private accounting and tax professionals we spoke with also agreed that as the size of the business grows, the VAT compliance burden decreases per dollar of sales.

Businesses that operate in multiple countries face additional burden, as they would need to understand the rules and rates in each of the countries where they operate. Even if multiple countries had conceptually simple VATs, they would likely have different VAT rates, forms, and rules for remitting VAT to tax authorities. For example, businesses in the European

Union may operate in multiple member countries, and therefore would need to register with each relevant tax authority to collect and remit the VAT, increasing compliance burden.

Preventing fraudulent VAT refunds presents a trade-off between minimizing compliance burden and minimizing the risk of issuing a fraudulent refund. Although the risk of fraudulent refunds can be reduced by allowing tax inspectors more time to verify the validity of VAT refunds, legitimate businesses suffer financially if their VAT refunds are delayed. Businesses can face a competitive disadvantage and cash flow difficulties if valid VAT refunds are not paid promptly. In the countries we studied, tax administrators had a service standard for a specified number of days to process and pay VAT refunds before they were required to pay the business interest on the refund request. Some examples are shown in table 3.

Table 3. VAT Refund Timing and Performance for Three OECD Countries

	Australia[a]	Canada[b]	New Zealand[b]
Days allowed for returns and refund processing	14	21	15
Percent of refunds processed on time	93.6	98	96.2

Sources: Australian Taxation Office; Canada Revenue Agency; New Zealand Inland Revenue Department.

[a] Data are from tax years 2006-2007.

[b] Data are from tax years 2005-2006.

The compliance burden on businesses may be partially offset by certain features of a VAT. Businesses that usually operate in a net debit position, meaning they remit VAT to the government at each reporting period, have cash flow benefits for the period of time between VAT collection and remittance. A 1994 study by the National Audit Office in the United Kingdom estimated that the cash flow benefit of the VAT reduced the overall gross compliance burden by almost 40 percent. Some VAT experts have also suggested that VAT requirements can have a positive effect on small businesses by forcing the businesses to improve their internal accounting and record-keeping.

Adding Complexity through VAT Preferences, Including Exemptions, Exclusions, and Reduced Rates for Goods and Services, Decreases Revenue and Generally Increases Compliance Risks, Administrative Costs, and Compliance Burden

All of the countries we studied have added complexity to their VAT designs, mainly through the use of tax preferences. Tax preferences—also called tax expenditures—result in foregone tax revenue due to preferential provisions that generally shrink the tax base. Such preferences can also exist in other tax systems, such as income taxes or RSTs. Countries' use of preferences—such as exemptions and reduced rates— generally results in reduced revenue and greater compliance risks, administrative costs, and compliance burden.[16] However, some preferences, such as thresholds for businesses, may not increase administrative costs and compliance burden because they reduce the number of entities subject to VAT requirements.

Table 4. VAT Design Choices and Their Use in Study Countries

Design choice		Definition	Australia	Canada	France	Study country use of design choices[a]	
						New Zealand	UnitedKingdom
Tax base	Exempt good or service (input taxed)	Exempt goods and services are not charged VAT when sold. Businesses that sell exempt goods or services neither collect VAT on the sale nor recover VAT paid on inputs.	5categories Example:Residential rent	16 Example:Legal aid	18 Example: Hospital and medical care	4 Example:Donated goods and services sold by a nonprofit organization	21 Example:Education
	Exclude good or service (zero-rate or tax free)	Zero-rated goods are wholly excluded from the tax base. Businesses apply a zero rate to the sale of the good or service and reclaim VAT paid on inputs.	13categories Example:Child care	7 Example:Basic groceries	0	4 Example:Certain sales of gold, silver, or platinum	13 Example:Children'sclothing
	Exempt businesses (thresholds)	Thresholds are a minimum level of sales activity a business can generate before being required to collect and remit the VAT. In practice, thresholds exempt smaller businesses from the VAT system.	A$75,000[b]	Can$30,000	€76,300	NZ$40,000	£64,000
			$53,426 USD[c]	$24,406	$85,995	$27,038	$103,243
Tax rate	Multiple tax rates	Multiple tax rates include a standard rate and one or more other non-zero rates that are applied to specific goods or services. Typically higher rates are typically applied to luxuries and reduced rates are often applied to necessities.	10% standard rate	5%	19.6%	12.5%	17.5%
			N/A reduced rates	N/A	5.5% 2%	7.5%[d]	5%

Sources: OECD, GAO analysis.

[a] For a list of which goods and services are subject to exemption, zero rating or reduced rating, see appendix II.

[b] The thresholds listed are the standard threshold for each country as of January 1, 2008 and are expressed in each country's domestic currency. Some countries have other thresholds that apply to specific types of organizations, such as nonprofit organizations.

[c] Thresholds shown in 2008 U.S. dollars were calculated using purchasing power parity conversion rates.

[d] Long-term stays in a commercial dwelling, such as a hotel or nursing home, are taxed at the standard rate on 60 percent of the total sale, making an effective reduced rate of 7.5 percent.

Additionally, in most study countries, certain financial services and real estate transactions are exempt for administrative purposes. Table 4 describes some VAT design choices and their application in our five study countries.

An exempt good or service is not taxed when sold and businesses that sell exempt goods or services cannot claim input tax credits for inputs used in producing the exempt output. By exempting a good or service, the government still collects tax revenue throughout the other stages of production because only the exempt sale is not taxed. Tax is paid and collected on inputs. On the other hand, excluding a good or service, more commonly referred to as zero rating, removes it from the tax base by charging an effective tax rate of zero on the final sale to the consumer. For goods and services that are zero-rated, VAT that was paid in the production of a good or service that is not subject to VAT when sold to the final consumer can be fully recovered through input tax credits. As a consequence, no net VAT revenue is actually collected by the government from the sale of zero-rated goods and services.

A threshold is a type of exemption that excludes certain businesses from collecting and remitting the VAT and from being able to claim input tax credits. Businesses with sales below the threshold do not charge VAT on their sales and do not claim input tax credits for VAT paid on purchases. Businesses with annual sales above the threshold level are required to register with the tax agency, and collect and remit the VAT.

Countries Vary in the Application of VAT to Specific Sectors, Including Food, Health Care, the Public Sector, Financial Services, and Real Estate

In our study countries, some economic sectors, such as certain consumer essentials like food and health care and public sector organizations are often provided VAT preferences because of social or political considerations. Other sectors, such as financial services, insurance, and real estate, are provided exemptions or exclusions because they are inherently hard to tax under a VAT system. Tables 5 through 9 show how each of our study countries has applied a VAT to various economic sectors.

Table 5. VAT Treatment of Select Consumer Essentials—Food and Health Care

	Australia	Canada	France	New Zealand	United Kingdom
Food	Basic and unprocessed food is zero-rated.	Basic groceries are zero-rated.	Most food and nonalcoholic beverages are taxed at the reduced rate of 5.5%.	Food is taxed at the standard rate of 12.5%.	Food is zero-rated.
Health Care	Most health care is zero-rated.	Medicines and medical devices are zero-rated. Medical and hospital care are exempt.	Medicines are subject to a reduced rate of either 5.5% or 2.1%. Medical and hospital care are exempt.	Health care is taxed at the standard rate of 12.5%.	Prescription drugs and medicines are zero-rated. Medical and hospital care are exempt.

Sources: OECD, GAO Analysis.

Table 6. VAT Treatment of Public Sector, Nonprofit, and Charitable Entities for Selected Countries

Australia	Canada	France	New Zealand	United Kingdom
Public sector entities (including subnational governments)				
VAT treatment of goods and services is the same as the private sector.	Partial exemptions applied depending on goods and services supplied. Subnational governments are granted a full to partial rebate of input taxes paid on exempt sales depending on the type of organization.[a]	Complex rules apply when determining whether certain goods or services are taxable or exempt when provided by the public sector.[b]VAT rules in EU countries must follow the VAT 6th Council Directive.[c] Partial rebates of input taxes paid on certain exempt activities.	VAT treatment of goods and services is the same as private sector.	Complex rules apply when determining whether certain goodsor services are taxable or exempt when provided by the public sector.[b]VAT rules in EU countries must follow the VAT 6th Council Directive.[c] Local authorities eligible for rebates on certain exempt activities.
Nonprofit and charitable organizations				
VAT treatment of goods and services is the same as the private sector. Subject to a special registration threshold of A$150,000 (US$106,853). Certain activities, such as sale of donated or undervalued goods and services, are zero-rated.	Partial exemptions applied depending on goods and services supplied. Subject to a special registration threshold of Can$50,000 (US$40,676). Qualifying organizations are entitled to a 50 percent rebate for input VAT for exempt activities.[a]	Exemptions granted for certain goods and services such as health care and education.	VAT treatment of goods and services is the same as the private sector. Certain activities, such as sale of donated or undervalued goods and services, are exempt.	Exemptions granted for certain goods and services such as health care and education.

Source: GAO analysis of information from selected countries and academic research.

[a] Canada's treatment of the public sector and nonprofits is similar to that of Australia and New Zealand; however, unlike those countries Canada exempts large sectors of the economy, such as health care and education. It provides rebates to certain subnational and nonprofit entities to offset some of the VAT paid on goods and services purchased to provide these exempt activities.

[b] Public bodies are required to charge VAT on business sales, which are sales that are determined to be competing with the private sector. According to Schenk, Oldman, *Value Added Tax: A Comparative* Approach, 2007, and Note from the *National Audit Office of the United Kingdom: Value-added Tax in the Public Sector* much of the complexity in applying VAT to the public sector in EU countries occurs when differentiating between business and nonbusiness activities of public sector entities.

[c] State, regional and local government authorities in EU countries do not charge VAT on their supplies of goods and services, except where it would lead to significant distortions of competition, or when the government carries out certain specified activities such as the supply of telecommunication services.

According to some VAT experts we spoke with, consumer essentials, such as food and health care, are often provided VAT preferences for social policy reasons. Study country data indicate that zero-rating basic groceries and food reduced VAT revenues by approximately 11 percent in Canada and 12 percent in the United Kingdom in 2004. Another way Canada offsets the burden of the VAT on low-income households is through rebates that are administered through the income tax system, whereby individuals or families with income that falls within certain limits receive quarterly payments aimed at relieving their overall VAT burden.

In many cases, the goods and services supplied by public sector, nonprofit, and charitable organizations are treated as final consumption by the organization itself rather than consumption by consumers. Consequently, these entities often charge no VAT on outputs but pay VAT on purchases. As described below, the treatment is sometimes due to the lack of a transaction and sometimes because of choices to exclude socially desirable goods or services from tax. The activities of all these entities can, typically, be placed in one of the three following categories:

Transfer payments redistribute income and wealth. Such transfers do not involve a sales transaction, and therefore, do not constitute a taxable supply of a good or service. However, public sector or nonprofit organizations that manage these transfer mechanisms would, absent a VAT preference, pay VAT on their acquisition of taxed goods and services.

Provision of goods and services that is not transaction-based often occurs when it is difficult or impossible to measure consumption by the individual. Examples of these types of goods and services include national defense, street lighting, and environmental protection. Like transfer payments, the purchases made to produce these goods and services are measurable and would be subject to VAT, absent VAT preferences.

Provision of goods and services that is transaction-based includes toll roads, libraries, museums (when entrance fees are charged), electric and water utilities, postal services, and health care and education services. In some cases, such goods and services may not be taxed because they are seen as socially desirable. In other cases, they may be taxed in order to avoid unfair competition with other entities.

The study countries differ in how they treat the public sector under the VAT. For example, France and the United Kingdom exempt governments, taxing only those activities that are in direct competition with commercial businesses. They apply the basic rule that if the activity is taxable when it is provided by private firms, it should similarly be taxable when provided by governmental units. New Zealand and Australia, on the other hand, tax the purchase and sale of all goods and services by governments, unless explicitly exempted or zero-rated.

There are some differences in how the study countries treat the nonprofit sector under the VAT. Unlike Australia and New Zealand, Canada, France, and the United Kingdom exempt certain goods and services that nonprofit organizations often provide such as education and health care. Therefore, these organizations must pay VAT on purchases but are unable to charge VAT on sales. A rebate mechanism is used in Canada, through which qualifying organizations recoup fifty percent of the VAT paid on purchases used to produce exempt goods ands services. For additional specific examples of Australia and Canada's treatment of government entities and nonprofit organizations, see appendix III.

Financial services and insurance are generally considered hard to tax because it is difficult to distinguish between the provision of a service (consumption) and return on investment. For example, deposits represent deferred consumption and interest earned on a deposit account is generally considered return on investment, not consumption.[17] The intermediary services of a bank are consumed and should be subject to VAT; however, there is often no explicit charge for the financial intermediation services that are provided. Instead, banks often pay depositors less interest than they charge borrowers and the difference covers the cost of the intermediation service. Some of the countries studied exempt financial services and have apportionment method guidelines for banks to recover some of the VAT paid on inputs. New Zealand allows zero rating of business-to-business financial services. The United Kingdom estimated the exemption of financial services and insurance reduced net VAT revenues collected by approximately 5 percent in 2006. For additional information about financial services and insurance, see appendix IV.

Table 7. VAT Treatment of Financial Services and Insurance

	Australia	Canada	France	New Zealand	United Kingdom
Financial services	Financial services are exempt. Australia has apportionment guidance for banks.	Financial services are exempt. Canada has proposed apportionment guidance for banks. Québec's provincial VAT zero rates financial services.	Financial services are exempt.	Certain business-to-business financial transactions are zero-rated. Other financial services are exempt. New Zealand has apportionment guidance for banks.	Financial servicesare exempt.
Insurance and reinsurance	Insurance and reinsurance are taxed at the standard rate of 10%, except health and life insurance which are zero-rated.	Insurance and reinsurance are exempt.	Insurance and reinsurance are exempt.	Life insurance and reinsurance are exempt. All other insurance policies are taxed at the standard rate of 12.5%.	Insurance and reinsurance are exempt.

Source: OECD, and GAO analysis.

[a]Apportionment guidance for banks and other financial services firms by tax authorities are usually approved methodologies for calculating the portion of the bank's or financial services firm's total input taxes paid that they can claim as credits.

Real estate, like other long-lived assets, is considered hard to tax under a VAT. Long-lived assets, such as residential housing, are a mix of consumption, as the residence is currently lived in, and savings, as the residence provides future housing consumption. Since consumption occurs over many years, taxing the full price of a new house would amount to taxing the present value of the stream of future housing services the house will provide. Consequently, taxing the full price of future sales of existing residential houses without providing input tax credits to homeowners would result in double taxation on the house. In such a situation, exempting the sale of existing residential property would not be a tax preference under a VAT.

Value-Added Taxes: Lessons Learned from Other Countries...   69

Table 8. VAT Treatment of Real Estate

	Australia	Canada	France	New Zealand	United Kingdom
Commercial property	Sales and leases of commercial property are taxed at the standard rate of 10%.	Sales and leases of commercial property are taxed at the standard rate of 5%.	Leases of commercial property are taxed at the standard rate of 19.6%. Sales of commercial property are exempt.	Sales and leases of commercial property are taxed at the standard rate of 12.5%.	Newly constructed commercial property is taxed at the standard rateof 17.5% for the first 3years from completion date. Sales and leases of existing commercial property are exempt, but the supplier retains the option to tax.
Residential property	Newly constructed residential property is taxed at the standard rate of 10%. Sales and leases of existing residential property are exempt.	Newly constructed or substantially renovated residential property is taxed at the standard rate of 5%. Sales and leases of existing residential property are exempt.	Sales of existing residential property are exempt. Sales of newly constructed (in past 5 years) or substantially renovated residential property are taxed at the standard rate of 19.6%. Leases of residential property are mostly exempt.	Leases of residential property are exempt. Sales of residential property by registered entities are taxed at the standard rate of 12.5%.	Sales of residential property are zero-rated. Leases of residential property are exempt.

Source: OECD, and GAO analysis.

Table 9. VAT Treatment of Select Socially Desirable Goods and Services

	Australia	Canada	France	New Zealand	United Kingdom
Books	Books are taxed at the standard rate of 10%.	Books are taxed at the standard rate of 5%. (The Québec provincial VAT effectively zero rates books.)	Books are subject to a reduced rate of 5.5%.	Books are taxed at the standard rate of 12.5%.	Books are zero-rated.
Fee-for - service cultural and religious services	Cultural services are taxed at the standard rate of 10%, with the exception of religious services which are zero-rated.	Cultural and religious services are exempt.	Cultural and religious services are exempt.	Cultural and religious services are taxed at the standard rate of 12.5%.	Cultural and religious services provided by publicand nonprofit organizations are generally exempt.

Source: OECD, and GAO analysis.

Tax administrators and tax professionals we spoke with in Australia and New Zealand told us that they face compliance challenges with real estate transactions because the rules are complex and some businesses are unfamiliar with them, as real estate transactions are not a part of their normal business operations. A particular challenge arises with dual use properties, such as a building with both commercial and residential space, that are subject to different sets of VAT rules. According to IRD officials in New Zealand, one quarter of all tax and VAT discrepancies involving small and medium businesses in 2007 arose from property transactions. For additional information on real estate, see appendix IV.

Similar to preferences in an income tax that are intended to promote certain activities, countries can exempt, exclude, or subject to a reduced rate goods and services that are deemed socially desirable. New Zealand does not exempt or zero rate cultural services, including religious services, but often these services do not involve sales and, therefore, no VAT would be charged.

Tax Preferences Decrease VAT Revenue in the Study Countries

One measure of VAT performance being developed by the OECD is the C-efficiency ratio (CER). The CER is expressed as a percentage and is calculated by dividing total VAT revenues by national consumption times the standard rate for each country. The CER provides an indication of how much of potential VAT revenue is actually collected, so it reflects the extent to which both tax preferences and noncompliance reduce the efficiency. A high CER is usually indicative of a VAT with few preferences and high compliance, while a low CER usually suggests an erosion of the tax base through some combination of preferences and low rates of compliance. Figure 4 shows the CERs for our five study countries and the average among OECD countries.

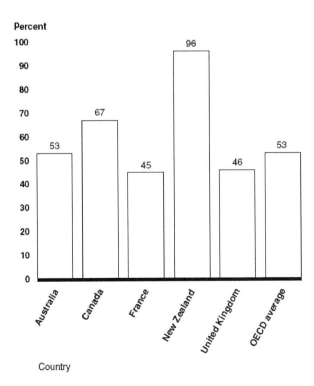

Source: OECD.

Figure 4. C-Efficiency Ratios of Five Study Countries and the Average for OECD Countries.

Of all of Canada's and the United Kingdom's tax preferences, zero rating basic groceries and food have had the largest impacts on VAT revenues, and therefore the CER. For example, in 2004-2005, zero rating food in the United Kingdom cost approximately £10.2 billion, representing a reduction of 12 percent in total VAT revenue collected that year. In Canada, zero rating basic groceries in 2004 was estimated to cost approximately Can$3.7 billion, reducing VAT revenues by approximately 11.3 percent that year. New Zealand's CER is higher than average likely due to the VAT's broad base and few tax preferences. Although tax preferences are a large contributing factor to the CER, the CER should be viewed with caution as other factors contribute to the overall calculation, primarily revenue loss from noncompliance. Furthermore, not all VAT preferences negatively impact the CER. For example, although exemptions generally decrease the CER by decreasing the tax base, the CER may increase due to tax cascading from exemptions, which increases overall VAT revenue collection.

VAT Preferences for Goods and Services Generally Increase Compliance Risks, Administrative Costs, and Compliance Burden

Although we were not able to find any direct quantitative evidence of how VAT complexity impacts administrative costs, tax officials and VAT experts said that complexity increases administrative costs and compliance burden and creates opportunities for noncompliance. VAT preferences introduce rules that apply only to a specific set of goods or services. Such preferences create the need to define the boundaries between goods and services getting different tax treatments, and may result in businesses misclassifying certain goods or services purchased or sold and reducing VAT revenue. Preferences that add complexity to the tax code also increase the time and resources needed for audits and education activities. Exemptions, reduced rates, and zero-rating also add to compliance burden by increasing the time and resources businesses must spend on accounting and record-keeping activities, in order to categorize their sales and purchases as fully taxable, reduced rated, zero-rated, or exempt. In the case of a business making both taxable and exempt sales, the business must also apportion its use of inputs and claim input tax credits only for inputs in taxable sales.

In Canada, basic groceries are zero-rated. Basic groceries include unflavored milk, bread, and other nonprepared foods, but do not include items such as snacks. These distinctions between goods are not always intuitive. Changes in ingredients, packaging, and temperatures can lead to different VAT treatment. In Canada salted peanuts are taxable and plain peanuts are zero-rated. The sale of five or fewer donuts in a single transaction is taxable, but the sale of six or more is zero-rated. In Australia takeout food is taxable if it is served as a single item for consumption away from the place of purchase. However, hot fresh bread is not subject to VAT unless it has a sweet filling or coating, or is sold in combination, such as sausage and onion on a slice of bread. Businesses that sell groceries have the additional burden of correctly categorizing their sales and face the compliance risk of charging the wrong VAT rate on their sales. The Australian Taxation Office and Canada Revenue Agency spend administrative resources on maintaining the list of groceries that fit into the definition of zero-rated sales, and on enforcement efforts to ensure grocers and other businesses are properly charging the VAT on appropriate sales. Like the VAT, a RST also has similar classification problems when certain goods and services are exempted.

For another example, in France catered food is subject to a reduced rate while restaurant food is taxed at the standard rate. Restaurants have the additional burden of categorizing their sales. According to French tax administrators, some restaurants overstate the catering portion of their business to fraudulently reduce their VAT liability. French tax administrators address this compliance risk through increased scrutiny of VAT returns filed by restaurants.

Thresholds

Businesses below a threshold that do not register with tax authorities pay VAT on inputs but do not collect VAT on sales. A threshold exempts certain categories of businesses from the VAT and creates compliance risks by making distinctions between businesses. Businesses with sales slightly above the threshold may have an incentive to underreport sales activities to avoid being required to collect and remit VAT. But unlike other VAT preferences, a threshold can decrease administrative costs and compliance burden. Since thresholds reduce the number of businesses in the system, they reduce the number of returns the tax agency processes, the number of businesses seeking services, and the number of businesses that are subject to audit. A high threshold can eliminate a large amount of VAT administrative costs while retaining much of the VAT revenue. Small businesses, by their nature, would generate a relatively small portion of revenue in the countries we studied, but account for a large portion of VAT returns filed. Smaller businesses often face a proportionally higher burden than larger businesses in complying with the VAT. Exempting them from VAT collection and filing requirements reduces the net burden a VAT imposes.

Although thresholds are intended to keep small businesses outside the VAT system, all of the countries we studied allow businesses with sales below the threshold to voluntarily register to collect and remit the VAT. Table 10 shows the percentage of registered businesses in Australia and Canada that are below the threshold but voluntarily register for the VAT. Tax administrators in Australia and New Zealand told us that businesses volunteer for a number of reasons, including wanting to claim input tax credits or misunderstanding the threshold requirements. In Australia, approximately one third of all VAT-registered businesses are below the stated threshold. They voluntarily register so that they can do business with larger companies. Tax officials told us that many larger companies will only conduct business with other VAT-registered businesses to make record-keeping easier. By purchasing goods or services only from businesses that charge VAT, these larger businesses can calculate input tax credits simply as a fixed percentage of all input costs. If they were to also purchase from a business that does not charge VAT, they must maintain more detailed records to calculate which inputs carry input tax credits and which do not.

Table 10. VAT-registered Businesses with Sales below the Threshold

	Australia[a]	Canada[b]
Threshold (in domestic currency)	A$75,000	Can$30,000
Total VAT registered businesses	1,963,907	2,834,360
Percentage of registered businesses with sales below the threshold	31.7%	34.5%

Sources: Australian Bureau of Statistics; Canada Revenue Agency.
[a] Data as of June 2006. [b] Data as of 2004.

Risk-Based Audit Selection

All of the countries we studied devote a significant amount of resources to audit activities and all used a risk-based audit selection approach in the administration of their VAT. Risk-based audit selection is intended to assist tax authorities with targeting administrative resources on noncompliant businesses and minimizes compliance burden on compliant businesses by reducing their chances of facing an audit. Generally, risk is assessed based on automated processes that compare the values on the VAT return to a series of thresholds, supplemented by information provided by business's interactions with tax administrators. For example, many of our study countries told us that refunds above a certain threshold amount are automatically flagged as risky. The automated process is adjusted periodically to account for changes in compliance trends or VAT filing behavior. Several of our study countries calculate normal VAT activity averages and limits by industry to further strengthen risk assessment tools. For example, if most restaurants remit taxes each time they file a VAT return, a restaurant that requests a VAT refund will receive extra scrutiny. French officials told us that approximately 88 percent of the returns identified as risky and audited are ultimately reassessed.

Because one of the major risks in VAT administration is issuing undeserved refunds, tax administrators pay particular attention to refund requests. Canadian tax administrators told us that if a fraudulent refund is paid, the refund recovery rate is close to zero if the error is later identified. When a refund request triggers an audit, the refund payment is delayed. This payment delay imposes additional burden on compliant businesses, but allows tax administrators more time to prevent fraudulent refunds from being issued.

Tax administration officials in Australia and Canada told us that preventing fraudulent refunds is their primary enforcement focus. Australia anticipated performing over 84,000 audits, including desk and field audits, on the approximately 2.1 million requests for VAT refunds in 2004-2005. Table 11 shows the average percentage of gross VAT collections that is paid back to businesses in the form of refunds in some of our study countries from 1998 to 2001.

United States Government Accountability Office

Table 11. Average VAT Refund Level as a Percentage of Gross VAT Collection (1998-2001)[a]

	VAT refunds as a percentage of gross VAT collection
Canada	50.3%
France	21.2
New Zealand	35.5
United Kingdom	40.9

Accounting and Filing Requirements

Tax administrators and VAT experts in several of our study countries told us that making the filing of forms and accounting for VAT easier on businesses can improve compliance. All of our study countries offer small businesses options in how often they file their VAT returns or how they calculate their VAT liability to address the differing administrative needs of businesses of various sizes. Large businesses are often required to file and remit VAT monthly, but small businesses often have the option to file and remit less frequently, such as quarterly or annually. Longer filing periods often reduce the burden on small businesses, while shorter filing periods for larger businesses maintain a steady monthly VAT revenue flow. By allowing small businesses to file VAT returns less frequently than larger businesses, tax administrators can save processing costs by reducing the number of returns they receive each month.

Tax administrators in all of our study countries also allow small liabilities as a way to further reduce compliance burden. Australia, Canada, and New Zealand offer three accounting options to address the diverse needs of businesses of different sizes, while the United Kingdom and France also offer more than one accounting option to small businesses. Based upon the amount of annual sales, businesses may select the accounting option that creates the least amount of bookkeeping and compliance burden. By allowing certain businesses to use methods that approximate their tax liabilities instead of calculating it for every transaction, they may be able to decrease their compliance burden. Tables 12 and 13 show the accounting options available to businesses in New Zealand and Canada.

Table 12. VAT Accounting Options in New Zealand

New Zealand	Accounting options and description		
	Invoice basis GST is accounted for when an invoice is issued or payment is made, whichever comes first.	Payments basis GST is accounted for in the taxable period in which a payment is made or received.	Hybrid basis GST is accounted forby using the invoice basis for sales and payments basis on purchases.
Eligible businesses	All	Businesses with annual sales of NZ$1.3million (US$878,728) or less	All

Source: New Zealand Inland Revenue Department.

Table 13. VAT Accounting Options in Canada

Canada	Accounting options and description		
	Regular method Businesses collect 5% VAT on eligible sales and pay 5% VAT on eligible purchases. At the end of the reporting period, the businesses net total VAT collected with total input tax credits and remit the difference to the government, or request a refund if they are so entitled.	Simplified method Businesses collect 5% VAT on eligible sales and pay 5% VAT on eligible purchases. At the end of the reporting period, the businesses multiply eligible expenses by (5/105). This figure is then subtracted from total VAT collected to calculate total VAT liabilities.	Quick method Businesses collect 5% on eligible sales and pay 5% VAT on eligiblepurchases. At the end of the reporting period, businesses total their sales and multiply by a sector-specific rate thatis below the standard 5% rate. Businesses are not allowed to claim input tax credits, but the sector-specific rate incorporates the approximate value of input tax credits they would otherwise claim.
Eligible businesses	All	Businesses with less than Can$500,000 (US$406,762) or less in sales in the latest fiscal year	Businesses with less than Can$200,000 (US$162,705) or less in annual sales

Source: Canada Revenue Agency.

Import Deferral Program

Australia and New Zealand have programs that allow some importers to defer VAT payment on imports, reducing compliance burden. In both Australia and New Zealand, the customs agency is responsible for collecting VAT on imports. With a deferral program, importers can establish a relationship with the customs and revenue agencies and pay their VAT liabilities to the revenue agency during normal filing intervals instead of paying customs on a per shipment basis. Deferral programs decrease some administrative costs and compliance burden by reducing the number of individual payments made by the business to the customs agency. Businesses must apply for this program, and use of the deferral scheme is limited to businesses with an established history of compliance with the tax administration agency.

Reverse Charge on Intangible Imported Goods and Services

Many countries, including all of our study countries, use a reverse charge mechanism to tax certain imported goods or services that are otherwise difficult to tax. For example, imported intangible services, such as marketing or accounting, do not physically cross borders where a customs agency would normally assess VAT. A reverse charge requires the importing business to self-assess the VAT on these imported goods or services. The self-assessed VAT generally is offset by an input tax credit claim if the good or service was used in the production of other taxable sales. Our study countries use the reverse charge mechanism for several goods and services, including intangible property, or advertising, consulting, accounting, and telecommunication services. The United Kingdom uses a specific reverse charge mechanism for cellular phones and computer chips to address the risk of carousel fraud, which is discussed further in appendix V.

Integrated Tax System

Logically, integrating tax administration and compliance activities across taxes, such as joint administration of a VAT and an income tax, would be beneficial both to tax administrators and businesses. Integrated tax administration would seem to reduce both administrative costs and compliance burden by decreasing the number of interactions between the business and the tax administrators and improve compliance by increasing the amount of information available to tax auditors for review. In an integrated system, a business would face a single audit for all taxes, whereas in a nonintegrated system a business could face a separate audit The countries we studied faced specific challenges that have prevented them from either fully integrating their tax administration or from systematically sharing information across tax programs. Until recently, Canada could not share information automatically across tax programs due to the limitations of its legacy computer systems. Generally, skill sets required by VAT auditors and income tax auditors are different, making separate audits sometimes a more practical approach. Canadian and French tax auditors are now starting to perform joint audits on a limited basis. For example, in Canada corporations and proprietorships reporting less than Can$4 million (US$3.3 million) in revenue are subject to a joint income tax and VAT audit.[18] New Zealand has been undertaking integrated audits of VAT and other taxes since 1990.

VAT Compliance Estimates

All of our study countries dedicate significant administrative resources to addressing VAT compliance risks, but actual or estimated compliance rates generally are not well documented. Of the countries we studied, only the United Kingdom annually estimates a tax gap and VAT revenue losses due to noncompliance. The United Kingdom estimates a VAT Theoretical Tax Liability (VTTL) using national consumption data, and compares it to actual VAT receipts. The difference is considered to be the VAT tax gap. From 2002 to 2007, the VAT tax gap ranged from 12.4 percent to 16.1 percent of the VTTL.[19] Other European countries have made less rigorous estimates of VAT losses which indicate that VAT losses from fraud are about 10 percent of total VAT gaps. For comparison, the 2001 gross tax gap in the United States was estimated as 17 percent of federal revenues.

Of the total VAT tax gap in the United Kingdom for 2006-2007, up to 16 percent is estimated to be attributed to Missing Trader Intra-Community (MTIC) fraud, which includes acquisition fraud and carousel fraud. Acquisition fraud occurs when a business imports a good and goes missing without paying the required VAT. Carousel fraud, a problem that is mostly contained to the European Union, is an extension of acquisition fraud whereby the original imported good is sold multiple times in the importing country before being exported again. The same goods can go through the carousel multiple times. Carousel fraud is difficult to detect because of the number of transactions involved and the frequent use of small, high value goods, such as cellular phones or computer chips. See appendix V for additional discussion of carousel fraud.

Tax officials in our other study countries told us they do not estimate VAT gaps the way the United Kingdom does, but Canadian tax administrators do have some VAT compliance measures. Some measures of VAT compliance in Canada, defined as registering as required, filing all forms on time, paying all VAT amounts when due, and reporting full and accurate information, are over 90 percent. New Zealand tax officials stated that while they do not measure a VAT gap, they estimate their VAT compliance problems are no worse than those of Australia, Canada, or the United Kingdom.

In Canada—One of Several Federal Countries with a VAT—Tax System Complexity and Compliance Burden Vary among Provinces Depending on Level of Coordination with a Federal VAT

Of the eight federal countries we identified with national VATs, Canada is the only one with multiple arrangements for administering the federal and subnational consumption taxes. Table 14 describes the VAT administrative arrangements for several countries with national VATs and subnational governments.

Table 14. National and Subnational VATs in Federal Countries

Country	National VAT	Subnational consumption tax	Administrative arrangement
Argentina	Yes	Yes	VAT administered at the national level alongside state sales taxes with states receiving a share of the national VAT revenue.
Australia	Yes	No	VAT administered at the national level with all revenue going to the states.
Austria	Yes	No	VAT administered at the national level with revenue shared by the national and state governments.
Belgium	Yes	No	VAT administered at the national level.
Brazil	Yes	Yes	VAT administered at the national level alongside state sales taxes.
Canada	Yes	Yes	Four administrative arrangementsthat include a VAT administered at the national level alongside provincial VATs or RSTs.
Germany	Yes	No	VAT administered at the national level with revenue shared by the national and state governments.
Switzerland	Yes	No	VAT administered at the national level.

Source: Bird and Gendron, University of Toronto.

As the table shows, some countries administer a federal VAT and then distribute all or a portion of the tax revenues collected to subnational jurisdictions, such as states and territories. For example, Australia has a federal VAT, but almost all revenues from that tax are distributed to the Australian states and territories. The VAT in Australia replaced a series of inefficient state taxes that were thought to be impeding economic activity. The federal and subfederal governments agreed that the federal government would administer the VAT on behalf of the states and territories. In exchange for federal VAT administration, the states and territories reimburse the federal government for the costs incurred for administration, but otherwise receive almost all of the revenues collected. Changes in the base and rate or amendments to the original agreement require unanimous support of the states, a federal government endorsement, and agreement by both houses of Parliament.

Canada is the only country that we studied that has both a federal VAT and subnational consumption taxes. Tax system complexity and compliance burden vary among the provinces in Canada, depending on the level of coordination between the federal VAT and subnational consumption taxes. Canada has four different arrangements with the provinces for administering the federal VAT and provincial consumption tax systems:

- separate federal and provincial VATs administered by a province (Québec),
- joint federal and provincial VATs administered by the federal government,
- separate federal VAT and provincial RSTs administered separately, or
- federal VAT only.

Table 15 shows the main features of Canada's four arrangements for VAT administration.

Table 15. Summary of Federal/Provincial Consumption Tax Arrangements

Consumption tax arrangement	Jurisdiction & rate	Type of taxes	Administration
Québec sales tax	•Québec – 7.5% (Applied to VAT inclusive price)	Separate federal VAT and provincial VAT	Provincial
Harmonized federal VAT and provincial VATs	•Newfoundland & Labrador – 8% •New Brunswick – 8% •Nova Scotia – 8% (Combined VAT/HST – 13%)	Joint federal and provincial VATs	Federal
Federal VAT alongside provincial sales taxes	•British Columbia – 7.5% •Manitoba – 7% •Ontario – 8% •Prince Edward Island – 10% •Saskatchewan – 7%	Separate federal VAT and provincial RST	VAT: Federal RST: Provincial
Federal VAT only	Provinces •Alberta – N/A Territories •Northwest Territories – N/A •Yukon Territory – N/A •Nunavut – N/A	Federal VAT	Federal

Source: GAO analysis.

Québec Sales Tax Arrangement (QST)

In 1992, the government of Québec agreed to administer the federal VAT on behalf of the federal government alongside a provincial VAT, called the QST. The federal government and Québec split the cost of joint administration. Although allowed some flexibility, Québec must follow the same basic rules that the federal government follows when selecting businesses for audit; conducting enforcement activities; and applying registration, payment, and dispute resolution procedures. This ensures consistent treatment of businesses regardless of geographic location in Canada.

The QST and VAT have almost the same tax base. However, there are a few key differences which create some additional administrative costs and compliance burden because affected entities have to comply with two sets of requirements when determining tax liabilities. For example, certain financial services that are exempt from the federal VAT are zero-rated under the QST. Québec also requires businesses to obtain both a provincial registration number and federal registration number.

Harmonized Sales Tax Arrangement (HST)

Beginning in April 1997, three Canadian Atlantic provinces—New Brunswick, Nova Scotia, and Newfoundland & Labrador—abolished their provincial RST systems and created the HST. The HST was the same as the federal VAT, except a tax rate of 8 percent was added to the federal VAT rate. Currently, the combined tax rate is 13 percent. The federal government agreed to administer the HST at no charge to the three provinces and distribute HST revenues back to the provinces. When the three Atlantic provinces chose to replace their provincial RSTs with the HST, they were able to reduce their tax administration costs. Figure 5 shows the administrative cost reductions achieved in New Brunswick just prior to harmonization. Tax administration costs dropped nearly 43 percent from about Can$11.6 million to just over Can$6.6 million.

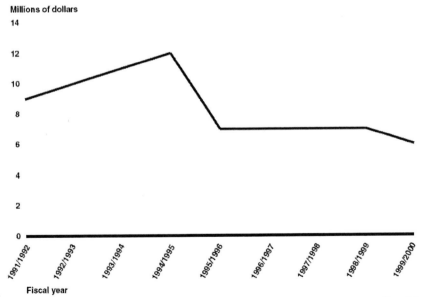

Source: New Brunswick cost data gathered by Robertson of Fasken Martineau DeMoulin LLP.

Figure 5. Tax Administration Costs in New Brunswick Before and After Harmonization.

However, the three provinces also anticipated a revenue loss because the HST rate of 8 percent was less than the RST rate that had been levied previously. For example,

Newfoundland & Labrador had an effective RST rate higher than 12 percent prior to HST implementation. The federal government agreed to pay the provinces a total of Can$961 million over 4 years—Can$349 million in each of the first 2 years, Can$175 million in the third year and Can$88 million in the fourth year—to offset part of the losses in provincial revenues.

Separate VAT and Provincial Sales Tax Arrangement

Five provinces levy RSTs alongside, yet independent of, the federal VAT. Retail businesses that operate within provinces with a RST are required to register for both systems, file returns in both systems, and are subject to separate audits within both systems. There are several notable effects of administering both taxes. Unlike the VAT, very few services are subject to the provincial sales tax. There are also a number of exemptions within the RST system. For example, some provinces do not tax children's clothing, some unprepared foods, or energy resources, such as natural gas. These goods are either fully taxed or defined differently under the federal VAT.

Further, the federal VAT zero rates certain goods or services whereas the RST uses exemptions. This is an important distinction and has administrative and bookkeeping implications. For example, a grocery store would be required to determine which goods are zero-rated under a VAT system, but are exempted under a RST. Under this scenario, the business will have to keep track of purchases and sales and determine separately how they are treated under each tax system.

Some businesses in RST provinces are disadvantaged compared to their counterparts in the HST and QST provinces because they must comply with two consumption tax systems. For example, businesses that operate retail operations in these provinces are required to file both a federal VAT and provincial RST return.

VAT-only Arrangement

Alberta and all three of the Canadian territories do not have a consumption tax at the subnational level. Therefore, purchases in these provinces are only subject to the federal VAT. Businesses that operate in these areas have a smaller compliance burden than those in provinces where a RST is also administered. Tax administration officials told us that one issue that arises from these areas is interprovincial sales, because some Canadians who live in one province will travel to Alberta or the territories to make purchases in order to avoid paying the provincial RST or VAT in their home province. This results in lost tax revenue.

VAT IMPLEMENTATION IN AUSTRALIA, CANADA, AND NEW ZEALAND BUILT ON PREEXISTING ADMINISTRATIVE STRUCTURES AND INVOLVED CONSIDERABLE RESOURCES TO EDUCATE, ASSIST, AND REGISTER BUSINESSES

Multiple agencies in Australia, Canada, and New Zealand were involved in VAT implementation. Each of these countries also developed multiple strategies for educating and assisting businesses, but getting some to register for VAT in advance of implementation was still a challenge.

Developing the VAT Administration in Several Study Countries Involved Multiagency Coordination, Development of New Policies and Processes, and Additional Staff

VAT implementation in Australia, Canada, and New Zealand involved multiple agencies, the development of new policies and processes, and hiring of additional staff. All three countries built on preexisting administrative structures to initially implement a VAT. Since the 1930s all had a national consumption tax before the VAT was adopted. For example, the Manufacturer's Sales Tax (MST) in Canada was a single-stage sales tax generally applied to the manufacturer's sales price of goods produced in Canada and to the customs value of goods imported into Canada. Wholesalers and retailers would pay the tax when they purchased certain goods.

Building up the administrative structure for the VAT in Australia, Canada, and New Zealand involved coordination among several government agencies. In all three countries this also involved the establishment of interagency committees to facilitate and coordinate implementation efforts. In Canada the former Customs and Excise division was responsible for administering the Excise Tax Act and the Department of Finance was responsible for sales tax policy and legislation. New Zealand's implementation involved coordination among five government agencies. The Ministry of Finance in New Zealand held public meetings and managed correspondence from constituents. The New Zealand Treasury's primary responsibility was the development of VAT policy, while the Inland Revenue Department was responsible for VAT registration and compliance. The Ministry of Social Welfare was responsible for managing the benefit increases associated with VAT implementation and the overall tax reform efforts. The Customs Service was responsible for terminating the wholesale sales tax and collecting VAT on imports. Also during implementation, all three countries gave agencies specific responsibility for monitoring the transition and its impact on consumer pricing. These offices worked to ensure businesses did not artificially inflate prices to take advantage of uncertainty during implementation.

Introduction of the VAT also involved efforts to develop and test forms and returns. According to International Monetary Fund guidance on VAT implementation, development of forms early in the implementation process is important because they are a key part of the education effort. Australia's implementation showed that if VAT implementation also involves an overhaul of business tax payment and filing procedures, new legislation would be necessary and more time would likely be needed for forms development. Australia coupled

VAT implementation with new business accounting and reporting requirements that had to be detailed on a Business Activity Statement (BAS). The BAS was intended to capture information on multiple business taxes in the country. Government officials in Australia told us that the BAS was responsible for the majority of VAT-related compliance burden at implementation due to the increased filing requirements and information reporting. Forms development took about 2 to 3 months in New Zealand, where both the VAT and VAT forms are relatively simple. Canada allocated 12 months to develop, test, print, and distribute its forms.

All three countries had some staff in place for administering the VAT; however, all also hired and trained large numbers of additional staff. For example, Canada hired over 3,900 additional personnel at the time of transition. This more than tripled the total staff previously responsible for administering the MST. Of the staff Canada initially hired, about 1,500 were to perform various educational functions, which included providing walk-in services, seminars, written correspondence, business information sessions, advisory visits, and extensive distribution of printed material. Advisory visits—in which administration officials would travel to specific businesses to educate its employees on the VAT—were continued only through the first quarter after VAT implementation.

Time Taken to Implement VATs Ranged from 15 to 24 Months

The amount of time tax administrations in Australia, Canada, and New Zealand had to implement a VAT ranged from 15 to 24 months due to the varying circumstances leading up to initial implementation in each of these countries. Australia and its states and territories reached agreement on a VAT in April 1999, 15 months prior to the effective implementation date of July 1, 2000. In Canada, much of the planning and early efforts to prepare for VAT implementation occurred before legislation was actually passed. According one Canadian official involved in implementation, planning began nearly 2 years in advance, but Canadian tax authorities had only 2 weeks between final passage of legislation and implementation. New Zealand originally allowed for 18 months between the publication of a policy paper on the VAT and actual implementation. However, because of delays in education activities, implementation was delayed an additional 6 months.

Government Agencies Used a Variety of Methods to Educate and Assist Entities Subject to VAT Requirements

Before entities subject to VAT requirements can be expected to comply, they must know what those requirements are and what they mean to specific economic and industry sectors. For Australia, Canada, and New Zealand, this resulted in the development and administration of extensive education and outreach efforts through a variety of direct and indirect assistance. Although all three countries implemented education and outreach efforts, Australia's approach is the most recent and provides the most detail on the strategies and programs that were in place.

According to officials involved in the initial implementation of the VAT in Australia, a major part of the education and outreach strategy was to target specific players in the various industry sectors and get them involved in educating others. The Australian government spent approximately A$500 million (US$464 million) on education efforts at transition. Australia established a Start-up Assistance Office within the Department of Treasury to assist small and medium-sized businesses and the community sector in preparing for and implementing VAT requirements. This office established and administered the programs described in table 16.

Industry partnerships were important to the education strategy implemented by the Australian Taxation Office and Treasury. According to Australian officials and others with knowledge of implementation, education materials produced by industries were well-received by businesses. In addition, industry partnerships established lines of communication that allowed the government to understand industry concerns about the VAT. For example, one concern was about the costs businesses needed to incur to come into initial compliance with the VAT. VAT experts in several of Australia's professional services and accounting organizations told us that corporations with large and diverse inventory items incurred significant transition costs. According to tax administration officials, one benefit of the industry partnership strategy is that many of the partnerships formed during VAT implementation still exist.

Table 16. Strategies Used in Australia to Educate and Assist Businesses

Grants to community groups and organizations	Program issued over 220 grants to a variety of community organizations, industry groups, and other organizations that worked with or on behalf of specific economic sectors. For example, grants were given to state chambers of commerce to develop and administer education programs to member businesses.
Advisor education	Program provided a series of tax education classes and seminars to a large network of informal advisors, such as accountants and tax preparers, who could then pass on their knowledge to the businesses or community and educational institutions with which they were affiliated.
Business skills education	Program developed and distributed a range of products and services to interested businesses that would be subject to VAT requirements. This included a telephone helpline, two VAT-specific Web sites, over 16 publications covering many topics ofinterest to VAT businesses, and specialized assistance to non-English speaking businesses.
Direct assistance to small businesses	Program delivered a A$200 (US$186) certificate to qualifying small business and community groups. The certificate could be redeemed with a registered supplier for goods or services that would assist the registrant in preparing for the VAT. The certificate could be redeemed to provide computer hardware, computer software, stationary, training courses, and financial advice. Over 1.9 million certificates were issued and could be redeemed at over 14,000 suppliers.

Source: GAO analysis of Australian Taxation Office documents.

Canada also made informing the public about the VAT and registering businesses subject to the tax an important part of the implementation effort. The Canadian Revenue Agency launched an extensive program to provide information to the business community on the VAT through seminars, publications, and telephone support. Tax administration officials also conducted widespread consultation programs to seek input from businesses, trade associations, and professionals on how to disseminate information and develop administrative procedures. A publication committee was also formed to steer the development of guides, information pamphlets, and technical memoranda. Consultants were retained to conduct focus testing to review some of the publications and make them more understandable.

The budget for education and outreach activities during the implementation of the VAT in Canada was substantial. According to one study, the Canadian government spent more than Can$85 million (US$98.5 million). To put this in context, this exceeded the amount spent by the nation's largest private-sector advertiser at the time by nearly Can$30 million (US$34.8 million). The VAT education and outreach campaign in Canada drew on the resources of several government agencies, which were coordinated by a cabinet-level committee on communications. Table 17 provides additional details on the agencies that were involved, the activities they conducted, and their associated costs.

Table 17. Summary of Education and Outreach Activities for VAT Implementation in Canada

Agency	Activity	Cost (Can$millions)1989-92
Department of Finance	Print, radio, and television advertising	11.6
	Direct mailings to 10 million households and over 500,000 industry group members Production and broadcasting of video on the VAT	5
	Operating costs for a Communications Working Group, including a toll-free hotline which, at peak, handled 6,000 calls a day	5
Canada Revenue Agency	General advertising	10.6
	Direct mailings to businesses and consumers	9.2
	Efforts to educate households on the VAT credit that would be administered through the income tax system	2.8
Consumer Information Office	Operating and advertising costs for a special office that was established to "limit confusion among consumers" about the GST. The office planned to spend $7.4 million on advertising in 1990-1991, another $6.9 million on the production of material, and $19.6 million for its costs of operation. The budget for these activities in 1991-1992 amounted to $8.4 million.	42.3
Approximate total		86.5

Source: Alasdair Roberts and Jonathan Rose, Queen's University.

Canada, like Australia, also provided assistance to small businesses during the implementation. For example, qualifying small businesses received one-time credits of up to Can$1,000 (US$1,159) to help them adapt to the VAT. The Canadian government also helped certain businesses offset the burden of double taxation created by transitioning from one type of consumption tax to another. Specifically, certain wholesalers' and retailers' inventories consisted of some goods on which the old MST had already been paid. The Canadian government provided refunds to offset payments made under the old tax. Determining the exact amount of tax that each individual business paid was difficult because the MST was a hidden tax and not identifiable for specific items in a business's inventory. Therefore, to

Australia and Canada Had Difficulty Getting Businesses to Register Early for VAT Prior to Implementation

Despite efforts to educate and reach out to businesses, both Australia and Canada still had difficulty in getting all businesses to register to collect and remit VAT prior to implementation. In Canada, the tax administration assumed it would have 12 months from the time the proposed VAT legislation was enacted to the date the tax would take effect. However, the legislation for the proposed VAT was enacted only 2 weeks before the effective date of January 1, 1991. Until the legislation was enacted, the requirement to register was neither mandatory nor enforceable. According to tax administration officials, the delay in passage of the legislation may have led potential registrants to question whether the VAT would indeed come into effect. Others may have refused to register voluntarily before the legislation became effective.

Despite having little authority to enforce registration until the VAT was passed, tax administration officials recognized they needed to identify and register businesses anyway if they were to be effective in administering the tax. The first step in the registration process was to identify and contact potential registrants. Because the VAT had an expansive reach, the Canada Revenue Agency was tasked with contacting every business and organization in Canada to determine whether or not they were required to register. To do this the agency prepared a master list for an initial mailing from information contained in four income tax system databases: (1) corporate, (2) individual, (3) payroll deduction, and (4) charitable organization. Second, it mailed approximately 1.9 million registration kits to potential registrants, followed by two sets of reminder notices. An additional 180,000 registration kits were sent to newly identified potential registrants identified using updated information in the income tax database. Third, a final registration kit was sent to potential registrants who had not yet responded.

Three months prior to implementation there were 500,000 registrants— one-third less than the administration's goal. To increase registrations, the Canada Revenue Agency began contacting potential registrants by telephone. Upon passage of the legislation, registration requests increased and continued to increase in January 1991. Four months after the VAT went into effect, the targeted goal of 1.6 million registrants was achieved.

Though the circumstances were different, the Australian Taxation Office also had difficulty getting businesses to register in advance of VAT implementation. Officials said that ensuring timely business registration was an important aspect of VAT implementation. Following an examination of registration times in other countries, tax officials tried to register as many businesses as possible prior to July 1, 2000. The tax administration was successful in getting most businesses to register before the VAT was implemented. However, according to officials involved in implementation, many registrations were filed close to the deadline, creating significant workload just before the VAT was to go into effect.

Tax administration officials also said they experienced some challenges registering nonprofit and charity organizations because these organizations were not included in other tax systems.

CONCLUDING OBSERVATIONS

Administering a VAT presents the same fundamental challenges as other tax systems, including the current U.S. income tax. They all have compliance risks, administrative costs, and compliance burden. While these challenges may differ in some specifics, they exist for all tax systems, including even simple VATs.

One overriding lesson about VAT design is that, like our income tax system, adding tax preferences to the system may satisfy economic, distributional, or other policy goals but at a cost. Tax preferences—in the form of exemptions, zero rates, or reduced rates—often reduce revenue, add complexity, and increase compliance risks. To mitigate the increased risk, countries have imposed additional record-keeping and reporting requirements on businesses, delayed refunds, and done more auditing of businesses. The end result is an increase in compliance burden for businesses and administrative costs for the government.

The choice of tax type is typically heavily influenced by criteria other than administrability. Revenue needs, impact on economic performance, and distributional consequences are prominent considerations and have been at the forefront of the debate in the United States about tax reform. Administrability and the details of how a new tax would be implemented often get less attention. However, administrability and design details do matter. The benefits of a new or reformed tax system, in terms of revenue, economic performance, or equity, would be at least partially offset by poor design that unnecessarily increased compliance risks, administrative costs, and compliance burden.

As agreed with your staff, unless you publicly announce the contents of this report earlier, we plan no further distribution of it until 30 days from the date of this letter. At that time, we will provide copies of this report to interested congressional committees and other interested parties. Copies of this report will also be made available to others upon request. In addition, the report will also be available at no charge on GAO's Web site at http://www.gao.gov.

If you or your staff has any questions about this report, please contact me at (202) 512-5594 or whitej@gao.gov. Contact points for our Offices of Congressional Relations and Public Affairs may be found on the last page of this report. Key contributors to this report are listed in appendix VI.

James R. White
Director, Tax Issues Strategic Issues Team

APPENDIX I: OBJECTIVES, SCOPE, AND METHODOLOGY

The objectives of this report were to describe for selected countries important lessons learned from experiences on (1) how value-added tax (VAT) design choices have affected compliance, the cost of administration, and compliance burden; (2) how countries with federal systems administer a VAT in conjunction with subnational consumption tax systems; and (3) how countries that recently transitioned to a VAT implemented the new tax.

In choosing the countries to study, we interviewed a number of VAT experts, including academics, private practice tax practitioners, researchers at the Organization for Economic Cooperation and Development (OECD), and government officials. We reviewed academic articles, books, and government publications on VAT compliance risks, administrative costs, compliance burden; federal and subnational tax coordination issues; and the topic of VAT implementation to identify these VAT experts. We contacted those experts who had a broad understanding of VAT issues related to our research objectives, who were recommended by other experts, and who were available to speak with us.

Based on our research and expert recommendations, we selected Australia because it implemented a VAT more recently; Canada because it has a federal system with a number of subnational consumption taxes; France because it is has the oldest VAT system; New Zealand because it has a simple system with a broad tax base; and the United Kingdom because of its work on VAT noncompliance and fraud. Like the United States, all of the countries we selected are members of OECD and are modern industrial nations for which a broad set of comparative economic and tax data were available.

We performed an in-depth literature review of government and academic literature related to each selected country's VAT. We visited Australia, Canada, France, and New Zealand and interviewed government officials and private practice tax professionals. In each country we visited we interviewed officials with the tax administration agency and the national audit institution; and VAT professionals from global taxation and audit firms. In Australia, Canada, and New Zealand, we also interviewed officials in their treasury departments and customs agencies, and academics. In Australia and Canada we also interviewed officials at relevant provincial and state agencies. For the United Kingdom, we communicated with appropriate officials in the National Audit Office and reviewed government documents on VAT administration and compliance. To obtain further information on our study countries, we met with VAT experts from the OECD, the European Commission, and the International Monetary Fund.

We conducted an extensive number of interviews for this report and corroborated as much testimonial evidence as possible with official government reports and documents, or published academic articles. We indicated in the report when evidence was based solely on the testimony of government officials or experts.

We collected and analyzed data on the countries and their VAT systems, including VAT revenue trends, administrative and compliance activities and costs, and the size and distribution of economic activity within the study countries. We gathered these data mostly from the OECD and government agencies in our study countries, including the national statistics agencies and national revenue agencies, but also from academic articles. In most cases the data used in this report come from the OECD or international government agencies. We determined the data were sufficiently reliable for the purposes of our report. We considered the OECD information we reviewed to be a reliable source of comparable statistical, economic, and social data and confirmed the data with government officials in our study countries. Most of the data used from international government agencies, including tax administrations, were publicly reported by these agencies. To provide additional assurance that these and all other data reported in our report were sufficiently reliable we discussed this information with the appropriate government officials, tax experts, and OECD officials. Additionally we provided the national audit institutions and the tax administration agencies of our study countries a copy of our report to verify data and specific factual and legal statements about the VAT in those countries. We made technical corrections to our report based on these reviews.

We conducted this performance audit from December 2006 through April 2008 in Atlanta, Ga.; Boston, Mass.; San Francisco, Calif.; and Washington, D.C.; Canberra and Sydney, Australia; Brussels, Belgium; Montreal, Ottawa, Québec, and Toronto, Canada; Paris, France; and Wellington, New Zealand, in accordance with generally accepted government auditing standards. Those standards require that we plan and perform the audit to obtain sufficient, appropriate evidence to provide a reasonable basis for our findings and conclusions based on our audit objectives. We believe that the evidence obtained provides a reasonable basis for our findings and conclusions based on our audit objectives.

APPENDIX II: GOODS AND SERVICES IN STUDY COUNTRIES SUBJECT TO EXEMPTIONS, ZERO RATING, OR REDUCED RATING

Table 18 lists the broad categories of goods and services that are subject to exemptions, zero-rating, or reduced rating in our study countries. Exports are not included in the list of zero-rated goods or services because this is included in the definition of the destination principle.

Table 18. Exempt, Zero Rated, and Reduced Rated Goods and Services in Study Countries

	Exempt	Zero rate	Reduced rate
Australia	financial services; residential rent and premises; certain supplies of precious metals; school canteens operated by nonprofit bodies; fund raising events conducted by charitable institutions	most food and beverages; health care (including health insurance); education; child care; religious services; activities of charitable institutions; water sewage and drainage; going concerns; precious metals; international travel; international mail; farm land; cars for use by disabled people	N/A
Canada	transport of sick or injured persons; hospital and medical care; human blood, tissues, and organs; dental care; charitable work; education; noncommercial activities of nonprofit making organizations; sporting services; cultural services; insurance and reinsurance; letting of immovable property; financial services; certain fund-raising events; legal aid; ferry; road and bridge tolls	medicine; basic groceries; certain financial services; certain agricultural and fishing products; medical devices; precious metals; international organizations and officials	N/A

Value-Added Taxes: Lessons Learned from Other Countries...

Table 18. (Continued).

	Exempt	Zero rate	Reduced rate
France	postal services; hospital and medical care; human blood, tissues and organs; dental care; charitable work; education; noncommercial activities of nonprofit making organizations; sporting services; cultural services; insurance and reinsurance; financial services; betting, lotteries, and gambling; supply of land and buildings; certain fund-raising events; construction, improvement, repair and maintenance work on monuments; cemeteries and graves commemorating war victims undertaken for public authorities and nonprofit bodies, new industrial waste and recyclable material; commodity futures transactions carried out on a regulated market; services rendered by resource consortia to their members composed of natural or legal persons that are VAT exempt or not subject to VAT	N/A	most food, nonalcoholic beverages; medicine; equipment for disabled; books; hotels; entertainment; author's rights; museums; transport; accommodation; agriculture; catering; newspapers; water; work on dwellings over 2 years old
New Zealand	financial services (including life insurance policies); supply of residential accommodation in a dwelling; fine metal; supply by a nonprofit body of donated goods and services	businesses as a going concern; fine metal; specific supplies by local authorities; supply of financial services to registered GST businesses	long term accommodation in a commercial dwelling (taxed at 60% of the value of the sale foran effective reduced rate)
United Kingdom	postal services; transport of sick or injured persons; hospital and medical care; human blood, tissues and organs; dental care; charitable work; education; noncommercial activities of nonprofit making organizations; sporting services; cultural services; insurance and reinsurance; letting of immovable property; financial services; supply of land and buildings; certain fund-raising events; burials and cremations; investment gold; sports competitions; certain luxury hospital care; works of art; some gambling activities	children's clothing; food, passenger transport, books; newspapers; sewerage and water; prescribed drugs; medicine; certain aids and services for disabled people; new housing; residential and some charity buildings; alterations to listed buildings; certain services and goods supplied to charities	fuel and power for domestic andcharity use; installation of certain energy saving materials; certain installations of heating equipment or security items; women's sanitary products; children's car seats; residential renovations; contraceptives; welfare advice; installation of mobility aids for elderly; smoking cessation products

Source: OECD.

APPENDIX III: SPECIFIC VAT TREATMENT OF PUBLIC SECTOR ENTITIES AND NONPROFIT ORGANIZATIONS IN AUSTRALIA AND CANADA

In Australia, public sector entities must pay VAT on taxable supplies just as a business would. However, they are also able to fully recover VAT paid for creditable purchases. Public sector entities are required to be registered for the VAT and file VAT returns just like private entities in order to remit VAT and claim credits.

Similar to Australia, Canadian federal government agencies also pay VAT on purchases from external suppliers. These agencies account for VAT paid on purchases throughout the year and, in March, present the account to the federal tax administration. The government is responsible for collecting VAT and, therefore, must file a tax return and remit funds on a monthly basis to meet this obligation.

Canada uses a rebate mechanism, rather than zero-rating, to refund VAT paid on inputs to tax-exempt sales by subnational and government-funded entities such as municipalities, universities, schools and hospitals. These organizations often provide tax-exempt services, and therefore, are unable to claim input tax credits for VAT paid on purchases used to provide those services. However, they are entitled to full to partial rebates on VAT paid on purchases. The percentage of recoverable tax paid varies by type of organization. For example, hospitals receive 83 percent of the total VAT paid to provide exempt goods and services while universities receive 67 percent. The rebate ratios were established to ensure that the sales tax burden of these entities did not increase as a result of moving to the VAT system from the previous consumption tax system.

Canada also provides VAT rebates of 50 percent to certain charities and nonprofits. Registered charities are eligible to claim a 50 percent rebate of VAT paid on purchases that are not used to produce taxable goods and services. Other nonprofit organizations may also claim the rebate, provided they receive at least 40 percent of their funding from the government.

APPENDIX IV: APPLYING THE VAT TO HARD-TO-TAX SECTORS

Some sectors of the economy, specifically financial services, insurance, real estate, and second hand goods, are inherently difficult to tax under conventional value-added tax (VAT) rules. For financial services and insurance, there is often no clear distinction between the provision of a service and a return on investment. For some real estate transactions and the sale of secondhand goods, it is difficult to calculate the implied input taxes.

Financial Services

Applying a VAT to financial services has proved challenging to many of the countries that implement a VAT. Determining the value added for each financial service is not a clear calculation. While some financial services, such as renting a safety deposit box, are fee based and therefore have a price that can be considered taxable consumption, others such as financial intermediation in the form of accepting deposits and making loans, do not. Rather than charging a fee for a specific service, the institution pays lower interest rates on deposits and charges higher rates on loans than they otherwise would. To tax these services, the value of the services would have to be imputed. The interest on deposits or loans is considered a return on investment and not the price for goods or services sold, and is therefore not subject to VAT. Taxing interest earned on deposit accounts results in a tax on savings rather than a tax on consumption.

Exempting

As a condition of membership, European Union (EU) member states are required to employ a partially harmonized VAT that follows the rules set forth in the Sixth Council Directive. As outlined in the Sixth Council Directive, EU member states are required to exempt from their VATs a series of specific financial services that include services related to credit, deposits, transfers, payments, debts, checks, and other negotiable instruments; transactions involving legal currency; transactions in shares, interests, debts, or other securities; and management of special investment funds. Many countries around the world have taken the EU approach and have opted to exempt financial services from their VAT base, but exemptions have created further complexities in how the VAT is ultimately applied. Of our study countries, only New Zealand has changed from exempting to zero rating some business-to-business financial services.

Input Tax Apportionment

Exempting financial services requires businesses to accurately calculate the amount of their overall inputs that are used for providing exempt financial services. In the case of inputs that are used for making both exempt and taxable services, such as computers, businesses must apportion what percentage of the input taxes of the dual-use input are associated with taxable sales to be able to claim proper input tax credits.

Some countries have specific apportionment guidelines for banks and financial services firms. These apportionment guidelines set methodologies for calculating VAT paid on business inputs that can be claimed as input tax credits.

Impacts on Outsourcing Decisions

By exempting financial services, as is done in most countries with a VAT, businesses have an incentive to vertically integrate as much as possible to reduce their noncreditable VAT paid on supplies. For example, a financial services firm that purchases pamphlets from an outside printer pays VAT for the printing services but does not claim input tax credits to reclaim the VAT paid. The firm would benefit financially if it could produce the pamphlets in house for less than the VAT inclusive price charged by the printer. To address this issue, countries use apportionment agreements or other VAT specific rules.

Tax Cascading

Exempting financial services also can create tax cascading. Tax cascading occurs when an exempt good or service is later used in the production of a taxable good or service, leading to a tax being levied on a tax. When a financial service is exempt, the supplier cannot recover the VAT paid on inputs, and therefore passes the VAT paid on inputs onto the consumer in the final price of the financial service. If the exempt financial service is then used in the production of a taxable service, the VAT is levied on the final price of the taxable service, which includes the input taxes passed on by the exempt financial service, resulting in a tax on a tax.

Zero Rating

While most VAT systems exempt financial services, some have more recently opted to zero rate them. New Zealand began applying a zero rate to business-to-business financial services in 2005. Zero rating business-tobusiness financial transactions effectively eliminates any distortions tax cascading would have created, but it does not eliminate the need for apportionment agreements with banks because sales to final consumers are still exempt. In Canada, Québec's provincial VAT applies a zero rate to financial services. Officials we spoke with indicated that zero rating financial services increased Québec's ability to attract and retain banks within the province.

Insurance

Insurance poses the same challenges to VAT taxation as financial services, and many countries include insurance into their definition of exempt financial services. While insurance and reinsurance are exempt in most countries, a few have designed methods to tax them. For example, New Zealand exempts life insurance policies, but levies the VAT on the margin between premiums collected and claims paid on all other types of insurance policies. Consumers pay the VAT when purchasing the policy and insurance companies receive input tax credits when paying out on a policy. For example, if a consumer purchases an automobile insurance policy for $500 annually, he/she is charged the 12.5 percent VAT rate, for a total of $562.50. If the consumer has an accident and claims $500 for the cost to repair the vehicle, the insurance company pays the policyholder $562.50 and claims $62.50 as input tax credits. The net VAT revenue collected on the policy is $0. Australia taxes property and casualty insurance but employs a different mechanism for allowing VAT registered policyholders to claim input tax credits.

Real Estate

Real estate transactions are considered difficult to tax due to the inherent challenges in determining input tax credits and the consumption value of long-lived assets, such as real property. If a VAT is intended to tax current consumption, taxing the purchase of a new home is in effect taxing future consumption, as the purchaser may live in the home and "consume housing" for several years. Charging a VAT on real estate can also create problems at the time of transition to a VAT. For example, in Australia, where new residential housing is taxed at the standard rate but existing housing is exempt, new residential housing prices increased at the time of transition as a result of the new tax. The Australian government developed a program that gave new home buyers a grant of A$7,000 (US$6,497) to help offset the increase in housing prices. Similarly, Canada has a housing rebate that allows for individuals to reclaim some VAT paid on purchases of a new house or on substantial renovations to an existing house.

Margin Scheme

Australia uses a margin scheme for certain real estate transactions to address the sale of existing property. In general, under the margin scheme the VAT is paid on the difference between the selling price and the value of the property on July 1, 2000—therefore taxing the value added since the introduction of the VAT. The seller cannot claim input tax credits from the original purchase. Similar margin schemes are used in other countries on the sales of high-value secondhand goods, such as works of art or antiques.

APPENDIX V: CAROUSEL FRAUD IN THE EUROPEAN UNION

Carousel fraud is mainly a compliance challenge in the European Union, where trade borders between member countries no longer exist. With no customs or border agency collecting value added tax (VAT) at the border, fraudulent businesses take advantage of VAT-free imports. Since companies do not pay input VAT on imported goods and services at the time of importation, it opens up the opportunity for stealing the entire amount of VAT collected on sales.

Figure 6 shows how carousel fraud can occur using as examples two European Union (EU) countries. Company 1 exports cell phones to Company 2, and does not charge a VAT, as exports are zero-rated by the destination principle. Because there are no physical trade borders between EU countries, Company 2 is supposed to self-assess and remit VAT upon importing the cell phones. Company 2 does not self-assess a VAT but does collect VAT on the sale to Company 3. Because Company 2 does not remit the VAT collected to the government, Company 2 can charge a lower price to Company 3 than what was paid on the import and still make a profit. The lower priced cellular phones then can continue through the carousel until Company 1 imports them again, beginning the process anew.

The United Kingdom employs a VAT Compliance Strategy (VCS) aimed at closing the tax gap. One main objective of the VCS is curbing carousel fraud within its borders, including requiring businesses that sell specific goods that are often used in carousel fraud, such as cellular phones and computer chips, to use a specific reverse charge. The specific reverse charge on these items requires each business purchasing cellular phones or computer chips to self-assess VAT on their purchase. Because businesses selling these goods to other businesses will claim an input tax credit equal to the self-assessed VAT, the only collection of VAT by the government is at the final retail stage, similar to a retail sales tax. Since implementation of VCS in 2002, HM Revenue & Customs estimates the VAT gap has decreased by almost 2 percentage points.

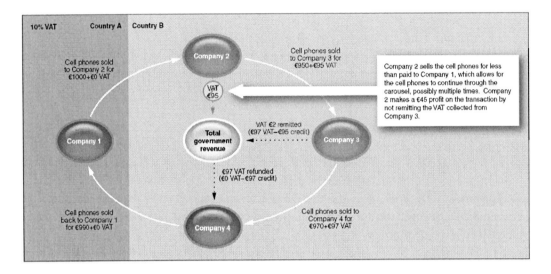

Figure 6. Carousel Fraud.

Canadian officials told us that carousel fraud, which they refer to as asset flipping, does occur to a limited extent in used automobile sales. Tax officials in Australia and New Zealand told us they have not had significant problems with carousel fraud because almost all imported goods are verified and assessed VAT at the border by their customs agencies.

APPENDIX VI: DISTRIBUTION OF ECONOMIC ACTIVITY BY INDUSTRY SECTOR IN SEVERAL STUDY COUNTRIES

Figure 7 shows the mix of economic activity in the United States, Australia, France, and the United Kingdom, countries for which the Organization for Economic Cooperation and Development (OECD) value-added data were available. Data for Canada and New Zealand were not available.

Gross value added is defined as output minus intermediate consumption and equals the sum of employee compensation, gross operating surplus, and taxes less subsidies on production and imports, except for net taxes on products. The shares of each sector are calculated by dividing the value added in each sector by total value added. Total gross value added is less than the gross domestic product (GDP) because it excludes VAT and similar product taxes.

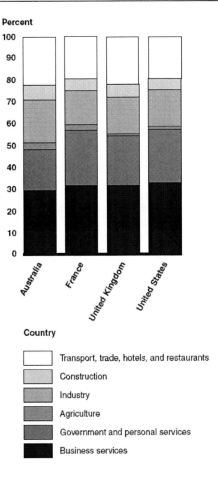

Figure 7. Value-added by Economic Sector in Select OECD Countries.

Industry consists of mining and quarrying, manufacturing, and production and distribution of electricity, gas, and water; trade consists of retail and wholesale trade and repair services; real estate covers rents for dwellings including the imputed rents of owner-occupiers; and government includes public administration, law and order, and defense.

End Notes

[1] United States Department of the Treasury, Approaches to Improve the Competitiveness of the U.S. Business Tax System for the 21st Century, (Washington, DC: Dec. 20, 2007).

[2] The 30 OECD member countries represent countries that have attained a relatively high level of development and share a commitment to the market economy and pluralist democracy. Its members account for 60 percent of world gross national product, three-quarters of world trade, and 14 percent of the world population.

[3] For examples, see Tax Reform for Fairness, Simplicity, and Economic Growth: The Treasury Department Report to the President (November 1984) and Congressional Budget Office, The Economic Effects of Comprehensive Tax Reform, (July 1997).

[4] GAO, Implications of Replacing the Corporate Income Tax with a Consumption Tax, GGD-93-55 (Washington, D.C.: May 1993).

[5] In most instances, we use the term 'businesses' in this report to refer to the corporations, businesses, partnerships, proprietorships, organizations, government agencies, and other entities that are required to collect and remit VAT. We refer to specific types of entities, as appropriate.

[6] Australia, Canada, and New Zealand refer to their VAT systems as a Goods and Services Tax (GST). For the purposes of this report, we will use the term VAT when referring to the GST systems of these countries.

[7] Of the 29 OECD countries that have a VAT, 28 use the credit-invoice VAT. One country, Japan, employs a type of subtraction method VAT which taxes the difference between a business's net outputs and net inputs. Invoices are used to show proof of purchases and sales, but not proof of VAT paid on inputs. For the purpose of this report, we focus only on the credit-invoice method.

[8] In theory, a VAT could be designed as an income tax by not allowing businesses to subtract investment purchases from sales, that is, by not allowing businesses to expense investments. Under an income tax, businesses would be allowed depreciation deductions that account for the loss in value of investments over time. In practice, VATs generally are designed as consumption taxes.

[9] The VAT was not a mandatory method for calculating tax obligations in France until 1968, according to Restructuring the French Economy by William James Adams.

[10] GAO, Tax Policy: Summary of Estimates of the Costs of the Federal Tax System, GAO-05-878 (Washington, D.C.: Aug. 26, 2005).

[11] GAO, Understanding the Tax Reform Debate: Background, Criteria, and Questions, GAO-05-1009SP (Washington, D.C.: September 2005).

[12] None of our study countries have a VAT as simple as shown in table 1, but New Zealand's VAT—which has a broad base with few exceptions—is generally considered by VAT experts to have the simplest VAT design among OECD countries.

[14] Carousel fraud is a form of missing trader fraud that involves a series of contrived transactions, including imports and exports, with the aim of creating large unpaid VAT liabilities and fraudulent VAT repayment claims.

[15] GAO Tax Policy: Value Added Tax: Administrative Costs Vary With Complexity and Number of Businesses, GAO/GGD-93-78 (Washington, D.C.: May 3, 1993).

[16] In some instances where an exempt good or service is used in the production of a taxable good or service, exemptions can produce a cascading effect, whereby a good or service is sold with an imbedded tax in the price, resulting in a tax on the tax. In this case, the exemption may lead to an increase in tax revenue.

[17] Because interest is not consumption, it is not considered to be a tax preference under a consumption tax.

[18] Wherever we provide foreign currency values converted to U.S. dollars, they represent 2008 dollars.

[19] HMRC's estimates of the VTTL are based on the best available data at the time the estimates are calculated, and are therefore subject to a broad range of uncertainties. HMRC's analysis concludes that the margin of error in these estimates could be as high as +/- 4 percentage points.

In: Value-Added Tax (VAT) and Flat Tax Proposals
Editors: D. B. Andrews and A. M. Davis

ISBN: 978-1-61324-191-2
© 2011 Nova Science Publishers, Inc.

Chapter 5

FLAT TAX: AN OVERVIEW OF THE HALL-RABUSHKA PROPOSAL[*]

James M. Bickley

SUMMARY

The concept of replacing the current U.S. income tax system with a flat rate consumption tax is receiving congressional attention. The term "flat tax" is often associated with a proposal formulated by Robert E. Hall and Alvin Rabushka (H-R), two senior fellows at the Hoover Institution. This report analyzes the idea of replacing the U.S. income tax system with this type of consumption tax. Although the current tax structure is referred to as an income tax, it actually contains elements of both an income and a consumption-based tax. A consumption base is neither inherently superior nor inherently inferior to an income base.

As of March 22, 2010, four bills have been introduced in the 111th Congress that include a flat tax based on the concepts of H-R. On February 12, 2009, Representative Michael C. Burgess introduced H.R. 1040, the *Freedom Flat Tax Act*. On May 4, 2009, Senator Lamar Alexander introduced a companion bill, S. 963, the *Optional One Page Flat Tax Act*. These bills would authorize an individual or a person engaged in business activity to make an irrevocable election to be subject to a H-R flat tax (in lieu of the existing tax provisions). On March 30, 2009, Senator Arlen Specter introduced S. 741, *Flat Tax Act of 2009*. On April 30, 2009, Senator Richard C. Shelby introduced S. 932, the *Simplified, Manageable, and Responsible Tax Act*. S. 741 and S. 932 would levy a flat tax modeled after the H-R proposal as a replacement for the individual and corporate income taxes, and the estate and gift taxes.

The combined individual and business taxes proposed by H-R can be viewed as a modified value-added tax (VAT). The individual wage tax would be imposed on wages (and salaries) and pension receipts. Part or all of an individual's wage and pension income would be tax-free depending on marital status and number of dependents. The business tax would be a modified subtraction-method VAT with wages (and salaries) and pension contributions subtracted from the VAT base, in contrast to the usual VAT practice.

---

[*] This is an edited, reformatted and augmented version of Congressional Research Services publication 98-529, dated March 22, 2010.

The analysis of the flat tax proposal is covered by the following four topics that sometimes overlap: broad economic issues, narrow sectoral economic issues, simplicity, and international comparisons. *First*, broad economic issues relate to economic effects of the flat tax on the entire economy: equity, efficiency, international trade, price level, interest rates, and revenue. *Second*, sectoral economic issues deal with specific industries or sectors of the total economy: differential effects on businesses, charitable organizations, housing, financial services, pensions and insurance, health care services, and state and local governments. *Third*, tax economists, government leaders, and taxpayers are interested in the simplicity of a tax system, and the current income tax system is complex. A positive aspect of the proposed flat tax is the ease with which the individual and corporate tax systems could be integrated. But, the complexity of the current tax code is partially due to attempts to achieve greater equity or to improve economic efficiency, and there are often tradeoffs between simplicity, equity, and efficiency. It can be argued that it may be "unfair" to compare the current income tax system with some form of a "pure" consumption tax; by the time a consumption tax becomes enacted, it may become complicated. *Fourth*, there are major distinctions between recent consumption tax proposals for the United States and the current tax systems of other developed nations. Numerous aspects of the H-R flat tax proposal have not been fleshed out and many important policy issues have yet to be analyzed.

INTRODUCTION

Some Members of Congress have indicated interest in the concept of replacing our current federal income tax system with some form of a consumption tax, including proposals with a flat rate. The term "flat tax" is often associated with a proposal formulated by Robert E. Hall and Alvin Rabushka (H-R), two senior fellows at the Hoover Institution at Stanford University. In 1981, they proposed the replacement of the federal individual income tax and the federal corporate income tax with a flat rate consumption tax. In early 1995, Hall and Rabushka published the second edition of their book titled simply *The Flat Tax*.[1] In 2005, Dr. Hall provided some additional insights into his flat tax proposal.[2] This report explains and evaluates the HallRabushka proposal for three reasons. First, as of March 22, 2010, four bills have been introduced in the 111th Congress that include a H-R flat tax.[3] Second, the Hall-Rabushka proposal concerns many issues relevant to other tax reform proposals. Third, unlike a number of other reform plans, the H-R proposal has sufficient detail to permit examination, although numerous aspects of the proposal have yet to be fleshed out.[4]

The report begins with discussions of congressional interest in the flat tax, the concept of an income tax base versus a consumption tax base, and three types of broad-based consumption taxes. Next, the justification and operation of the proposed H-R flat tax are explained. Lastly, selected policy issues are examined, including both broad and narrow economic issues, simplicity, and international comparisons. The broad economic issues relate to the economic effects of the flat tax on the entire economy, for example, equity, efficiency, and international trade. The more narrow economic issues deal with specific industries or sectors of the total economy, such as housing or charitable organizations.

In the 111th Congress (as of March 22, 2010), four bills for fundamental tax reform include a flat tax based on the concepts of H-R. On February 12, 2009, Representative Michael C. Burgess introduced H.R. 1040, the *Freedom Flat Tax Act*. On May 4, 2009, Senator Lamar Alexander introduced a companion bill, S. 963, the *Optional One Page Flat*

Tax Act. These bills would authorize an individual or a person engaged in business activity to make an irrevocable election to be subject to a H-R flat tax (in lieu of the existing tax provisions). On March 30, 2009, Senator Arlen Specter introduced S. 741, *Flat Tax Act of 2009.* On April 30, 2009, Senator Richard C. Shelby introduced S. 932, the *Simplified, Manageable, and Responsible Tax Act.* S. 741 and S. 932 would levy a flat tax modeled after the H-R proposal as a replacement for the individual and corporate income taxes, and the estate and gift taxes.

INCOME VERSUS CONSUMPTION TAXATION

Although our current tax structure is frequently referred to as an income tax in popular discussions, it actually contains elements of both an income and a consumption-based tax. For example, it excludes some income that goes to savings, such as pension and individual retirement account (IRA) contributions, which is consistent with a tax using a consumption base. Overall, however, the return to new investment is taxed, which is consistent with an income tax.

The easiest way to understand the differences between the income and consumption tax bases is to define and understand the economic concept of income. In its broadest sense, income is a measure of the command over resources that an individual acquires during a given time period. Conceptually, an individual can exercise two options with regard to his income: he can consume it or he can save it. This theoretical relationship between income, consumption, and saving allows a very useful accounting identity to be established; income, by definition, must equal consumption plus saving.

Should the tax base be income or consumption? Is one inherently superior to the other? How do they stack up in terms of simplicity, equity, and efficiency? There appears to be insufficient theoretical or empirical evidence to conclude that a consumption-based tax is inherently superior to an income-based tax or vice versa.

Types of Consumption Taxes

The three general types of consumption-based taxes are: a retail sales tax, a value-added tax (VAT), and a consumed-income tax.[5] A broad-based consumption tax, however formulated, is equal to a tax on wages plus a lump sum tax on old capital in existence at the time the tax is imposed.

Retail Sales Tax
A retail sales tax (RST) is a consumption tax collected only at the retail level by vendors. A RST equals a set percentage of the retail price of taxable goods and services. Retail vendors collect the RST and remit tax revenue to the government.

Value-Added Tax

The H-R flat tax can be considered a modified value-added tax. Hence, an examination of specific aspects of a VAT is particularly important in explaining the operation of the proposed flat tax.[6]

Concept of a Value-Added Tax[7]

A value-added tax is levied at each stage of production on firms' value added. The value added of a firm is the difference between a firm's sales and a firm's purchases of inputs from other firms. In other words, a firm's value added is simply the amount of value a firm contributes to a good or service by applying its factors of production (land, labor, capital, and entrepreneurial ability).[8]

The prevailing procedure is to treat the purchase of capital inputs (plant and equipment) the same way as the purchase of any other input; that is, the purchase price is deducted at the time of purchase. This tax treatment of capital purchases is equivalent to expensing.

Methods of Calculating VAT

Three alternative methods of calculating VAT are the credit method, the subtraction method, and the addition method. Under the *credit method*, the firm calculates the VAT to be remitted to the government by a two-step process. First, the firm multiplies its sales by the tax rate to calculate VAT collected on sales. Second, the firm credits VAT paid on inputs against VAT collected on sales and remits this difference to the government. Under the *credit-invoice method*, a type of credit method, the firm is required to show VAT separately on all sales invoices and to calculate the VAT credit on inputs by adding all VAT shown on purchase invoices. Under the *subtraction method*, the firm calculates its value added by subtracting its cost of taxed inputs from its taxable sales. Next, the firm determines its VAT liability by multiplying its value added by the VAT rate.

Under the *addition method*, the firm calculates its value added by adding all payments for untaxed inputs (e.g., wages and profits). Next, the firm multiplies its value added by the VAT rate to calculate VAT to be remitted to the government.[9]

Consumed-Income Tax

A consumed-income tax would have a tax base that includes all sources of income but allows deductions for saving. This base would result in the taxation of only consumption. Taxpayers would deduct contributions to qualified savings accounts (equivalent to individual retirement accounts, with unlimited contributions permitted). All withdrawals from qualified savings accounts would be taxable at the time of withdrawal. Policymakers would have the option of applying a progressive rate structure to the level of consumed income. In contrast to a RST or VAT, each individual would be responsible for calculating his level of consumed income and paying his tax obligation.[10]

HALL-RABUSHKA FLAT TAX

Justification

Hall and Rabushka argue that replacing the existing individual income tax with their flat tax would be a major improvement for three reasons: the flat tax would be much simpler than the current income tax, consumption is a better tax base than income, and the flat tax would be much more efficient than the current income tax system.

First, Hall and Rabushka maintain that there is a need for tax simplification. They argue that the complexity of the current federal individual and corporate income tax systems results in excessive administrative and compliance costs.[11]

Second, Hall and Rabushka argue that a consumption tax is superior to an income tax because " ... individuals would be taxed on what they take out of the economy (when they spend money to consume), not on what they produce (reflected in working and saving)."[12] They claim that

> By exempting investment from taxation, consumption taxes encourage investment and discourage spending. (Over time, each act of investment traces back to an act of saving; thus exempting investment from the tax base amounts to exempting saving.)[13]

Third, Hall and Rabushka assert that the current tax system results in an inefficient use of resources. They argue that their flat tax proposal would improve the allocation of resources, which would result in higher economic growth and a rise in living standards.

As will be discussed in more detail, some economists dispute H-R's justifications for a flat tax.

Operation

With a standard VAT, firms collect the tax and remit it to the Government. The H-R flat tax is essentially a *modified VAT*. The H-R flat tax proposal breaks the VAT into two parts: "an individual wage tax" (to collect tax on wages and pension receipts) and "a business tax" (to collect tax on old capital).[14] The principal effects of the H-R flat tax are like those of a standard VAT. In 1995, Hall and Rabushka published the second (and most current) edition of their book about their flat tax proposal. Hence, their analysis utilizes data from 1991, and their presentation of their proposal is for 1995. From 1991 through 2008 and from 1995 through 2008, according to the Bureau of Labor Statistics, the consumer price index rose 58.08% and 41.27%, respectively.[15] Thus, these rises in the price level should be considered in examining the data in their proposal.

The proposed bill in the 111th Congress based on the H-R concept includes much higher "personal allowances" for taxpayers and dependences than proposed by H-R for 1995, as described in the subsequent sections of this report. As previously indicated, on March 30, 2009, Senator Arlen Specter introduced S. 741, the Flat Tax Act of 2009. This bill's individual wage tax includes a "basic standard deductions" (equivalent to H-R's "personal allowances") of $25,000 for a joint return, $25,000 for a surviving spouse, $18,750 for a head of household, $12,500 for a married taxpayer filing separately, and $12,500 for a single taxpayer. The Flat Tax Act of 2009 also includes a deduction for each dependent of the taxpayer of $6,250. The dollar value of these deductions are indexed for inflation.

Individual Wage Tax

The individual wage tax would be imposed on wages (and salaries) and pension receipts at a 19% rate. Part or all of an individual's wage and pension income would be tax free depending on marital status and number of dependents. For tax year 1995, the personal allowance for a married couple filing jointly would be $16,500 and the personal allowance for each dependent would be $4,500. Thus, for a family of four (husband, wife, and two dependents) the first $25,500 in wage and pension income would not be taxed. All current income tax deductions would be eliminated including those for charitable contributions, mortgage interest, and state and local income and property taxes. An individual's Social Security contributions would not be deductible and his Social Security benefits would not be taxable. The current partial taxation of benefits for higher-income taxpayers would be eliminated.[16] H-R estimate that 80% of taxpayers do not run businesses, and consequently, they would only have to file this simple individual wage-tax form.[17]

Business Tax

The business tax would be a modified subtraction method VAT at a 19% rate with wages (and salaries) and pension contributions subtracted from the VAT base. (Under a standard subtraction-method VAT, a firm would not subtract its wages and pension contributions when calculating its tax base.)

Except for pension contributions, all fringe benefits would be included in the firm's tax base. "The employer's [Social Security] contributions would be treated like other fringe benefits—it would not be deductible from the business tax."[18] Government employees and employees of nonprofit organizations would have to add to their wage tax base the imputed value of their fringe benefits, because activities of government entities and tax-exempt organizations would be exempt from the business tax.

All purchases of plant and equipment would be immediately expensed (deducted from gross income). There would be no depreciation expenses for previously purchased plant and equipment. There would be no recovery of cost of goods sold (existing inventory)—a firm selling off inventory would not be able to deduct the cost.

A standard subtraction-method VAT would rebate negative amounts of VAT that might occur when a firm's subtractions exceed its revenue—for example, when a firm invests a large amount but has low sales. Under the H-R business tax, any negative tax would be carried forward to the next year with interest paid on the carry-forward.

Self-employed individuals would *usually* find it advantageous to file both a business tax return and an individual tax return. From their business operations, they would be able to pay themselves a salary, and thus use the personal allowance to exclude some income from taxation. For example, a married couple operating a business could exclude up to $16,500 in salary from taxation.

All owners of rental real estate would be required to file the business tax return.[19] "The purchase price [of rental property] would be deducted at the time of purchase, and the sale price would be taxed at the time of sale."[20]

SELECTED POLICY ISSUES

The H-R tax presented policy issues that fall into four broad categories: broad economic issues, more narrow sectoral economic issues, simplicity and international comparisons.

Broad Economic Issues

Broad economic issues concern the economic effects of the flat tax on the entire national economy. There are six: equity, efficiency, international trade, price level, interest rates, and revenue.

Equity

Policymakers are concerned about the distributional (or equity) effects of taxation; the proposed flat tax is no exception. A tax change has both a horizontal effect and a vertical effect on equity. Horizontal equity concerns the equal treatment of households with the same ability-to-pay. Vertical equity concerns the tax treatment of households with different abilities-to-pay. The most common measure of ability-to-pay is some measure of income, but some prefer a measure of consumption. Tax incidence usually is measured by using a one-year time period although a lifetime period sometimes is considered.[21]

Hall-Rabushka Analysis

Hall and Rabushka acknowledged that their proposed flat tax would cause some taxpayers to pay more taxes and some to pay less in the short run, but in the long run, they claimed that a higher rate of economic growth would cause many taxpayers who initially lost to eventually benefit.[22]

For 1991, H-R compared taxes on adjusted gross income consisting only of wage income with a hypothetical tax payments from the wage tax for a typical family (a married couple with 1.1 dependents). H-R concluded that currently the typical family with wage income below about $10,000 does not pay significant individual income tax on that income and would pay no flat tax on wages. The typical family with wage income between $10,000 and $30,000 would pay less under the flat wage tax than they currently pay in income tax. But, the flat wage tax would be slightly higher on average for the typical family in the $30,000 to $90,000 range. The typical family with wage income over $100,000 would pay less under the flat wage tax.[23]

But, H-R pointed out that there are limits to the preceding comparison.

> The individual wage tax component of the flat tax, however, will raise less revenue than the personal income tax, and, correspondingly, the business tax component of the flat tax will raise more revenue than the existing corporate income tax.[24]

The comparison above only covered wage income. For 1991, the average tax rate on wage income under the flat tax would have been only 8.5% because personal allowances would have excluded one-half of wage income from taxation.[25] In contrast, for 1991, the average tax rate on wage income under the individual income tax was 10.4%.[26]

Because of the substantial data problems in attempting to measure the incidence of the flat tax compared to the current individual tax, H-R conclude that

> We can't tell if there are any income groups who would pay significantly higher taxes, including the wage taxes they would pay directly and the business taxes they would pay indirectly. This group could not include the poor, who receive almost no business income.[27]

U.S. Treasury's Analysis

The U.S. Treasury analyzed the incidence of the proposed Armey-Shelby flat tax, which is based on the Hall-Rabushka concept.[28] The Treasury used a broad-based income concept called Family Economic Income (FEI): a concept that includes, for example, employer-provided fringe benefits and the imputed rent on owner-occupied housing.[29] In order for the Armey-Shelby flat tax to be revenue neutral, the U.S. Treasury maintained that a 20.8 percentage rate would have to be levied. The Treasury calculated the incidence of the change to the flat tax on eight different FEI classes. The Treasury concluded that only the highest income class (FEI of $200,000 or more) would pay less in taxes; other classes would pay more.[30] These distributional effects are partially the result of assumptions concerning the incidence of different components of the flat tax.[31]

Gravelle's Analysis

Jane G. Gravelle, a Senior Specialist at CRS, emphasized that if a flat tax is passed, and the Federal Reserve did not change the money supply, then the flat tax would be shifted backwards onto owners of equities (old capital) and wage earners. Gravelle also assesses the lifetime and intergenerational incidence of a consumption tax:

> The consumption tax tends to shift the burden to holders of old assets, who are likely to be old. The young tend to benefit if they are likely to do a significant amount of lifetime saving, but the young who do little lifetime saving can be made worse off if tax rates are much higher. Those who do little lifetime saving are likely to be the lifetime poor. At the same time, very wealthy individuals with accumulated assets who consistently pass on wealth across the generations may also avoid the tax and may find their tax burdens lowered indefinitely compared to an income tax. Thus, these generational shifts probably contribute to a less progressive tax.[32]

Gravelle's analysis raises the issue of horizontal equity since the flat tax would shift the tax burden from the young to the old. It should also be noted that old capital and thus the old will bear a consumption tax regardless of whether the money supply is altered. Accommodating the tax with a price change will cause the burden to be shared by debt claimants—the cost of physical assets would rise resulting in the net of tax sales proceeds being fixed, but the purchasing power would fall and cause proceeds of both debt and equity holders to effectively bear the tax. If price is not changed, and there is no reason to believe it will be under the flat tax except for a minor revision to reflect the cost of fringe benefits, prices of goods will not rise, and the net of tax sales proceeds would fall by the amount of this tax. This tax will fall solely on equity since the value of outstanding debt is fixed. This tax could be very high for heavily leveraged assets that are recently purchased.

In summary, the current income tax system is progressive but the incidence of the H-R flat tax is uncertain. There is no general agreement concerning the vertical incidence of the proposed shift to the H-R flat tax—whether it would reduce or increase tax progressivity.

Efficiency

In public finance, the more *neutral* is a tax, the less the tax affects private economic decisions; and, consequently, the more efficient is the operation of the economy.

For households, two out of three major decisions would not be altered by this hypothetical consumption tax. First, this consumption tax would not alter choices among goods because all would be taxed at the same rate. Thus, *relative* prices would not change. In contrast, other taxes, such as excise taxes, which change relative prices, would distort household consumer choices by encouraging the substitution of untaxed goods for taxed goods. A hypothetical income tax on all income would be neutral in this respect.

Second, a flat tax does not affect the relative prices of present and future consumption. In contrast, the individual income tax affects the relative prices of present and future consumption because the income tax is levied on income which is saved, and then the returns on saving are taxed.

A household's work-leisure decision, however, would be affected by a flat tax or any other tax on either consumption or income. Since leisure would not be taxed, any tax increase would fall on the returns to work. Hence, under either an consumption or an income tax the price of leisure is reduced relative to the consumption an individual could finance with an extra hour of labor.

For a firm, the flat tax would not affect decisions concerning method of financing (debt or equity), choice among inputs, type of business organization (corporation, partnership, or sole proprietorship), and goods to produce. Other types of taxes may affect one or more of these types of decisions.

Because consumption is a smaller base than income, to raise the same amount of tax revenue, a consumption-based tax would require a larger increase in marginal tax rates than would an income tax. Distortions caused by these higher marginal rates could offset (or even exceed) other neutral advantages of the flat tax. Hence, whether an income tax system or a flat tax system is more efficient is unknown.[33]

Savings

H-R argue that taxing only consumption rather than all income (saving and consumption) would increase the savings rate. H-R predict that in consequence, a flat tax would cause an increase in the capital stock that would increase gross domestic product (GDP) by 2% to 4% within seven years.[34]

National saving consists of government saving, business saving, and personal saving.[35] Any tax increase or reduction in federal expenditures would be expected to reduce government dissaving, and consequently, raise national saving.[36] Thus, whether a flat tax increases or reduces revenue is relevant to its effect on national saving.

Another issue concerns the personal savings rate. But there is no conclusive theoretical or empirical evidence that a consumption tax will increase the savings rate and consequently the level of national savings.[37] According to economic theory, a rise in the after tax rate of return would have two conflicting effects. *First*, each dollar saved today results in the possibility of a higher amount of consumption in the future. This relative increase in the return from saving causes a household to want to substitute saving for consumption out of current income (substitution effect). *Second*, a higher rate of return on savings raises a household's income; consequently, the household has to save less to accumulate some target amount of savings in the future (income effect). Thus, this income effect encourages households to have higher current consumption and lower current saving. These two conflicting effects mean that economic theory cannot determine the effects of the rate of return on the savings rate.

Highly stylized life-cycle models show that a flat tax would cause a substantial increase in the savings rate, but these models are extremely controversial.[38] These stylized models add a *third* effect for a consumption tax. Unlike a mere exclusion of tax on the return, the consumption tax allows an up-front deduction for savings, but requires the payment of tax on both principal and return when consumption occurs in the future. Thus, individuals need to save today to pay these taxes due in the future; they can do so while still consuming more today because of their large tax cuts. Thus, while the young may consume some part of their tax cut, the old reduce their consumption by much more, and the overall effect is to increase aggregate savings in the economy. But these stylized life-cycle models rely on somewhat idealized assumptions, such as all taxpayers having perfect information and certainty that the tax system will not change during their lifetimes. If these idealized assumptions are relaxed, then the results are not conclusive that switching from an income tax to consumption tax would increase savings.[39]

Work Effort

H-R maintain that their flat tax would reduce the marginal tax rate of most taxpayers. Taxpayers would have a marginal rate of either zero or 19%. H-R estimate that as a result, their flat tax would increase total hours of work in the U.S. economy by 4%.[40] Hence, "total annual output of goods and services in the U.S. economy would rise by about 3%, or almost $200 billion."[41]

Whether a revenue neutral flat tax increases or reduces a household's marginal tax rate, it would have conflicting effects on the number of hours worked by that household. Households with a lower marginal tax rate would have an incentive to substitute work for leisure because of the relative rise in the value of work to leisure (substitution effect). Conversely, a household would have an incentive to reduce its hours worked because it needs to work fewer hours in order to achieve a given standard of living (income effect). For households with a higher marginal rate, the substitution effect would tend to decrease work effort but the income effect would tend to increase work effort. A household's marginal rate affects its substitution effect but its average tax rate affects its income effect. Thus, as assessed by current economic theory, a flat tax could decrease, increase, or not change a household's hours worked. In any case, many economists believe that, on the basis of theoretical considerations and empirical studies, the current income tax system does not significantly affect the aggregate number of hours worked.

Investment

H-R maintain that taxing all investment at a uniform rate would improve the efficient allocation of capital and raise the return on capital investment. The current system does have major distortions in the taxation of capital income such as the double taxation of corporate income, the preference for debt financing, and the favorable treatment of owner occupied housing. In addition, H-R cite an analysis by Alan J. Auerbach, an economics professor at the

University of California at Berkeley, that the current tax system has a bias in investment toward equipment and away from structures, and consequently, eliminating this bias would raise gross national product (GNP) by 0.8%.[42]

H-R argue that currently tax-favored entities such as pension funds prefer investing in low risk activities often secured by readily marketable assets. H-R maintain that their flat tax would eliminate tax preferences including the interest deduction, and therefore, redirect investment into innovative enterprises based on new ideas.[43]

But in response to all the efficiency arguments, it can be argued that it is not appropriate to compare a perfect consumption tax in concept with an imperfect real income tax system. There are steps that might improve the present system that stop short of a flat tax—for example, the current individual income tax and the corporate income tax could be integrated or, current tax preferences could be eliminated or curtailed, thus producing a more neutral income tax.

Growth
According to H-R,

> Tax reform along the lines of our simple tax will influence the American economy profoundly: Improved incentives for work, entrepreneurial activity, and capital formation will substantially raise national output and the standard of living.[44]

H-R estimate that their flat tax would raise annual output by 6% after the economy has fully adjusted to the tax change which would be a period of seven years.[45] This 6% increase in output would consist of a 3% rise due to increased work effort and a 3% rise due to a combination of added capital formation and better entrepreneurial incentives.[46]

But H-R provide no model on which their estimate is based. As discussed in preceding sections, many tax economists do not believe that changes in the tax code can significantly affect either the savings rate or the work-leisure decision. Also, most capital accumulation models have a much longer period to return to steady state than seven years. For example, to increase net output by 3% through increased savings, the capital stock would have to increase by about 12%. Since the capital stock tends to grow at the growth rate of the economy—say 2% a year—the savings rate would have to nearly double for that seven-year period to increase the capital stock by that much.

International Trade
The Hall-Rabushka flat tax is not border adjustable. That is, unlike a credit-invoice method value-added tax, for example, the H-R tax is not levied on all imports and rebated on all exports. Popular perception holds that this lack of border adjustability would increase this nation's balance-of-trade deficit. Economic theory, however, holds that border tax adjustments have little current effect on the balance-of-trade because the balance-of-trade is, in part, a function of international capital flows. Any changes in the product prices of traded goods and services brought about by border tax adjustments would usually be offset by exchange rate adjustments.[47]

Price Level

The H-R flat tax proposal would not require any change in the price level. Wage income and pension receipts are taxed at the individual level while capital income minus net investment and fringe benefits (except pension contributions) are taxed at the firm level. Thus, the flat tax proposal would not *require* a change in the price level to prevent an economic contraction (unlike a VAT), except for the small effects due to taxing fringe benefits.[48]

Interest Rates

Most economists believe that the H-R flat tax (or a similar proposal) would lower interest rates, but a minority of economists maintain that interest rates could rise.[49]

Revenue

Policymakers are concerned about three aspects of a tax's revenue yield: adequacy, stability, and countercyclical effects.

Adequacy

The H-R flat tax would replace the personal income and corporate income taxes. This drastic change raises the issue of the adequacy of the revenue yield. Revenue forecasting is, at best, a necessary but inexact government undertaking. Revenue forecasts of income tax revenues often have been too low or too high. Thus, there is a justifiable concern that in an abrupt transition to a flat tax the initial revenue yield could be far too low or too high compared with the amount forecasted. Any drastic unexpected decline or rise in tax revenue could be destabilizing to the economy.

Stability

Consumption is more stable than personal income since people attempt to maintain their living standards during recessions (save less) and save more during periods of prosperity. Business income (and hence business income taxes) usually rises dramatically during an economic expansion, but usually declines precipitously during a recession. Because the flat tax excludes business income, it would result in more stable total tax revenues over the business cycle than an income tax system.

Countercyclical Effects

The current income tax system is an automatic stabilizer; that is, without any discretionary action by policymakers, the income tax system tends to maintain aggregate demand in the economy (by reducing tax revenues) during recessions and curtailing aggregate demand (by increasing tax revenue) during booms. The countercyclical effects of a flat tax would be much weaker since revenues would be more stable over the business cycle. But the importance of these tax effects are diminished in the modern world of highly mobile capital.

Sectoral Issues

As previously indicated, more narrow economic issues deal with specific industries or sectors of the total economy. Seven are discussed in the subsequent sections: differential effects on businesses, charitable organizations, housing, financial services, pensions and insurance, health care, and state and local governments.

Differential Effects on Businesses

As noted previously, if there is no price accommodation, the general burden of the H-R flat tax will fall on wages and old capital. At a more discrete level, the business tax proposed by H-R would have differential effects among corporations depending on their financial characteristics and their industry.[50] Many large, established, slow-growing corporations with large depreciation expenses and high interest expenses would be collect much higher business taxes than they pay under the current corporate income tax. These corporations would be unable to deduct depreciation for plant and equipment purchased prior to the enactment of the flat tax. Also, they would be unable to deduct interest costs on their outstanding debt. Furthermore, existing inventory costs would not be recovered. Firms selling off inventory or selling assets would face a large tax burden especially if debt financed.[51]

In contrast, young, fast growing corporations with little debt and low depreciation expenses would collect less under the business tax than they pay under the current corporate income tax. All new investment in plant and equipment would be immediately expensed. Because of their low level of outstanding debt, the loss of the interest expense would be of little concern to these corporations.

H-R use examples to demonstrate that there would be a dramatic change in the amount of taxes collected by different corporations. According to H-R, in 1993, General Motors (GM) paid about \$110 million in corporate income taxes. In 1993, GM's interest expense and depreciation outweighed its new investment: GM had interest expenses of \$5.7 billion and depreciation deductions for past investment of \$9 billion but only about \$6 billion in new investment. Thus, under the H-R flat tax, for 1993, H-R estimate that GM would have remitted taxes of \$2.72 billion, over 24 times its actual corporate tax liability.[52]

In contrast, H-R examined the corporate income tax return of the Intel Corporation. In 1993, Intel paid \$1.2 billion in corporate income taxes. Intel had no debt and thus no interest expenses and invested heavily in new plant and equipment. Thus, under the proposed flat tax, Intel would have remitted only \$277 million for 1993, less than one-fourth its actual corporate income tax liability.[53]

The elimination of depreciation expenses would create a special transitional problem. Managers of a business would be reluctant to purchase plant and equipment in the year before the flat tax would go into effect because they would be able to write off only one year of depreciation. If managers of this business simply waited a year, the entire investment outlay could be written off, that is, expensed. Hence, the approval of the flat tax could result in a sudden decline and then a sharp rise in investment after the flat tax was operational. Furthermore, managers of many existing businesses may consider it "unfair" to change the rules and deny depreciation expenses for past investment.

H-R offer, as an option, allowing managers of businesses to continue depreciating investments made before the introduction of the flat tax. This would require, however, a higher tax rate to offset the resulting loss in revenue, and there would be a reduction in economic efficiency.[54] But, the higher tax rate would be temporary, since depreciation expenses would diminish over time.[55] Furthermore, the flat tax would be more complicated if depreciation was permitted.

Also, the flat tax would eliminate tax preferences available to specific industries. For instance, oil producers currently receive a tax break on "intangibles" which allows them to write off most of their drilling costs. In addition, oil independents use the percentage depletion allowance to write off a percentage of their receipts. Thus, the oil producing companies probably would collect more under the business tax than they currently pay in corporate income taxes.

Hence, the financial structure and tax preferences of different industries would result in differential shifts in tax liabilities between the current corporate income tax and the proposed business tax.

Charitable Organizations

Currently, taxpayers who itemize can deduct the value of contributions they make to qualifying charitable organizations.[56] The H-R flat tax would eliminate this charitable deduction which would likely cause charitable donations to decline. But H-R claim that the decline in charitable contributions would be small.[57] Their claim, however, is controversial.[58] For example, Professor Charles T. Clotfelter and Richard L. Schmalbeck estimated that the Armey flat tax proposal (which is based on the H-R proposal) would significantly reduce charitable contributions.[59]

Housing

The flat tax would eliminate the mortgage interest deduction and the property tax deduction.[60] These deductions are controversial. Supporters argue that they promote home ownership and home improvement, which have positive spillover effects. Opponents argue that these preferences have little effect on the rate of home ownership and primarily benefit higher income families.[61] Furthermore, critics claim that these preferences have led to an overinvestment in housing. For example, the Competitive Policy Council, a bipartisan panel established by Congress, warned that Americans are hurting their competitiveness "by overinvesting in their houses and underinvesting in the kinds of new products and technologies that generate higher wages and salaries."[62]

Hall and Rabushka argue that interest rates would decline, and consequently the loss of these tax advantages could be offset by homeowners refinancing their mortgages. H-R predict that their flat tax would reduce interest rates by "at least a fifth."[63] H-R point out that in 1994 interest rates on municipal bonds were about one-sixth less than comparable taxable bonds. But H-R assert that taxable bonds also receive tax preferences; for example, if they are held in pension funds, the tax is deferred on interest income.[64] Hence, H-R assert that "interest rates could easily fall to three-quarters of their present levels after tax reform; rates on tax-free securities would then fall a little as well."[65] H-R maintain that their flat tax would encourage new investment which could cause some rise in interest rates, therefore, "as a safe working hypothesis ... [they] assume interest rates [would] fall in the year after tax reform by about a fifth."[66]

But their analysis did not incorporate the expanding influence of international movements of capital. Today's capital markets are truly global. Owners of financial capital can quickly transfer their funds among countries in order to maximize their expected returns. Consequently, whether or not the flat tax would lower interest rates is unknown.

Hence, many families with large interest payments and property tax payments might be unable to continue making their mortgage payments. These families might be forced to sell their homes. Furthermore, the sudden elimination of these preferences might cause a sudden drop in the value of the average house.[67] A decline in housing values would be a loss for sellers but a benefit to buyers.

H-R acknowledge that the elimination of interest deductions would result in winners and losers during transition. They state:

> If Congress decides that a transition measure to protect interest deductions is needed, we suggest the following. Any borrower may choose to treat interest payments as a tax deduction. If the borrower so chooses, the lender must treat the interest as taxable income. But the borrower's deduction should be only 90% of the actual interest payment, while the lender's taxable income should include 100% of the interest receipts.[68]

This transition option would grandfather in existing interest deductions; thus, borrowers would benefit at the expense of lenders. The proposal also would apply to new loans. For the housing industry, many homeowners would be protected from the forced sale of their homes, but mortgage lenders would suffer financially. Furthermore, this transition proposal would add complexity to the flat tax. It is important to recognize that part of the effect of H-R in discouraging demand for housing arises from the opportunities for a higher return from other investments.[69]

Financial Services

The primary service of financial institutions (banks, savings & loan associations, credit unions, etc.) is intermediation; that is, aggregating funds of depositors and providing credit to borrowers by making loans or purchasing debt instruments. Core services provided by financial institutions are not identified by explicit fees. Instead these services are implicit in the interest spread between the rates paid depositors and the rates charged on loans to borrowers or received on purchased debt instruments. For an insurance company, the value-added is approximately equal to premiums received from policyholders for risk protection. But life insurance often includes a savings component, which is difficult to separate from risk protection.[70]

Hall and Rabushka claim that it would be easy to measure the value-added of financial intermediaries and insurance companies.[71] But, developed nations have found that it is so difficult to measure value-added of financial institutions and insurance companies that they generally exempt these businesses from their VATs.[72]

Pensions and Insurance

Pensions are favored under current tax law because they are effectively tax exempt (treated on a consumption-tax basis). While firms would still have reasons to provide pensions, proposals that would extend this treatment to all investments would make pensions relatively less attractive, and might discourage their use. If some individuals now save more through a pension plan than they would on their own, overall savings could be adversely affected as well.[73] Currently tax-favored insurance policies (e.g., whole life insurance) would also become relatively less attractive.[74]

Health Care

Under current law, there are numerous tax preferences for health care spending. The most significant is that "an individual is entitled to an itemized deduction for expenses paid during the tax year for the medical care of the individual, the individual's spouse, or a dependent to the extent that such expenses exceed 7.5% of adjusted gross income."[75] Under the H-R flat tax, all tax preferences for health care would be eliminated including the itemized deduction.

Under the H-R flat tax, firms would have less of an incentive to provide compensation in the form of health care for employees. Furthermore, individuals with catastrophic health care needs (in excess of 7.5% of adjusted gross income) would not receive a tax preference.

Hence, the H-R flat tax would tend to reduce the rate of growth in the demand for health care which in turn would lower the rate of inflation of health care services from what would otherwise occur.

State and Local Governments

State and local governments would be affected by the proposed H-R flat tax. These effects fall into three categories: municipal bonds, deductibility of state and local taxes, and states' tax structures.[76]

Municipal Bonds

Currently, interest on municipal (state and local) bonds is exempt from federal corporate and individual income taxes. This tax exemption has raised the market value of municipal bonds. As noted above, the effect of the H-R proposal on interest rates is disputed. But, if interest rates decline only slightly, or not at all, the H-R proposal would cause outstanding municipal bonds to decline sharply in value because of the elimination of the tax exemption.

The mere possibility of passage of the Armey flat tax plan, which was similar to the H-R proposal, reduced the value of outstanding municipal bonds at that time.[77] Many managers of municipal bond funds blamed discussions about flat taxes for the negative cash flow which "plagued municipal bond funds throughout 1995."[78] Thus, if the H-R flat tax becomes law, individuals owning municipal bonds may experience large capital losses. Furthermore, state and local governments may have to pay higher interest rates on new debt issues because municipal securities would no longer have a tax advantage over other debt issues.

Some economists dispute the wisdom of providing a tax subsidy to municipal bonds. Thus, the flat tax's removal of the subsidy may be beneficial.

Deductibility of State and Local Taxes

Currently, individuals who itemize can deduct most state and local taxes. This is a form of revenue sharing. For example, if a state raises its income tax, individuals who itemize save on their federal income taxes an amount equal to their marginal federal income tax rate multiplied by the increase in their state income tax payments. The H-G flat tax would eliminate this tax preference. This tax preference is particularly valuable to high income individuals in high tax states such as New York. This tax preference has been controversial, and some tax economists have recommended that it be curtailed or eliminated.[79]

States' Tax Structures

Since the flat tax is a consumption tax, the federal government would be competing directly with states' sales taxes, their primary revenue source. But most states also levy an income tax which is their second main source of revenue. States with income taxes generally base their tax bases on the federal income tax base, with slight variations. If the federal government replaces its income taxes then the continuation of current state income taxes would impose high compliance costs on individuals and businesses since these taxpayers would have to continue to calculate their income tax liabilities. States would also have high administrative costs. But states probably would react by dropping their taxes on net income and adopting a consumption-based tax that would piggyback on the new federal consumption tax base, thereby retaining the administrative and compliance benefits that flow from conforming to the federal tax base.[80]

Simplicity

H-R argue that their flat tax proposal would reduce drastically the current complexity of the U.S. tax system. Tax preferences would be eliminated. Tax integration and simple returns would result from their consumption tax.

Integration and Measuring Capital Income

Since new investment would no longer be taxed, the flat tax would also eliminate problems the current system encounters with measuring capital income: capital gains, attempts to distinguish between real and nominal income, depreciation procedures, and debt versus equity financing. A positive aspect of the proposed flat tax is the ease with which the individual and corporate tax systems could be integrated. Thus, a change that economists have long advocated for its economic efficiency could be accomplished in a simple way.

But it would be possible to levy a flat tax with an income base, simply by retaining depreciation and inventory accounting. The corporate and individual income tax systems could be integrated while retaining an income base—what makes integration simple is the flat rate.

Simple Returns and Other Simplicity Issues

H-R emphasize that, because their flat tax system is simple, the two tax forms "can fit on postcards."[81] The flat tax returns require little information and only a few simple calculations, but critics argue that there are numerous underlying complications.

Six additional issues are relevant to the complexity of the proposed flat rate tax. *First*, the current income tax system is complex. The federal tax code and the federal tax regulation are lengthy and continue to expand. Many taxpayers spend much time, money, and effort complying with the current income tax system. The complexity of the tax code and the fear of the Internal Revenue Service (IRS) have caused many taxpayers to pay for professional assistance.

For tax year 2000, a microsimulation model developed jointly by IBM and the IRS estimated the amount of time and money that individuals spend on federal tax compliance.[82] The authors found that "in tax year 2000, 125.9 million individual taxpayers experienced a total compliance burden of 3.21 billion hours and $18.8 billion."[83] This translates into an average burden of 25.5 hours and $149 per taxpayer.[84] Furthermore, for tax year 2003, 78.75 million individuals paid for the preparation of their returns.[85]

The complexity of the income tax, however, should not be overstated. For example, for tax year 2006, the Internal Revenue Service reported that only 49.12 million returns out of 138.39 million returns were filed by individuals who itemized their deductions."[86] Also, the complexity of the current tax code is partially due to attempts to achieve greater equity or improve economic efficiency, and there are often tradeoffs between simplicity, equity, and efficiency.

Second, complexity may contribute to the gross income "tax gap"—the difference between income taxes owed and the amount voluntarily paid in a timely manner—which the Internal Revenue Service estimated is $350 billion for 2001.[87] In addition, widespread tax avoidance reduces tax revenues which, in turn, necessitates higher tax rates to raise a given amount of revenue. But, enforcement efforts and late payments reduced the gross tax gap by $55 billion for 2001. Furthermore, it can be argued that, in comparison to other developed nations, current U.S. tax compliance is satisfactory. Finally, a tax gap of unknown magnitude would occur under the flat tax.

Third, in comparison to the current income tax, a flat *rate* does little to reduce complexity because most taxpayers simply look up their tax liability in a table.

Fourth, it can be argued that it may be "unfair" to compare the current income tax system with some form of a "pure" consumption tax. By the time a consumption tax becomes enacted, it may become complicated, in part, because of lobbying by special interest groups. Furthermore, an initially simple tax may become complicated over time as it is revised.

Fifth, as an alternative to the flat tax, the current income tax system could be simplified by expanding the tax base which would require eliminating tax preferences and reducing marginal rates.

Sixth, the flat tax can, in some instances, be more complicated (rather than simpler) than the tax it replaces. For example, federal government employees and employees of non-profits would have to add to their wage base the imputed value of their fringe benefits.[88] Hence, a separate individual wage tax form would be necessary for these employees. The actual calculation of the imputed value of fringe benefits would be complicated. Another example is that H-R have not discussed tax issues concerning multinational corporations.

International Comparisons

There are three major distinctions between recent consumption tax proposals for the United States and the current tax systems of other developed nations. *First*, although the United States is the only developed nation without a broad-based consumption tax at the national level, other developed nations adopted broad-based consumption taxes as adjuncts rather than as replacements for their income based taxes. Congressional proposals would replace our current income taxes with consumption taxes, rather than use consumption taxes as adjuncts to our current income based system. Despite what is sometimes claimed, the United States would thus be moving into unchartered waters.

Second, all developed nations with VATs, except Japan, calculate their VATs using the credit-invoice method. The H-R flat tax proposal, however, would use the subtraction method of calculation for the business tax. The General Agreement on Tariffs and Trade (GATT Agreement) requires that for a consumption tax (including a VAT) to be rebated on exports, the tax must be levied on an item by item basis. Furthermore, the business tax is not levied on wage income. In contrast to most VATs, the business tax would not be border adjustable. Consequently, domestic firms would collect the business tax on their products sold domestically or exported but the business tax would not be collected on imported products. But, as previously discussed, economic theory has long recognized that border tax adjustments have no effect on the balance-of-trade because the balance-of-trade is a function of international capital flows.

Third, most other developed nations have much larger public sectors (government spending as a percentage of gross domestic product) than the United States. These countries offer a wider range of social benefits (such as national health care) in order to reduce inequality and lessen economic insecurity. Hence, these nations need greater tax revenues, and consequently, levy both broad-based consumption taxes and income taxes.

CONCLUSION

The concept of replacing our current federal income tax system with a flat rate consumption tax is receiving congressional interest. The term "flat tax" is often associated with a consumption tax proposal formulated by Robert E. Hall and Alvin Rabushka, two senior fellows at the Hoover Institution. As of March 22, 2010, four bills have been introduced in the 111th Congress that include a flat tax based on the concepts of H-R. On February 12, 2009, Representative Michael C. Burgess introduced H.R. 1040, the *Freedom Flat Tax Act*. On May 4, 2009, Senator Lamar Alexander introduced a companion bill, S. 963, the *Optional One Page Flat Tax Act*. These bills would authorize an individual or a person engaged in business activity to make an irrevocable election to be subject to a H-R flat tax (in lieu of the existing tax provisions). On March 30, 2009, Senator Arlen Specter introduced S. 741, *Flat Tax Act of 2009*. On April 30, 2009, Senator Richard C. Shelby introduced S. 932, the *Simplified, Manageable, and Responsible Tax Act*. S. 741 and S. 932 would levy a flat tax modeled after the H-R proposal as a replacement for the individual and corporate income taxes, and the estate and gift taxes. This report discusses the idea of replacing the current U.S.

income tax system—which is a hybrid of an income and a consumption tax—with a pure consumption tax formulated by H-R.

The combined individual and business taxes proposed by H-R can be viewed as a modified value-added tax (VAT). The individual wage tax would be imposed on wages (and salaries) and pension receipts. Part or all of an individual's wage and pension income would be tax free depending on marital status and number of dependents. The business tax would be a modified subtraction method VAT with wages (and salaries) and pension contributions subtracted from the VAT base. (Under a standard subtraction-method VAT, a firm would not subtract its wages and pension contributions when calculating its tax base.)

Hall and Rabushka argue that replacing the existing individual income tax with their flat tax would be a major improvement for three reasons: the flat tax would be much simpler than the current complex income tax, consumption is a better tax base than income, and the flat tax would be much more efficient than the current income tax system.

This report's examination of the H-R flat tax proposal and their arguments supporting it looked at *four* topics: broad economic issues, narrow sectoral economic issues, simplicity, and international comparisons.

The broad economic issues concern the economic effects of the flat tax on the entire national economy. The flat tax would be shifted backwards onto owners of equities (old capital) and wage earners. The current income tax system is progressive but the incidence of the H-R flat tax proposal across income classes is unknown. The flat tax would reduce the tax burden on the young but increase it on the old.

Whether the proposed flat tax would be more or less efficient than the current income tax system is unknown. There is no conclusive theoretical or empirical evidence that the flat tax proposal would significantly affect savings, work effort, investment, or growth. A consumption base is neither inherently superior nor inferior to an income base.

The H-R flat tax would not be border adjustable. Current economic theory holds that border tax adjustments have little effect on the balance-of-trade because the balance-of-trade is largely a function of international capital flows.

The H-R flat tax proposal would not require any change in the price level. Most economists believe that the H-R flat tax would lower interest rates, but a minority of economists maintain that interest rates could rise.

Revenue forecasting is an inexact, if necessary, science; hence, there is a considerable concern that the initial revenue yield from the flat tax could be far too low or too high. Over the business cycle, total tax revenues would be more stable under a flat tax than under an income tax system.

Narrow sectoral economic issues concern specific industries or sectors of the total economy. The six microeconomic issues discussed were differential effects on businesses, charitable organizations, housing, financial services, health care, and state and local governments. Most of these discussions related to the elimination of an existing income tax preference.

The *simplicity* of the proposed flat tax is emphasized by Hall and Rabushka. A positive aspect of the proposed flat tax is the ease with which the individual and corporate tax systems could be integrated.

The complexity of the current tax code is partially due to attempts by policymakers to achieve greater equity or improve economic efficiency. In comparison to the current income tax, a flat rate, per se, does little to reduce complexity because most taxpayers simply look up their tax liability in a table. It can also be argued that it may be "unfair" to compare the current income tax system with some form of a "pure" consumption tax. By the time a consumption tax can be enacted it may become complicated. As an option to the flat tax, some observers maintain that the current income tax system could be simplified by expanding the tax base.

International comparisons of tax systems indicate that there are major distinctions between recent consumption tax proposals for the United States and the current tax systems of other developed nations. Although the United States is the only developed nation without a broad-based consumption tax at the national level, other developed nations adopted broad-based consumption taxes as adjuncts rather than as replacements for their income based taxes. Notably, all developed nations with VATs, except Japan, calculate their VATs using the credit-invoice method. The H-R flat tax proposal, however, would use the subtraction method of calculation for the business tax. Finally, most other developed nations have much larger public sectors (government spending as a percentage of gross domestic product) than the United States. These nations need greater tax revenues, and consequently, levy both broad-based consumption taxes and income taxes.

It is worth noting that numerous aspects of the H-R flat tax proposal have not been fleshed out and important policy issues have yet to be analyzed.

APPENDIX. TAX FORMS UNDER THE FLAT TAX

Form 1	Individual Wage Tax		1995
Your first name and initial (if joint return, also give spouse's name and initial)		Last name	Your social security number
Present home address (number and street including apartment number or rural route)			Spouse's social security no
City, town, or post office, state, and ZIP code	Your occupation➤		
	Spouse's occupation➤		

1	Wages and salary	1	
2	Pension and retirement benefits	2	
3	Total compensation (line 1 plus line 2)	3	
4	Personal allowance		
	(a) ☐ $16,500 for married filing jointly	4(a)	
	(b) ☐ $9,500 for single	4(b)	
	(c) ☐ $14,000 for single head of household	4(c)	
5	Number of dependents, not including spouse	5	
6	Personal allowances for dependents (line 5 multiplied by $4,500)	6	
7	Total personal allowances (line 4 plus line 6)	7	
8	Taxable compensation (line 3 less line 7, if positive; otherwise zero)	8	
9	Tax (19% of line 8)	9	
10	Tax withheld by employer	10	
11	Tax due (line 9 less line 10, if positive)	11	
12	Refund due (line 10 less line 9, if positive)	12	

Source: Hall and Rabushka, *The Flat Tax*, p. 59.

Figure A-1. Individual Wage Tax.

Form 1   **Business Tax**   **1995**

Business Name   Employer Identification Number

Street Address   County

City, State, and ZIP Code   Principal Product

1	Gross revenue from sales	1	
2	Allowable costs		
	(a) Purchases of goods, services, and materials	2(a)	
	(b) Wages, salaries, and pensions	2(b)	
	(c) Purchases of capital equipment, structures, and land	2(c)	
3	Total allowable costs *(sum of lines 2(a), 2(b), 2(c)*	3	
4	Taxable income *(line 1 less line 3)*	4	
5	Tax *(19% of line 4)*	5	
6	Carry-forward from 1994	6	
7	Interest on carry-forward *(6% of line 6)*	7	
8	Carry-forward into 1995 *(line 6 plus line 7)*	8	
9	Tax due *(line 5 less line 8, if positive)*	9	
10	Carry-forward to 1996 *(line 8 less line 5, if positive)*	10	

Source: Hall and Rabushka, *The Flat Tax*, p. 59.

Figure A-2. Business Tax.

End Notes

[1] The complete citation of this book is Robert E. Hall and Alvin Rabushka, *The Flat Tax,* Second Edition (Stanford, California: Hoover Institution Press, 1995), 152 p. (The first edition of this book was published in 1985.)

[2] Robert E. Hall, "Guidelines for Tax Reform: The Simple, Progressive Value-Added Tax," in Alan J. Auerbach and Kevin A. Hassett, eds., *Toward Fundamental Tax Reform* (Washington, DC: The AEI Press, 2005), pp. 70-80.

[3] Three bills based on the Hall-Rabushka proposal were introduced in the 110th Congress: H.R. 1040, S. 1040, and S. 1081. Former House Majority Leader Richard K. Armey introduced flat tax legislation based on the Hall-Rabushka proposal, his most recent bill being introduced in the 107th Congress. His proposed flat tax bills have been frequently analyzed by economists. In 1996, presidential candidate Steve Forbes advocated a flat tax based on the H-R concept. For a explanation of his proposal, see Steve Forbes, *Flat Tax Revolution* (Washington, DC: Regency Publishing, Inc., 2005), 216 p.

[4] For a description of current tax reform proposals, see CRS Report R40414, *Tax Reform: An Overview of Proposals in the 111th Congress*, by James M. Bickley.

[5] For a comparison of the flat tax concept with other consumption tax concepts, see Joel Slemrod and Jon Bakija, *Taxing Ourselves: A Citizen's Guide to the Great Debate over Tax Reform*, 3rd ed. (Cambridge, MA: The MIT Press, 2004), pp. 233-271.

[6] Robert E. Hall refers to his flat tax as "the simple, progressive value-added consumption tax."

[7] For a comprehensive examination of the value-added tax, see CRS Report RL33619, *Value-Added Tax: A New U.S. Revenue Source?*, by James M. Bickley.

[8] These factors of production have specific meanings to an economist. Labor consists of all employees hired by the firm. Land consists of all natural resources including raw land, water, and mineral wealth. Capital is anything used in the production process, which has been made by man. The entrepreneur is the decision maker who operates the firm.

[9] For a comparison of the credit-invoice method and the subtraction method, see CRS General Distribution Memorandum, *Value-Added Tax: Methods of Calculation*, by James M. Bickley; available from the author.

[10] An analysis of the concept of a consumed income tax is presented in CRS Report 98-248, *A Federal Tax On Consumed Income: Background and Analysis*, by Gregg A. Esenwein. (Out-of-print report available from CRS on request.)

[11] For an examination of the administrative and compliance costs of the current income tax system and the flat tax, see William G. Gale and Janet Holtzblatt, "Measuring the Impact of Administrative Factors under Tax Reform," *Proceedings of the 1998 Annual Conference of the National Tax Association*, pp. 341-349.

[12] Hall and Rabushka, p. 40.

[13] Ibid., p. 41.

[14] Copies of tax forms for the individual wage tax and the business tax are shown in Appendix.

[15] Bureau of Labor Statistics, *CPI Inflation Calculator*, available at http://www.bls.gov/data/inflation_calculator.htm, visited Apr. 22, 2009.

[16] Hall and Rabushka, p. 77.

[17] Ibid., p. 59.

[18] Ibid., p. 77.

[19] Ibid., p. 72.

[20] Ibid.

[21] For a brief discussion of these equity issues, see CRS Report RL33619, *Value-Added Tax: A New U.S. Revenue Source?*, by James M. Bickley.

[22] Hall and Rabushka, p. 93.

[23] Ibid., p. 91.

[24] Ibid.

[25] Ibid., p. 92.

[26] Ibid.

[27] Ibid., p. 93.

[28] The flat tax proposal of former House Majority Leader Richard K. Armey would have repealed the earned income tax credit (EITC), thus the Treasury's study includes a repeal of the EITC. If the earned income tax credit (EITC) were repealed, there would have been an increase in taxes (loss in negative tax) for those who had an EITC in excess of their tax liability. Hall and Rabushka did not mention the EITC in their book, and consequently, whether or not their proposal included a repeal of the EITC is not known.

[29] For a definition of Family Economic Income, see U.S. Treasury, Office of Tax Analysis, "New Armey-Shelby Flat Tax Would Still Lose Money, Treasury Finds," *Tax Notes*, v. 70, no. 4, Jan. 22, 1996, p. 454.

[30] Ibid., pp. 453-455.

[31] For a presentation of these assumptions about incidence, see U.S. Treasury, Office of Tax Analysis, "New ArmeyShelby Flat Tax Would Still Lose Money, Treasury Finds," p. 453.

[32] CRS Report 95-1141, *The Flat Tax and Other Proposals: Who Will Bear the Tax Burden?*, by Jane G. Gravelle.

[33] For an analysis of the efficiency of a pure consumption tax versus a pure income tax, see Jane G. Gravelle, "Income, Consumption, and Wage Taxation in a Life-Cycle Model: Separating Efficiency from Redistribution," *American Economic Review*, v. 81, no. 4, Sept. 1991, pp. 985-995.

[34] Hall and Rabushka, p. 87.

[35] For an explanation of the components of national saving, see CRS Report RL32119, *Can Public Policy Raise the Saving Rate?*, by Brian W. Cashell.

[36] For a comprehensive analysis of the U.S. saving rate, see CRS Report RS21480, *Saving Rates in the United States: Calculation and Comparison*, by Brian W. Cashell.

[37] For an examination of this issue, see CRS Report RS22367, *Federal Tax Reform and Its Potential Effects on Saving*, by Gregg A. Esenwein.

[38] For example, see Don Fullerton and Diane Lim Rogers, "Lifetime Effects of Fundamental Tax Reform," in *Economic Effects of Fundamental Tax Reform*, Henry J. Aaron and William G. Gale, eds. (Washington: Brookings Institution Press, 1996), p. 321-352; and David Altig, Alan J. Auerbach, Laurence J. Kotlikoff, Kent A. Smetters, and Jan Walliser, "Simulating Fundamental Tax Reform in the United States," *American Economic Review*, v. 91, no. 3, June 2001, pp. 574-595.

[39] CRS Report RL32603, *The Flat Tax, Value-Added Tax, and National Retail Sales Tax: Overview of the Issues*, by Jane G. Gravelle.

[40] Hall and Rabushka, p. 84.

[41] Ibid., p. 86.

[42] Ibid., p. 87.

[43] Ibid., p. 88.

[44] Ibid., p. 83.

[45] Ibid., p. 89.

[46] Ibid.

[47] For an further explanation of this issue, see CRS Report RL32603, *The Flat Tax, Value-Added Tax, and National Retail Sales Tax: Overview of the Issues*, by Jane G. Gravelle.

[48] For a comprehensive analysis of this topic, see CRS Report 95-1141, *The Flat Tax and Other Proposals: Who Will Bear the Tax Burden?*, by Jane G. Gravelle.

[49] For opposing views on the effect of a flat tax on interest rates, see John E. Golob, "How Would Tax Reform Affect Financial Markets?," *Federal Reserve Bank of Kansas City Economic Review*, v. 80, no. 4, Fourth Quarter, 1995, pp. 19-39; and, Martin Feldstein, "The Effect of a Consumption Tax on the Rate of Interest," Working Paper No. 5,397, National Bureau of Economic Research, Cambridge, Massachusetts, Dec. 1995, 31 p. An analysis of various factors affecting interest rate changes is presented in CRS Report 96-379, *The Flat Tax and Other Proposals: Effects on Housing*, by Jane G. Gravelle. (Out-of-print report available from CRS on request.)

[50] For a comprehensive analysis of this issue, see Martin A. Sullivan, *Flat Taxes and Consumption Taxes: A Guide to the Debate* (New York: American Institute of Certified Public Accountants, 1995), pp. 125-149.

[51] This could be a quite a problem not only for many mature large corporations but also for many small businesses, farmers, and owners of rental properties.

[52] Hall and Rabushka, pp. 64-65.

[53] Ibid., pp. 65-66.

[54] Ibid., pp. 78-79.

[55] Ibid., p. 79.

[56] For an examination of this tax preference, see CRS Report RL34608, *Tax Issues Relating to Charitable Contributions and Organizations*, by Jane G. Gravelle and Molly F. Sherlock.

[57] Hall and Rabushka, *The Flat Tax*, pp. 99-101.

[58] For an article on this issue, see William C. Randolph, "Dynamic Income, Progressive Taxes, and the Timing of Charitable Contributions," *Journal of Political Economy*, v. 103, no. 4, Aug. 1995, pp. 709-738.

[59] Charles T. Clotfelter, and Richard L. Schmalbeck, "The Impact of Fundamental Tax Reform on Nonprofit Organizations," in *Economic Effects of Fundamental Tax Reform*, edited by Henry J. Aaron and William G. Gale (Washington, Brookings Institution Press, 1996), pp. 211-246.

[60] For an analysis of possible policy changes under fundamental tax reform concerning the mortgage interest deduction, see CRS Report RL33025, *Fundamental Tax Reform: Options for the Mortgage Interest Deduction*, by Pamela J. Jackson.

[61] U.S. Congressional Budget Office, *Budget Options*, (Washington, U.S. Govt. Print. Off., Feb. 2007), pp. 267-268.

[62] Steven Pearlstein, "Americans' Investing Focus Faulted," *Washington Post*, no. 284, Sept. 15, 1995, p. F3.

[63] Hall and Rabushka, p. 94.

[64] Ibid., p. 95.

[65] Ibid.

[66] Ibid.

[67] For a view that argues that there will be serious effects, see Roger E. Brinner, Mark Lasky, and David Wyss, "Residential Real Estate: Impacts of Flat Tax Legislation," DRI Analysis, Summary Prepared for the National Association of Realtors, Lexington, Massachusetts, May 1995, 19 p. Also, for a critical view of this DRI study, see Rebecca S. Schaefer, "Ganging Up Again at 'Gucci Gulch': A Look at the DRI Flat Tax Study," *Issues and Answers*, Citizens for a Sound Economy, Aug. 15, 1995, 3 p.

[68] Hall and Rabushka, p. 79.

[69] An analysis of this issue is presented in CRS Report 96-379, *The Flat Tax and Other Proposals: Effects on Housing*, by Jane G. Gravelle. (Out-of-print report available from CRS on request.)

[70] Charles E. McLure, Jr., *The Value-Added Tax, Key to Deficit Reduction?* (Washington: American Enterprise Institute, 1987), p. 135.

[71] Hall and Rabushka, pp. 74-75.

[72] McLure, pp. 135-138.

[73] CRS Report RL32603, *The Flat Tax, Value-Added Tax, and National Retail Sales Tax: Overview of the Issues*, by Jane G. Gravelle.

[74] For an overview of the taxation of life insurance products and life insurance companies, see CRS Report RL32000, *Taxation of Life Insurance Products: Background and Issues*, by Andrew D. Pike and CRS Report RL32180, *Taxation of Life Insurance Companies*, by Andrew D. Pike.

[75] For a comprehensive discussion of this tax preference, see Internal Revenue Service, *Publication 502—Medical and Dental Expenses, 2007.*

[76] An overview of the effects on the states of flat tax proposals is presented in CRS Report 95-1150, *Consumption Taxes and State-Local Tax Systems*, by Dennis Zimmerman (Out-of-print report available on request), and Robert P. Strauss, *Administrative and Revenue Implications of Alternative Federal Consumption Taxes for the State and Local Sector* (Washington: American Tax Policy Institute, July 6, 1997), 78 p.

[77] Michael Stanton, "Correction for Possible Tax Reform Has Run Its Course, Managers Say," *The Bond Buyer*, v. 313, no. 29,686, July 7, 1995, p. 7.

[78] Jon Birger, "Tax Reform Won't Do Much for State Funds, Moles Says," *The Bond Buyer*, v. 313, no. 29,717, Aug. 21, 1995, p. 6.

[79] For an examination of this tax preference, see U.S. Congressional Budget Office, *Budget Options*, p. 269.

[80] CRS Report 95-1150, *Consumption Taxes and State-Local Tax Systems*, by Dennis Zimmerman (Out-of-print report available from CRS on request).

[81] Hall and Rabushka, *The Flat Tax*, p. 52.

[82] John L. Guyton, John F. O'Hare, Michael P. Stavrianos, and Eric J. Toder, "Estimating the Compliance Cost of the U.S. Individual Income Tax," *National Tax Journal*, v. 66, no. 3, Sept. 2003, pp. 673-688.

[83] Ibid., p. 682.

[84] Ibid.

[85] Internal Revenue Service, *Statistics of Income Bulletin*, v. 25, no. 3, winter 2005-2006, p. 208.

[86] Internal Revenue Service, *Statistics of Income Bulletin*, v. 27, no. 4, spring 2008, available at http://www.irs.gov/tax_stats, visited Mar. 16, 2009.

[87] For an analysis of the tax gap, see CRS Report R40219, *Tax Gap, Tax Enforcement, and Tax Compliance Proposals in the 111th Congress*, by James M. Bickley.

[88] As already discussed, private businesses would pay the business tax on the fringe benefits of their employees except for pension contributions, which would be taxed at the individual level.

In: Value-Added Tax (VAT) and Flat Tax Proposals
Editors: D. B. Andrews and A. M. Davis

ISBN: 978-1-61324-191-2
© 2011 Nova Science Publishers, Inc.

Chapter 6

THE FLAT TAX, VALUE-ADDED TAX, AND NATIONAL RETAIL SALES TAX: OVERVIEW OF THE ISSUES[*]

Jane G. Gravelle

SUMMARY

The current income tax system is criticized for costly complexity and damage to economic efficiency. Reform suggestions have proliferated, including a national retail sales tax, several versions of a value-added tax (VAT), the much-discussed "Flat Tax" on consumption (the "HallRabushka" tax), the "USA" proposal for a direct consumption tax, and revisions of the income tax. The President has indicated that major tax reform will be a priority item in his second term, and his tax reform commission has included a modified flat tax as one of its options.

Most reform proposals are based on the notion that switching to a consumption tax base or exempting savings from tax would increase the savings rate and improve economic efficiency. Although theoretical inter-temporal models predict that saving and efficiency would increase, evidence from past tax cuts does not bear out this prediction. Any effect on savings would depend crucially on the transition provisions. It is also argued that these taxes could improve the country's trade balance. Trade balances, however, depend on capital flows and would be affected by these tax changes only if they do bring about an increase in the U.S. savings rate. There is no reason to expect trade benefits from any of the tax changes per se.

A broader tax base would have diverse effects on economic sectors. Sectors that might be adversely affected include the non-profit sector (loss of charitable contributions deductions), the state and local sector (loss of state tax deductions, change in their own tax structures), and the health care sector (taxation of fringe benefits). Shifting the tax base from income to consumption, while generally increasing business investment, would differentially affect firms, depending on their growth rate, capital structure, and employee benefit structure. Such a shift would also make investment in pensions, insurance policies, owner-occupied housing, and tax-exempt bonds relatively less attractive.

There are macroeconomic problems with a transition to a consumption tax, and these problems are extremely serious for transiting to a system that collects all revenue from

---

[*] This is an edited, reformatted and augmented version of Congressional Research Services publication RL32603, dated March 14, 2008.

business (VAT or retail sales tax). For these tax shifts, avoiding a serious economic contraction would be quite difficult. The flat tax would not have these problems but it can cause significant windfall losses in asset values.

A flat-rate tax is also intended to simplify the system and reduce compliance and administration costs. Many of the proposals, if kept simple while being enacted, would reduce costs; however, many individual taxpayers are currently under a flat-rate income tax, so their lot would not be much improved. An enacted law, however, might not be as simple as the proposals.

Consumption taxes also change the distribution of tax burdens, especially on generations. The old consume more of their incomes, and their burden would increase; younger people save more, and their burdens would fall. Higher income individuals would see a reduction in taxes. This report does not track current legislation and will not be updated.

INTRODUCTION

The current tax system, with its graduated tax on individual incomes, its separate tax on corporate profits, its gift and estate taxes on the transfer of wealth, and its separate wage tax to fund the Social Security and Medicare systems, has many critics. It is said to cost the country in lost time, economic efficiency, trade, and contentment. Reform proposals have proliferated, ranging from a broader-based, flatter-rate income tax to scrapping the system altogether in favor of a national sales tax or some other form of national consumption tax.

This report surveys some of the issues to be considered in debating such drastic tax changes, considering not only a broader based income tax but also three basic forms of consumption taxes: the Hall-Rabushka "flat tax," the value-added tax (VAT), and the national retail sales tax. After a brief overview of some of the current proposals, the sections that follow discuss economic efficiency issues, foreign trade issues, effects on different economic sectors, short-run adjustment costs, compliance and administration, and revenue and distributional implications.

PROPOSED ALTERNATIVES TO THE PRESENT TAX SYSTEM

The idea of replacing our current income tax system has been a topic of perennial congressional interest. Although many recent proposals are referred to as "flat taxes," most actually go much further than merely adopting a flat-rate tax structure and would change the tax base from income to consumption. More recently, the President has indicated some interest in such fundamental tax reform, and his advisory commission has proposed a modified flat tax.

Three Main Tax Bases

Theoretically, one could construct a tax system using one or a combination of three main tax bases: income, wages, or consumption. Income-and wage-based taxes are familiar and relatively easy to understand.

Under a comprehensive income tax, all income, whether from labor or capital, would be included in the tax base. A wage-based tax would be levied only on income from labor; income from capital would be excluded from the base. Obviously, wages provide a smaller tax base than income and would therefore require higher tax rates to raise the same revenue as a tax based on all income.

With the exception of sales taxes, the American people are not very familiar with other forms of broad-based consumption taxes and so there is some confusion about how they might be measured and levied. The easiest way to understand the basis of consumption taxes is to first define and understand the economic concept of income.

In its broadest sense, income is a measure of the command of resources that an individual acquires during a given time period. Conceptually, an individual has two options with respect to his income; he can consume it or save it. This relationship means that by definition income must equal consumption plus saving.

This relationship helps in understanding how a comprehensive consumption-based tax might be levied at the individual level. An individual would add up all his income as he does under the current tax system but would then subtract out his net saving (saving minus borrowing) or add net borrowing. The result would produce a tax based on consumption at the individual level.

A consumption tax could also be collected at the retail level as a retail sales tax on final consumption. (A retail sales tax exempts, in theory, the sale of intermediate goods including capital goods to be used in a business). Or it could be collected at each stage of the production process in the form of a value-added-tax (VAT). With the VAT, firms face a tax on gross receipts less purchases of materials, goods for resale and capital to be used in the business. A VAT can be implemented using either a credit-invoice method or a subtraction method.[1] Another way of collecting the tax, the Hall-Rabushka flat tax, would split the VAT base between firms and individuals. Firms would deduct wages from their tax base and individuals would pay a tax directly on their wages. Although the point of collection differs (individual level, retail level, or firm level), when defined comprehensively, the tax base is the same: consumption.

Regardless of the point or form of collection, however, a consumption tax is ultimately paid by the individual consumer. Because consumption is smaller than income, a comprehensive consumption tax would require higher tax rates than a comprehensive income tax to raise the same revenue, although with a low savings rate, the bases (and thus tax rates) are very close.

Other developed nations have VATs (of the credit-invoice type), but also have income taxes. Their VATs do not replace income taxes, but rather finance a higher level of government spending. Most of these nations do not have a retail sales tax, which is an important subnational tax in the United States.

Current Proposals

There is currently no serious proposal to shift the entire tax system to a wage-based tax as such. The current proposals are almost all based on a switch to some form of consumption taxation, either a national sales tax or some form of value-added tax. They differ principally in their point of collection rather than their tax base. These proposals include several versions of the value-added tax widely used in Europe, a national sales tax such as those used in the states, and more exotic variations, such as the "Flat Tax" devised by economists Robert Hall and Alvin Rabushka and the Unlimited Savings Account or "USA" tax originally introduced in the 104th Congress by Senators Dominici and Nunn. There is also some interest (and at least one serious proposal) in a broader-based, flatter rate income tax.[2] No bill for this type of fundamental tax reform has had sufficient detail to be operational, and no such bill has ever received a floor vote.

The President indicated that fundamental tax reform would be a major priority of his second term, although the shape of that reform is uncertain at this point. His advisory commission has included a modified flat tax (which included a tax on financial income) as one of the recommended options along with an income tax reform.[3] Many of the issues discussed in this paper, especially sectoral effects on currently favored industries would also apply to a broader based income tax.

CAN SWITCHING TO A DIFFERENT TAX SYSTEM HELP THE ECONOMY?

Probably the most often repeated argument in favor of switching to a flat-rate consumption tax is that it will make the economy more efficient and will increase private savings. When evaluating this argument, however, comparisons should not be made between the current income tax system and an ideal consumption tax.

Compared to a theoretically ideal tax (whether the base is consumption or income), the existing tax system will always appear flawed. For policy evaluation, therefore, a more appropriate comparison is between a theoretically pure consumption tax and a theoretically pure income-based tax.

Efficiency Issues

The economic efficiency or inefficiency of a tax system may be judged by its effects on behavior. To the degree that the tax system distorts economic behavior (from what it would be in the absence of the tax), it is economically inefficient. The distortion prevents the efficient allocation of resources. Basically, with the exception of lump-sum or head taxes, all taxes, regardless of whether they are based on income or consumption, distort behavior and affect the allocation of resources.

Both an income and a consumption tax distort the choice between labor and leisure. For example, under either tax, the price of leisure is reduced relative to the consumption an individual could finance with an extra hour of labor.

An income tax also distorts the choice between present and future consumption (saving). Under an income tax, the return to savings is subject to tax. This reduces the resources an individual will have available for consumption in the future, and hence raises the price of future consumption relative to the price of present consumption. In contrast, a tax on consumption is neutral with respect to the choice between present and future consumption.

The relative price of future consumption in terms of present consumption is the same as if there were no taxes.

In theory, adopting a consumption tax may or may not increase overall economic efficiency. Under a consumption tax which yielded revenue equal to an income tax, the tax rates would have to be higher than the tax rates on the income tax base because consumption is smaller than income. The higher tax rates under a consumption tax would increase the distortion between work and leisure choices. The efficiency gain from removing the present/future consumption distortions, therefore, might be offset by the efficiency loss inherent in the larger distortion between work and leisure decisions.

Many economists have argued, however, that a consumption tax is superior in achieving economic efficiency (i.e., in leading individuals to consume and work in a more optimal fashion) because of the elimination of the distortion between present and future consumption. They base this argument on the simulated outcomes of inter-temporal models, which virtually always predict a gain in efficiency from the shift from flat rate income to flat rate consumption taxes.[4] One reason for this predicted efficiency gain—which often does not occur with a shift from an income to a wage tax base—is that a consumption tax is the equivalent of a tax on wages and a lump sum tax on existing wealth. The lump sum tax allows tax rates to be much lower with a consumption base than with a wage base, even though neither tax the return to new investment. In fact, when an economy's saving rate is very low, the consumption tax base is quite close to the income tax base. (There are distributional consequences to this feature that will be discussed subsequently). Thus, even though tax rates may be higher under a consumption tax than under an income tax and increase the distortion between work and leisure, this increase is a relatively small effect—the lump sum tax on old wealth has made this efficiency gain possible.

The existence, and even the magnitude, of this efficiency gain, however, is not entirely clear under a less abstract modeling of the tax. First, under current law the income tax imposes higher marginal tax rates on capital income than on labor income (primarily because of the corporate income tax). To replace both corporate and individual revenues by a flat consumption tax would require a higher consumption tax rate and the tradeoff between the labor leisure distortion and the present and future consumption distortion is less clear. There may be potential gain from moving from graduated tax rates to flat rates, but such gains could be accomplished within an income tax reform; moreover many consumption tax proposals include some form of relief for lower income individuals.

Perhaps more importantly, there is a good deal of uncertainty about whether these intertemporal models actually reflect how people behave. The presumed sophistication and information requirements of such models is high and there is evidence and reason to believe that most individuals decide their savings behavior based on fairly straightforward rules of thumb that suggest savings does not respond positively to higher rates of return (although it could decline). There is even less evidence that individuals are able to shift their leisure (and therefore their working hours) over time, a behavior that is an important feature of many of these intertemporal models. If the behavioral responses are small, then the efficiency gains are small.

There are certain practical aspects of consumption taxes, however, that may give them some advantages over income taxes. For example, the problems and complexities of measuring income from capital are eliminated under a consumption tax. Eliminating the current law differential in the tax treatment of different forms of capital could improve resource allocation and economic efficiency. In practice, of course, there may be pressure for differential taxes on different types of consumption goods, a differential that is quite feasible with the retail sales tax and with some forms of the VAT, but much less likely under a tax on consumed income. Moreover, in some types of taxes (particularly the retail sales tax) it is very difficult to separate out intermediate purchases from final purchases and administer such rules. As a result, some final goods are likely to escape the tax and some intermediate goods and capital goods are likely to be subject to the tax.

It appears that, on the whole, switching from an income to a consumption tax would probably not produce great improvements in economic efficiency. Nonetheless, even small efficiency gains may be important because they continue year after year. However, similar gains might also be achieved though income tax reform.

Effects on Saving

Intertemporal models also tend to predict an increase in savings in switching from income to consumption taxes and this effect is often viewed to be a positive result of a consumption tax (separate from the efficiency gains described above). An increase in the savings rate, however, cannot be determined to be necessarily desirable, since it trades off current consumption for future consumption. Moreover, under a consumption tax the old (retirees who are dissavers because they are drawing down their accumulated capital to finance consumption) would pay higher taxes and the young would pay lower taxes. Because of their higher tax liabilities, retired workers would have to reduce their consumption (or return to the work force). Since some of the increase in savings, at least in these models, is the result of a windfall tax on assets of the old, it is even more difficult to determine the extent to which the savings effects are desirable.

For the young, a consumption tax is the equivalent of exempting the rate of return on savings from tax. Normally, the effect on savings of increasing the rate of return (via a tax cut) is ambiguous. There is a substitution effect—because the return is higher, one has to give up less consumption today in order to consume a given amount in the future. This lower "price" of future consumption encourages more of it. At the same time, there is an income effect—because the rate of return is higher one can actually consume more in the future, while saving less, allowing more consumption today. The net effect of these two forces is uncertain.

A consumption tax has another important feature, however, that overwhelms this income effect. Unlike a mere exclusion of tax on the return, the consumption tax allows an up-front deduction for savings, but requires the payment of tax on both principal and return when consumption occurs in the future. Thus, individuals need to save today to pay these taxes due in the future; they can do so while still consuming more today because of their large tax cuts. Thus, while the young may consume some part of their tax cut, the old reduce their consumption by much more, and the overall effect is to increase aggregate savings in the economy.

As with the case of efficiency gains, some of the results regarding the effects of a consumption tax on savings are based on intertemporal models which rely on somewhat idealized assumptions. For instance, they assume that all taxpayers have perfect information, and the sophistication to map out their consumption choices over a long period of time, and that they are certain that the tax system will not change during their lifetimes. If these idealized assumptions are relaxed, then the results are not conclusive that switching from an income tax to a consumption tax would increase savings.

In addition, the empirical evidence regarding the effect of tax incentives on savings is inconclusive. For example, the Economic Recovery Tax Act of 1981 significantly reduced marginal income tax rates, expanded the availability of individual retirement accounts (IRAs), and accelerated depreciation deductions. Life-cycle models would predict that these changes should dramatically increase private savings, but that did not happen.

Finally, it is critical to note that any transition rules that are enacted to mitigate the increased taxes on the elderly at the time of transition to a consumption tax would tend to reduce the stimulus to new saving. A crucial part of the savings effect is the reduced consumption of the old; moreover, any increase in taxes on the young would be more likely to come partly at the expense of savings. Indeed, if enough transitional relief were given to the elderly, the income effect could be reduced to a point where there may be no effect, or even a negative effect, on new saving, at least in the short run. In addition, the elderly, particularly those with high incomes, often do not exhibit the dissaving associated with life cycle model savings, and it then becomes crucial to determine their motive for leaving bequests.

Because of these ambiguities and the lack of conclusive empirical evidence, it cannot be determined definitively that a consumption tax would significantly increase the level of saving in the economy.

COMPETITIVENESS OF U.S. COMPANIES UNDER DIFFERENT TAX SYSTEMS

Among the arguments for switching from an income tax to a consumption tax is the assertion that a consumption tax would make U.S. industries more competitive and help the U.S. balance of trade.

When analyzing the effects of tax policy changes on international trade it is important to differentiate between a nation's perspective and a firm's perspective. A nation engages in trade because through trade it can obtain the goods and services its people want or need at a smaller resource cost than if it were to produce those goods and services itself. A nation exports its products as a means of paying for what it imports.

On the other hand, a firm's ultimate goals are to sell its products and maximize its profits. Exports provide a means to achieve these goals.

The Balance of Trade

Popular perceptions about trade tend to reflect a firm's perspective on trade. Most people believe that if the United States could produce goods at costs comparable to or lower than those abroad, our exports would increase and our imports decrease. This in turn would improve our trade performance and reduce our trade deficit.

In the aggregate, however, the United States is not like a firm that can continually capture larger shares of the world market by producing output at lower costs than foreign firms. A nation engaging in trade cannot be a market winner in all products.

Indeed, without borrowing and lending (international capital flows), trade between nations would always be balanced. The only way trade can be out of balance is if one nation lends another nation the resources to pay for the extra goods it imports but does not pay for with its current exports. Capital flows and trade balances are always mirror images of one another; a capital inflow produces a trade deficit while a capital outflow produces a trade surplus.

Hence, tax policy designed to reduce the cost of traded U.S. goods and services will have little effect on trade performance or the balance of trade.

Border Tax Adjustments

For example, consider the argument that if the United States were to replace its income tax with a border-adjustable VAT, then U.S. trade performance would improve and the trade deficit would diminish.

Under the World Trade Organization (WTO) rules, indirect taxes such as a VAT may be rebated on exports and imposed on imports. Direct taxes, such as income taxes, however, cannot be adjusted at the border. The existence of these border tax adjustments has led some to conclude that nations with VATs have a trade advantage over the United States.

On the surface, this appears to be a plausible argument; reduce the price of U.S. goods and exports will rise, increase the price of foreign goods and imports will fall. Trade, it is said, will move into balance.

A simple response to this argument is that most European countries with VATs also have income tax structures similar to the United States. Their VATs are not displacing income taxes; they are permitting a higher level of government spending.

But, at a more fundamental level, border tax adjustments don't matter, other than in the composition of trade (and in this case, they serve to preserve relative prices in each country in accord with that country's own consumption taxes). This is because the balance of trade is a function of international capital flows, not the flow of traded goods and services.

Therefore, in the absence of changes to the underlying macroeconomic variables affecting capital flows (for example, interest rates), any changes in the product prices of traded goods and services brought about by border tax adjustments are ultimately offset by exchange-rate adjustments. Border-tax adjustments would have no effect on a nation's balance of trade or its basic competitiveness.

The Effects of Tax Policy on Trade

That is not to say that changes in the tax structure could not influence trade levels or patterns. Changes in tax policy which affect the underlying macroeconomic variables that govern capital flows (for instance, by increasing either public or private savings, which in turn would lower interest rates, or by making investment in the United States more attractive) could affect the balance of trade. For example, if a tax policy change caused domestic savings to rise, then a likely outcome would be a fall in interest rates and a reduction in the net inflow of capital, which would reduce the level of imports relative to exports. This effect of capital flows is transitory, however. As foreigners adjust their portfolios these effects would reverse, as the smaller stock of capital would result in smaller earnings and an increase in the net inflow of payments (outside of trade). These last effects would be small but permanent and offset in present value the initial short run effect.

In addition, tax reforms which increase the overall efficiency of the U.S. economy will ultimately have a positive effect on this nation's terms of trade. Defined simply, terms of trade reflect the amount of domestic resources that have to be given up in order to acquire a given quantity of imported goods. If a nation's terms of trade improve, it gives up fewer domestic resources to acquire the same level of imports. If its terms of trade deteriorate, then it gives up more domestic resources to acquire the same level of imports.[5]

Taxes distort the allocation of resources in the economy. If tax reforms reduce the distorting effects of the tax system, then resource allocation will become more efficient which will increase domestic economic welfare.

When the allocation of domestic resources is less distorted, domestic goods can be produced at a lower total resource cost than they could before the tax reforms. So, to acquire the same amount of imported goods, the nation gives up fewer domestic resources, which represents an improvement in the U.S. terms of trade. The gain, however, is likely to be small.

Finally, tax policy can and does affect the composition of trade. For example, if the tax change increased the tax burden of some firms relative to others, then those firms with an increased tax burden might see their market share and their exports decline. On the other hand, those firms that experienced a relative decline in their tax burden might see their market share and their exports increase. These relative shifts in the inter-firm tax burdens, and the resultant shift in market output, could affect the composition of both exports and imports. Indeed, the purpose of allowing rebates of value added taxes is to prevent one country's pattern of differential consumption taxes from being imposed on another by stripping out the relative taxes on exports and allowing the importing country to impose their own pattern of taxes.

HOW WILL DIFFERENT ECONOMIC SECTORS BE AFFECTED

The proposed tax reforms would affect the allocation of economic resources. Some sectors, generally those that are capital intensive and growing, will gain. Slower growing firms will lose. Other sectors that might be adversely affected by broadening the base to more fully reflect income and by removing itemized deductions are the non-profit sector, the state and local sector, the residential real estate industry, and the health care sector. These are sectors that receive special benefits under the income tax.

Proposals to shift the tax base from an income base to a consumption base (most proposals), while generally increasing business investment, would differentially affect firms, depending on their growth rate, capital structure, and employee benefit structure. They would also make investment in pensions, insurance policies, owner-occupied housing, and tax-exempt bonds relatively less attractive, and investments in ordinary stocks and bonds more attractive.

Sector Effects

Firms and sectors that would be adversely affected by tax change may face a difficult transition period, which could lead to some economic disruption. Moreover, for certain types of tax structures, there would be a need for a major one-time price inflation to avoid an economic contraction. Some tax revisions present design challenges regarding the treatment of some industries, such as financial institutions.

These firms and sectors are likely to be opposed to this type of tax shift:

State and Local Governments

Most states rely on the federal government for income tax administration and compliance, and to some extent conform to the federal tax base. States would either face increased enforcement costs and lost revenues if they retained current rules, or they would have to adapt their systems to the federal system. Also, for the reform proposals that do not tax capital income, tax-exempt bonds would become less attractive, and borrowing by states and municipalities more costly. Also, proposals that disallow the deductibility of state and local taxes would make increases in these taxes more costly to taxpayers. Finally, for some proposals state and local governments would need to remit taxes on employee fringe benefits.

Owner-Occupied Housing

Generally, businesses include receipts in income and deduct costs. Owner-occupants of housing do not include the imputed income (rental value of living in the house), while mortgage interest and property taxes remain deductible. Thus, the federal income tax favors owner-occupied housing. Changes in the tax structure that restrict deductions of interest and taxes or that exempt income from new investments from tax would divert investment out of this sector and into the business sector. The likely magnitude of this effect is uncertain.

Non-Profit Institutions

Proposals that would eliminate the charitable contributions deduction could decrease charitable giving to some degree. The incentive for higher-income individuals (and, hence, charitable giving to the recipients of their contributions) would be most affected, since they are the ones who itemize. Non-profit institutions might also need to remit taxes paid on fringe benefits for their employees under some proposals.

Health Care

Health insurance fringe benefits are favored under current tax law, which allows firms a deduction for contributions but does not include benefits in employees' income. Flat-tax proposals that would eliminate the employer deduction might discourage firms from offering health insurance. Indeed, proposals that provide wage exemptions would make health plans overtaxed relative to wages for low-income individuals who have not exhausted a wage exemption.

Sales tax and VAT structures might, however, exempt medical care from the base, lowering its relative price. It is extremely difficult, however, to exempt a product under a subtraction-method VAT. A subtraction method VAT taxes income minus intermediate goods, so that any tax paid in the intermediate states of production would still affect the tax on the final product. Credit-invoice methods, where firms pay a tax (which could be zero) on total receipts and get a credit for previous taxes can be used to vary tax rates and exempt goods and services. The VAT proposals have been for subtraction method approaches.

Pensions/Insurance

Pensions are favored under current tax law because they are effectively tax exempt (treated on a consumption-tax basis). While firms would still have reasons to provide pensions, proposals that would extend this treatment to all investments would make pensions relatively less attractive, and might discourage their use. If some individuals now save more through a pension plan than they would on their own, overall savings could be adversely affected as well. Currently tax-favored insurance policies (e.g., whole life insurance) would also become relatively less attractive.

Differential Effects on Firms

A consumption tax would encourage investments in business equity capital. In the case of the flat tax, or a VAT, the firms would not be allowed interest deductions and new investments would be expensed rather than depreciated. Firms that are growing slowly, or contracting, would find expensing of new investment to be of little benefit over annual depreciation deductions. Firms that rely more heavily on debt would also find their tax bills rising. Investment would be favored under a sales tax because investment goods are exempt.

Some proposals would tax certain employee fringe benefits, which would increase the relative cost of compensation for firms that have a large share of these fringe benefits in their benefit package.

Growing firms that rely heavily on equity and offer few fringe benefits would be the beneficiaries of these tax revisions.

Special Problems

The financial sector (banks, insurance companies, investment brokers), currently accounting for substantial corporate tax, is difficult to tax under a consumption base. Owner-occupied housing cannot be taxed directly, but can be accommodated easily by leaving it out of the system.

TRANSITION COSTS AND MACROECONOMIC ADJUSTMENTS

One of the most difficult issues to address in considering a shift to consumption taxes is the transition from the current system to the new tax regime.[6] While all shifts to a consumption tax cause some common transitional disturbances and windfall gains and losses, the most serious problems arise from a shift to a national retail sales tax or to a value added tax. In these cases, a tax formerly largely collected from individuals is now collected at the firm level—either from retailers on total sales or from both final and intermediate producers' value added. Flat taxes avoid this problem but can result in confiscatory taxes on existing assets.

Price Accommodation and Short-run Contractions under a RetailSales Tax or VAT

Holding prices fixed, these firms would need to reduce payments to workers to retain profit levels. In fact, many firms would not have enough of a profit margin to pay the tax without something else—either prices or wages—adjusting. Consider, for example, a grocery retailer that may have a 1% or 2% profit margin now owing a tax equal to 20% of receipts. This firm simply does not have the cash to pay the tax. If it is difficult to lower wages (and presumably it would be), a significant one-time price inflation, to allow these costs to be passed forward in prices instead, would be required to avoid a potentially serious economic contraction. Note that the price increase, were it possible to implement correctly and precisely, would solve the transition problem because although prices would rise, individuals would have more income to purchase the higher priced goods—and demand would not fall. It is difficult, however, for the monetary authorities to engineer such a large price change. Moreover, even with the monetary expansion in place to do so, the imposition of such a tax would be disruptive if firms are reluctant to immediately raise prices, again leading to an economic contraction. That is, firms could contract their business, or even close down, until output had contracted enough to raise prices.

These disruptions are not minor in nature—imagine the difficulties of engineering and absorbing a one-time price increase that is likely to be close to 20% (the level, approximately, that might realistically be needed to replace the income tax).[7] Even if such an inflation could be managed, there are always concerns that any large inflation could create inflationary expectations—it's hard to manage a single one-year price increase. In fact, economists who judge a consumption tax to be superior to an income tax may nevertheless be skeptical about the advisability of making the change because of these transition effects.

Despite the extensive analysis of the economic effects of fundamental tax reform, however, little attention has been devoted to potential short-run contractionary effects, particularly of proposals that would shift the liability for tax payments from individuals to businesses. One may note, however, that when a major macroeconomic forecaster (Roger Brinner from DRI/McGraw-Hill) modeled a VAT replacement in a Joint Committee on Taxation study, he found output falling over the first five years, reaching a height of 12.5 % in the fourth year.[8] (The other forecaster did not simulate a VAT, but only a flat tax which does not require this price accommodation; the remaining modelers had full employment models).

Although the short run disruption from the retail sales tax and the VAT is most pronounced, any shift to a consumption tax will likely cause short term economic contraction due to sectoral shifts. In the Joint Committee on Taxation study, both macroeconomic modelers who used cyclical models (that permitted unemployment) projected the flat tax, which continues to tax individuals on their wages, to cause contractions (albeit smaller) in the short run.

Windfall Losses for Equity Investments Under the Flat Tax

The flat tax also produces some transitional effects on cash flow that can be quite severe for owners of assets because it does not require a price accommodation. A consumption tax can also be characterized as a wage tax plus a lump sum tax on old capital. That is, it taxes the sources of income used, sooner or later, for consumption purposes. (Individuals will eventually consume out of new assets but the cost of those new assets will also have been deducted from income when acquired.)[9]

One explicit manifestation of this effect is that businesses that have already purchased assets and inventories, in the expectation of being able to deduct their costs over a period of time (under a fixed depreciation schedule for plant and equipment and when sold for inventories), will no longer be able to take such deductions. If a firm is constantly growing, then the ability to deduct new investments in full will more than compensate for this loss of old deductions, on a cash flow basis (although the value of the firm will still fall). But for a firm that is not growing, or is liquidating, or for an investor who wishes to shift from a physical ownership (such as real estate) to financial asset, tax liability could rise dramatically.

Consider the following example. Suppose an investor purchases a building for $450,000, with a mortgage of 95% ($427,500). Two years later, the price has increased to $500,000 and he has taken $23,000 of depreciation deductions; to simplify suppose he has refinanced to maintain the same mortgage. He decides to sell and use the proceeds to buy a financial asset (such as a corporate stock). Under current law, he would measure gain subject to tax as the sales price of $500,000 less the basis (original cost of $450,000 less $23,000 in depreciation, or $427,000). This gain would amount to $73,000 which is the sum of the appreciation in the property of $50,000 and the depreciation he has already taken. Assuming for simplicity a 20% tax rate, he would pay capital gains tax of $14,600. He pays the mortgage of $427,500, and is left with net cash of $57,900.

Suppose, however, that a flat tax (consumption tax) had been enacted in the interim at the same rate. Under the flat tax, he would pay a 20% tax on $500,000, or $100,000. One can see that this tax is more than confiscatory: after repaying the mortgage of $427,500 and paying the tax of $100,000 he has a loss in cash flow of $27,500.

Why does this happen? It happens because the flat tax is collected in a way that does not require a price increase and the lump sum tax on assets falls solely on the equity claim to an asset. The holder of the mortgage has had no loss in value. With either a retail sales tax or a VAT and price accommodation, the investor would be left with $73,000 in cash, whose purchasing power has decreased by 20%.[10] The mortgage holder's asset would also lose 20% in value. Thus, the lump sum tax is allocated to both debt holders and equity holders.

The problem with the flat tax would not occur under another form of consumption tax that does not require a price accommodation—a direct tax on consumed income. Under this approach, individuals would begin with the income tax base, and deduct net investment or add net withdrawals of investments to income. With this type of tax, both financial and physical investments would be included in the calculation, and the individual would be able to deduct the mortgage repayment as an investment. The direct tax on consumed income has not proven to be very popular, however, as it would complicate rather than simplify tax calculations for the individual and require unfamiliar and probably unpopular tax rules, such as including loans in taxable income.

One could avoid this cash flow problem under the flat tax by allowing the recovery of depreciation, inventory and basis. Such revisions would be costly to include, and would require much higher tax rates, perhaps for a long period of time.[11] They would also zero out the tax for many firms. The lump sum tax on old capital is an important contributor to the projected efficiency gains for switching to consumption taxes, the major reason that so many economists favor a consumption base.

Stock Market Effects

Note also that these physical effects on capital, and their variations across types of assets, should also be transmitted to stock prices. If a tax is levied at a 20% rate, with inflation to fully accommodate, all consumption prices would rise by 25%. A dollar of financial (or physical) assets can purchase only 80% of the real consumption goods it could purchase in the past. If there is no inflation, the nominal price of consumption goods should be constant and debt retains its purchasing power, but since new assets can be purchased at a 20% discount, the value of a firm's old capital would fall by 20%. If the firm has no debt, the stock should fall by 20%; if a third of its assets are financed by debt (typical of the economy) the stock should fall by 30%; if half is debt, the stock should fall by 40%. Individuals who have borrowed to buy stock could be significantly affected.[12]

EFFECT ON TAX ADMINISTRATION
AND THE UNDERGROUND ECONOMY

The complexity and cost of the current tax system is one of the most potent arguments used by the tax reform advocates. Each of the proposals discussed in this paper is advertised to be simpler and less costly to comply with and to administer than the current income tax. Even tax evasion is sometimes blamed on the complexity of the income tax.

Taxpayer Compliance

Easing the burdens of taxpayers in complying with the tax system is one of the biggest selling points for the "flat tax" and other tax simplification proposals. The current system is said to be a nightmare of complexity, requiring taxpayers to read and understand volumes of tax law, regulations, and instructions, and to complete page upon page of complicated forms.

The Internal Revenue Service (IRS) itself says it takes taxpayers an average of 13 hours and 29 minutes to prepare an individual income tax return (Form 1040).[13] The cost in taxpayer time and expenditures for the individual income tax has been estimated at $67 billion to $99 billion.[14] Costs to big business have been estimated at $2 billion.[15] The complexity is accused of contributing to the perception of unfairness, since the rich are seen as able to hire experts to help them escape their fair share.

The Flat Tax, Value-Added Tax, and National Retail Sales Tax

Two issues immediately present themselves: (1) how much of a burden is the current system, and (2) to what extent would the tax reforms currently contemplated relieve this burden?

What is the Current Burden?

Certainly the current system is complex. The Internal Revenue Code is thousands of pages long, and the regulations interpreting it run to tens of thousands of pages. The taxpaying public must file hundreds of different types of forms and schedules; time spent on taxes has been estimated at 2-8 billion hours for individuals and 800 million hours for businesses.[16]

These kinds of numbers are a bit misleading, however, because they do not apply to most taxpayers.

Most of the complex issues are of no concern to most taxpayers. Fewer than 35% of individual taxpayers itemize deductions. (The "very popular" mortgage interest deduction is claimed on less than 29% of returns and the charitable contribution deduction on about 31%.)[17]

Fewer than 16% of individual returns report business or farm income or loss, fewer than 8% rental income or loss, and fewer than 5% partnership or S-corporation income or loss.[18] (These percentages overlap.)

Businesses do face more complexity and compliance burden under the tax system than do most individuals, but it is hard to know its real extent.

Would Tax Reform Relieve the Burden?

A national sales tax or value-added tax that collected all taxes from businesses would obviously relieve the compliance problems of individual taxpayers, since they would need to file no returns at all.

Business taxpayers would not necessarily have compliance costs reduced by a VAT, however; depending on how the taxes were structured, businesses might find themselves facing two largely incompatible accounting systems. For financial purposes, creditors and stockholders would still require net income calculations, with depreciation, inventories, and all the other accrual accounting conventions. At the same time, the tax system would require value-added computations on a cash-flow basis.

A flat tax with a single rate would not, by itself, do much to simplify things for most individual taxpayers. In fact, for many individuals, the current system *is* a flat tax with a single rate and a large exemption. Almost 41% of all individual income tax returns currently either owe no tax or are taxed at a 10% rate.

The flat tax, therefore, would not represent much of a simplification for many individual taxpayers, who are already subject to a similar system, nor for larger businesses, which would be relieved of only the marginal accounting costs associated specifically with the income tax. Its simplifications would mostly benefit smaller businesses and individuals with more complex income tax filings. Individuals with businesses, however, would be required to file two returns, one for the business and one for their wage income.

If a VAT or retail sales tax were to provide a mechanism to relieve the burden for the poor, though a credit system, as many propose, individuals would still have to file returns to claim the credit.

Administrative Costs

The current tax system relies heavily on the uncompensated ("voluntary") labor of the taxpaying public, which reduces the government's administrative costs considerably. In FY2003, IRS collected around $1.9 trillion with a budget of about $9.8 billion, or a cost of less than 1/2 cent per dollar collected (not counting costs to taxpayers).[19]

Most of the proposed tax reforms appear to rely even more heavily on "voluntary" taxpayer efforts. Many proposals contemplate a reduced IRS presence in taxpayers' lives, and some even suggest abolishing the IRS altogether. Except for the national sales tax proposals that would be collected by the states, no proposal has specified how collection and enforcement activity is to be reduced.

Many of the problems that create administrative costs in the income tax system, such as verifying inventory or depreciation accounting, would be reduced or eliminated under most proposals, but major ones would still exist. A VAT or partial VAT would involve every business entity, and businesses are the source of most of IRS's current enforcement costs. Administrative costs often arise from taxpayers' attempts to avoid paying taxes, and no tax reform will produce a system in which people do not wish to avoid taxes.

The Underground Economy

Another hope for the tax reform proposals is that a new tax structure would reduce transactions taking place outside the tax system. This may depend on what part of the "underground" economy is meant. The "informal" economy, which involves evading taxes on legal activities, is partly a function of tax rates. Reducing rates would reduce the rewards of evasion and thus the incentive to cheat (but some proposals would result in a *higher* marginal rate for most smaller taxpayers, 17% instead of 10%, for example). For the illegal economy, where tax evasion is normally a minor part of the criminal activity, there is no reason to expect any outcome except continued evasion, although a different tax structure would alter the way in and degree to which income avoids tax, and, depending on behavioral responses, the actual burdens. For example, under an income tax, producers in an underground market pay no taxes, while their customers who operate in the legal market do. Under a sales tax, producers effectively pay taxes on income when it is spent in the market; their customers pay no tax on the segment of income that reflects value added by the illegal part of the market (although tax is paid on intermediate inputs).

In many ways certain forms of value added taxes and, to a greater extent, retail sales taxes increase the incentive for firms to avoid tax. For a retailer with, say, a 2% profit margin, the benefit of avoiding a profits tax is less than one percent of profits. If the retailer stands to save 20% of each dollar, the incentive to avoid tax is much greater. That is the reason that many tax administrators would recommend the invoice credit form of the VAT used by Europeans (so that firms present evidence on their intermediate purchases which helps to monitor the behavior of the seller) rather than the subtraction method, where firms subtract from intermediate purchases from their tax base. It is also a reason that many tax scholars doubt that a high retail sales tax is feasible, and indeed no such high rate of the retail sales tax exists anywhere.

HOW WOULD THE DISTRIBUTION OF THE TAX BURDEN AND THE LEVEL OF TAX REVENUES BE AFFECTED BY A DIFFERENT TAX SYSTEM?

Many of the tax reform proposals have not been subject to detailed analysis. Based on those analyses that have been done, however, a number of the flat-tax proposals could, in their current form, lose revenue, perhaps substantial amounts. They would also reduce the progressivity of the tax.

Revenue Effects

Most proposals have been designed to be revenue neutral, but have not been evaluated by official revenue estimators. The Treasury Department, however, has analyzed a version of the flat tax with a proposed rate of 17%, finding a revenue shortfall. (This estimate, however, was made in 1995 before the major tax cuts were enacted.)

The Treasury found that the revenue-neutral flat-tax rate in the proposal, given the level of exemptions (ranging from about $10,000 for a single individual to about $30,000 for a family of four), would be around 21% (20.8%), about four percentage points above the proposed permanent rate of 17%.[20]

Alternatively, the 17% rate could be maintained and the exemptions cut by over half to maintain revenue neutrality. With neither revision, Treasury estimated the proposal would lose $138 billion annually.

There has been considerable dispute about whether the 23% tax rate proposed for the Fair Tax, a national retail sales tax with a rebate for low income families would be adequate to replace the income tax (and payroll tax). Reasons for the dispute include technical questions about the requirements to keep government spending fixed in real terms, the degree of evasion, the effects on economic growth, and whether the tax is replacing the current level of tax revenues following the recent tax cuts or the level after these tax cuts expire.[21]

Other proposals with lower rates and/or more exemptions would presumably lead to larger revenue losses. Adding deductions, such as the payroll tax deduction, or restoring itemized deductions, such as those for mortgage interest and charitable contributions, would cause larger revenue losses.

Value-added taxes or sales taxes (which are equivalent to the flat tax except that they have no exemptions) could presumably raise adequate revenue at lower rates if the base were kept broad. The required rates in other proposals will depend on the base.

Any revenue losses would either lead to higher deficits and debt or require spending cuts; generally the latter option has been proposed. Some proponents have incorporated in their plans the presumption that tax rates can be lowered in the future due to economic growth.

It is important to note that a number of these taxes have a consumption base; thus any growth that arises from increased savings would contract, rather than expand, the tax base in the short run. Increases in labor supply would increase the tax base. Our knowledge of the likely effects on labor supply and savings is very limited, however.

Distributional Effects

Any flattening of the tax rates would have distributional consequences across income classes. In addition, a switch from an income to a consumption base for taxation could cause large changes in the distribution of taxes across generations and family types as well as income classes.

Income Classes

Holding revenue constant, flat-tax proposals would reduce tax burdens on higher-income individuals; if the earned income tax credit (EITC) is repealed, the burden would rise on low-income individuals, as well as the middle class.

Based on the 21% tax rate, and using percentage change in disposable income as a measure, poor individuals would experience decreases of 6%-7% under the flat tax and middle income individuals decreases about 3% to 5%, while the highest income class will gain about 9%, according to the Treasury analysis (again based on estimates before the recent tax cuts).[22] These effects would be more pronounced if revenue neutrality were achieved through lower exemptions rather than a higher tax rate. There are, however, conceptual problems in assessing distribution of consumption taxes.[23]

Value-added and sales taxes would reduce tax progressivity further because they do not permit exemptions, unless a credit mechanism were introduced. Proposals with a graduated rate structure would be more progressive than other proposals, but they have not been closely examined by the Treasury or the Joint Committee on Taxation.

Generations

Proposals to shift the tax base from an income to a consumption base (most proposals) would shift the tax burden substantially across generations. The flat tax, for example, has a consumption base, although it appears to be a wage tax for individuals. The burden of tax would be shifted from wages and capital income to consumption, which is equivalent to wages and old capital (both principal and return). Since older individuals own capital, the burden would tend to be shifted to those individuals.

A Lifetime Perspective

The ways in which a consumption tax burdens old capital are complex, and the incorporation of generations as well as income in distributional analysis is limited at this time. In general, however, younger individuals who are in taxable status and who will save substantial sums over their lifetimes would benefit relatively from the tax, while middle and higher income older individuals consuming assets would bear a greater burden. Wealthy individuals would have their tax burdens reduced over their lifetime if they maintain and increase their assets. Poor individuals with little savings over their lifetime would be relatively unaffected by the change in the base, as long as transfer payments are indexed to changes in the price level needed by a tax revision. The rate structure is more important for these low-income individuals.

Marriage Neutrality

The marriage neutrality of the tax system is a function of the tax structure, not the choice of tax base -income or consumption. Hence, both an income and a consumption based tax can be marriage neutral if the accompanying tax structure is designed appropriately. Marriage penalties and/or bonuses can be avoided if taxes are levied on individual rather than family income or consumption and if standard deductions and tax rate brackets for married couples are twice the size of those for single taxpayers.

Under the current income tax when married couples are compared to single filers, marriage tax penalties are confined to very low-income married couples who claim the earned income tax credit and to high-income married couples above the 25% marginal income tax threshold. All other married taxpayers receive marriage tax bonuses, or at worst, a neutral tax treatment when compared to two singles with the same combined income.

A flat-rate consumption tax, with two filing statuses -married and single, and with a standard deduction for married couples that is twice the size of the standard deduction for a single individual would eliminate all marriage tax penalties and bonuses. The same result, however, could also be achieved under an income tax by adopting a single tax rate and standard deductions that are twice as large for married couples as for single individuals.

There are no marriage bonuses or penalties with a sales or value added tax.

End Notes

[1] Under the credit-invoice method, a firm pays the VAT on total output and receives a credit for taxes paid by its intermediate suppliers. Under the subtraction method a firm pays tax on total output less the costs of intermediate inputs. The credit invoice method is commonly used in other countries and because of multiple reporting tends to lead to a high level of compliance. The credit invoice method allows differential rates to be applied to final products based on the tax at the last stage, while the subtraction method is appropriate for a single uniform rate.

[2] For a summary of current bills and proposals, see CRS Report RL34343, *Tax Reform: An Overview of Proposals in the 110th Congress*, by James M. Bickley.

[3] The President's Advisory Panel on Federal Tax Reform, *Simple, Fair, and Pro-Growth: Proposals to Fix America's Tax System*, November 2005, which can be found at http://www.taxreformpanel.gov/.

[4] For a discussion of these models and their effects on savings, see CRS Report RL31949, *Issues in Dynamic Revenue Estimating*, and CRS Report RL32517, *Distributional Effects of Taxes on Corporate Profits, Investment Income, and Estates*, both by Jane G. Gravelle.

[5] See CRS Report RL32591, *U.S. Terms of Trade: Significance, Trends, and Policy*, by Craig K. Elwell, for a discussion of the concept.

[6] See CRS Report 98-901, *Short-Run Macroeconomic Effects of Fundamental Tax Reform*, by Jane G. Gravelle for a more detailed discussion of these issues.

[7] The rate would depend on whether and the extent of any family exemption. A 20% tax exclusive rate would correspond to a tax inclusive rate between 16% and 17%.

[8] U.S. Congress, Joint Committee on Taxation, *Tax Modeling Project and 1997 Symposium Papers*, committee print, 105th Cong., 1st sess., November 20, 1997, JCS-21-97 (Washington: GPO, 1997), p. 24.

[9] Physical business assets (equipment, structures, and inventories) would be deducted from income as an intermediate good under the flat and VAT approaches and not subject to the retail sales tax. Sales of business assets, whether new or used, would be taxed under the VAT and flat tax. Owner occupied housing would presumably be an exception because the stream of imputed rental income is not taxed; newly constructed housing would presumably be subject to the retail sales tax and the purchaser would not be allowed a deduction or credit under a flat tax or VAT. Existing housing would presumably be neither taxed nor eligible for deduction. The return to this new housing would still be exempt from tax, but the method of doing so would be different.

[10] The price level in the economy would increase by 25%. Why 25% rather than 20%? This is simply the difference between the tax inclusive rate of 20% and the tax exclusive rate of 25%. (The tax exclusive rate is $t/(1-t)$ where t is the tax inclusive rate). If prices go up by 25% you lose 20% of purchasing power. That is, an $80 basket of goods would now cost 25% more, or $100 and you spend $100 to purchase goods that are worth only $80—your $100 has lost 20% of its purchasing power. In our example, in the case of the retail sales tax, the individual keeps $72,500 (the $500,000 sales price less the mortgage repayment, which is $72,500). He implicitly pays a tax of 20% because this amount can only purchase $58,000 of goods before the application of a 25% retail sales tax. In the case of a VAT, the price of the building would rise by 25%, to $625,000, and after paying a 20% tax on receipts, the investor would have $500,000 less the mortgage payment—with the same results ensuing.

[11] The magnitude of these transition issues for the flat tax is discussed in CRS Report RL33545, *The Advisory Panel's Tax Reform Proposals*, by Jane G. Gravelle.

[12] Some people disbelieve that this price effect would occur, but if it did not, then in effect the tax is not acting as a consumption tax and none of the investment incentives would work. It is the fall in the price of stock that makes investment in corporate equity more attractive and it corresponds to the ability, when directly investing, to deduct the cost of capital acquisitions.

[13] Instructions for Form 1040 (2003), p. 77.

[14] Statement by Janet Holtzblatt in a presentation to the American Enterprise Institute, reported in Brandt, Goldwyn, "Tax Administration Service Estimates Tax Compliance Costs at $99 billion for Individuals in Year 2000," *Bureau of National Affairs Daily Tax Report*, no. 23, February 5, 2004, p. G-2. The range reflects a value per hour between $15 and $25.

[15] Joel B. Slemrod and Marsha Blumenthal, "The Income Tax Compliance Cost of Big Business," *Public Finance Quarterly*, vol. 24, October 1996, pp. 411-438.

[16] For a survey of estimates, see Joel Slemrod, "Which Is the Simplest Tax System of Them All?" in Henry J. Aaron and William G. Gale, eds., *The Economics of Fundamental Tax Reform* (Washington: The Brookings Institution, 1996), pp. 367-368.

[17] "Individual Income Tax Returns, Preliminary Data, 2002," *SOI Bulletin*, Winter-Spring 2003-2004, Internal Revenue Service, 2003.

[18] Ibid.

[19] U.S. Department of the Treasury, *The Budget in Brief FY2005*, February 2005. There are some additional costs budgeted under Treasury and Justice Departments and the Judiciary Branch.

[20] U.S. Department of the Treasury, Office of Tax Analysis, *Preliminary Analysis of a Flat Rate Consumption Tax*, March 10, 1995.

[21] Proponents arguments for these rates can be found in "The FairTax: Fundamentals and Facts," is cited and at the Beacon Hill Website http://www.beaconhill.org/. Others find that the rate must be much higher. See William G. Gale, "The Nastional Retail Sales Tax: What Would the Rate Have to Be?" *Tax Notes*, March 16, 2005, pp. 889-911, and President's Advisory Panel on Tax Reform's final report, 2005, Chapter 9: http://www.taxreformpanel.gov/final-report/.

[22] Ibid. Most analyses find that high-income individuals would gain from a flat tax. Some studies find a plan with a rebate would benefit very low-income individuals as well. See for example, Peter Mieszkowski and Michael G. Palumbo "Distributive Analysis of Fundamental Tax Reform," in *United States Tax Reform in the 21st Century*, George R. Zodrow and Peter Mieszkowski, eds., Cambridge, UK: Cambridge University Press, 2002; The President's Advisory Panel on Tax Reform's final report, Chapter 9: http://www.taxreformpanel.gov/final-report/, pp. 141-178.

[23] For a discussion of the conceptual problems relating to income distribution, see Leonard E. Burman, Jane G. Gravelle, and Jeff Rohaly, "Towards a More Consistent Distributional Analysis," http://www.taxpolicycenter.org/ publications/url.cfm?ID=411480.

In: Value-Added Tax (VAT) and Flat Tax Proposals
Editors: D. B. Andrews and A. M. Davis

ISBN: 978-1-61324-191-2
© 2011 Nova Science Publishers, Inc.

Chapter 7

VALUE-ADDED TAX:
A NEW U.S. REVENUE SOURCE?[*]

James M. Bickley

SUMMARY

Some form of a value-added tax (VAT), a broad-based consumption tax, has been frequently discussed as a full or partial replacement for the U.S. income tax system.

A VAT is imposed at all levels of production on the differences between firms' sales and their purchases from all other firms. For calendar year 2005, a broad-based VAT in the United States would have raised net revenue of approximately $50 billion for each 1% levied. Most other developed nations rely more on broad-based consumption taxes for revenue than does the United States. A VAT is shifted onto consumers; consequently, it is regressive because lower-income households spend a greater proportion of their incomes on consumption than higher-income households. This regression, however, could be reduced or even eliminated by any of three methods: a refundable credit against income tax liability for VAT paid, allocation of some of VAT revenue for increased welfare spending, or selective exclusion of some goods from taxation.

From an economic perspective, a major revenue source is better the greater its neutrality — that is, the less the tax alters economic decisions. Conceptually, a VAT on all consumption expenditures, with a single rate that is constant over time, would be relatively neutral compared to other major revenue sources. A VAT would not alter choices among goods, and it would not affect the relative prices of present and future consumption. But a VAT cannot be levied on leisure; consequently, a VAT would affect households' decisions concerning work versus leisure.

The imposition of a VAT would cause a one-time increase in this country's price level. But a VAT would not necessarily affect this country's future rate of inflation if the Federal Reserve offset the contractionary effects of a VAT with a more expansionary monetary policy. If the United States continued its policy of flexible exchange rates, then the imposition of a VAT would not significantly affect the U.S. balance-of-trade. There is no conclusive evidence that a VAT would change the rate of national saving more than

---

[*] This is an edited, reformatted and augmented version of Copngressional Research Services publication RL33619, dated January 3, 2008.

another type of major tax increase. The high revenue yield from a VAT would cause administrative costs to be low, measured as a percentage of revenue yield. In comparison to other broad-based consumption taxes, VATs have produced relatively good compliance rates. Whether or not a federal VAT would encroach on the primary source of state revenue, the sales tax, is subject to debate. A federal-state VAT could be collected jointly, but a state would lose some of its fiscal discretion.

CONCEPT OF A VALUE-ADDED TAX

A value-added tax is a tax, levied at each stage of production, on firms' value added. The value added of a firm is the difference between a firm's sales and a firm's purchases of inputs from other firms. In other words, a firm's value added is simply the amount of value a firm contributes to a good or service by applying its factors of production (land, labor, capital, and entrepreneurial ability).[7] Another method of calculating a firm's value added is to total the firm's payments to its factors of production.

Types of VAT

There are three types of VATs that differ in their tax treatment of purchases of capital inputs (plant and equipment). Under the *consumption VAT*, capital purchases are treated the same way as the purchase of any other input: the purchase price is deducted at the time of purchase. This tax treatment of capital purchases is equivalent to expensing. Under the *income VAT*, the VAT paid on the purchases of capital inputs is amortized (credited against the firm's VAT liability) over the expected lives of the capital inputs. Under the *gross product VAT*, no deduction for the VAT on purchases of capital inputs is allowed against the firm's VAT liability.

All 29 OECD nations with VATs use the consumption type. The consumption VAT is the type usually advocated for this country. Indeed, most VAT advocates intend to shift tax burdens from capital income to consumption. Furthermore, a consumption VAT is simpler to compute because firms do not have to separate expenditures for capital from other expenditures.

Methods of Calculating VAT

There are three alternative methods of calculating VAT: the credit method, the subtraction method, and the addition method.[8] Under the *credit-invoice method,* a firm would be required to show VAT separately on all sales invoices.[9] Each sale would be marked up by the amount of the VAT. A sales invoice for a seller is a purchase invoice for a buyer. A firm would calculate the VAT to be remitted to the government by a three-step process. First, the firm would aggregate VAT shown on its sales invoices. Second, the firm would aggregate VAT shown on its purchase invoices. Finally, aggregate VAT on purchase invoices would be subtracted from aggregate VAT shown on sales invoices, and the difference remitted to the government. The credit-invoice method is calculated on a transactions basis.

Under the *subtraction method*, the firm calculates its value added by subtracting its cost of taxed inputs from its sales. Next, the firm determines its VAT liability by multiplying its value added by the VAT rate.[10] Most flat tax proposals are modified subtraction method VATs. Under the *addition method*, the firm calculates its value added by adding all payments for untaxed inputs (e.g., wages and profits). Next, the firm multiplies its value added by the VAT rate to calculate VAT to be remitted to the government.

The credit-invoice method is used by 28 of 29 OECD nations with VATs. Tax economists differ in their classifications of the Japanese VAT. Both the credit-invoice and the subtraction methods have been discussed for the United States. The prevailing view of economists is that the credit-invoice method is superior. This method requires registered firms to maintain detailed records that are cross indexed with supporting documentation. A VAT shown on the sales invoice of one firm is the same as the VAT shown on the purchase order of another firm. Hence, the credit-invoice method allows tax auditors to cross check the records of firms. Also, each firm has a vested interest in insuring that the VAT shown on its purchase orders is not understated so the firm can receive full credit against VAT liability for VAT previously paid. Thus, the credit-invoice method would seem to be easier to enforce. Also, the credit-invoice method is probably the only feasible method if there are to be multiple tax rates.

Supporters of the subtraction method maintain that it would have low compliance costs because all necessary data could be obtained from records kept by a firm for other purposes. Still, a firm would have to make calculations based on these data. For example, deductible expenses would have to be separated from nondeductible expenses, and some data expressed on an accrual basis would have to be converted to a cash flow basis.

The credit-invoice method would have substantial compliance costs because the amount of VAT would have to be shown on every sales invoice (and, conversely, on every purchase invoice). On the plus side, however, the credit-invoice method would yield an additional data base to firms. Some firms might find these additional data useful in decision making. For example, records of purchase invoices and sales invoices may improve some firms' control over their inventories. Compliance costs of the credit-invoice method might be partially offset by the value of the VAT data base to firms, but this value has never been quantified.

The credit-invoice method would have greater administrative costs than the subtraction method because of its requirements for additional data, computations, and record-keeping. Although there are data on the administrative costs of a VAT calculated by the credit-invoice method, empirical data are not available on the subtraction method; consequently, a quantitative comparison of costs currently is not feasible. The subtraction method would not work administratively if many goods are exempt or if multiple tax rates are levied. Unless specified otherwise, this report will assume that the credit-invoice method is used and that the VAT is the consumption type.

Exemption Versus Zero-Rating

None of the VAT proposals would require all firms to collect the VAT. The two fundamental methods of giving special tax treatment to businesses in an industry under a VAT are exemption and zero-rating. An exempt business would not collect VAT on its sales and would not receive credit for VAT paid on its purchases of inputs. An exempt business would not register with tax authorities, and, consequently, would not be part of the VAT system. Hence, an exempt business would not have the usual VAT compliance costs and would not impose administrative costs on the government (except verification of its exemption, of course). An exempt business's costs, however, include any tax paid on inputs, because it receives no credit for previously paid taxes.

A zero-rated business would not collect VAT on its sales but would receive credit for VAT paid on its inputs. This is equivalent to the business being charged a zero tax rate. A zero-rated business would be a registered taxpayer, and, consequently, would involve the usual compliance and administrative costs. A zero-rated business, however, would receive a refund of any VAT paid on its inputs, so its costs would not include VAT paid at earlier stages. The effects on final prices and total VAT collected by the government caused by exempting or zero-rating firms would vary with the stage of production.

An exempt retailer would not charge any VAT on its sales but it would not receive any credit for VAT previously paid on its inputs, so its price to the final consumer would include all VAT paid except that on its own value-added. The government would have collected a tax on all the value added in the product except the retailer's.

A zero-rated retailer would not charge any VAT on its sales, but it would receive credit for all VAT previously paid on its inputs. A zero-rated retailer would not remit VAT to the government, but it would receive a refund for VAT previously paid by suppliers. Hence, the price of the commodity would not include any VAT, and the government would receive no revenue.

Exempting or zero-rating a retailer would not affect the linkage (or chain) of VAT collections and credits between different stages of production because retailers are the final stage of production and distribution. But exempting or zero-rating an intermediate stage, such as manufacturing of wholesaling, would break the chain between firms at different stages of production.

Exempting, however, causes a far more serious break than zero-rating. For example, an exempt manufacturer would not collect VAT on sales to a wholesaler and would not receive credit for VAT paid on inputs. A nonexempt wholesaler would not receive credit for the VAT paid on the manufacturer's inputs included in the price it paid the manufacturer. But the wholesaler would remit VAT collected on all of its sales, so some of the value added in the product would be taxed twice. Consequently, exempting a manufacturer or any other intermediate producer would increase total VAT collected by the government and the final retail price of the commodity.

A zero-rated manufacturer would not collect VAT on sales but would receive credit for VAT paid on inputs. The price paid by the wholesaler, therefore, would contain no VAT. The nonexempt wholesaler would collect VAT on sales and would not be eligible for any VAT credits, but the total VAT at that point would exactly equal what it would have been had there been no untaxed stage. Subsequent stages of production would charge VAT on sales and would receive credit for VAT paid on inputs as though there had been no break in the chain. Hence, zero-rating a manufacturer or other intermediate stage would change neither total VAT remitted nor the retail price on the commodity.[11]

If both zero-rated firms and exempt firms operate at the same level of production in the same industry, the zero-rated firms would have a competitive advantage, because their costs are less by the amount of the VAT.

Policy makers may be faced with a decision to either zero-rate or exempt a particular product.

> Zero-rating is desirable when the objective is to exclude the consumption of the product completely from tax, where an exemption is warranted when it is not regarded as feasible or desirable to tax the activity but some tax on final consumption is considered desirable....
>
> There are two major objections to exemption. First, cascading results as the exempt firms and their business customers cannot receive input tax credit. Secondly, firms producing both exempt and taxable (including zero-rated) items must allocate inputs between exempt and non-exempt categories, and this is difficult to accomplish in any non-arbitrary way and to control.[12]

REVENUE YIELD

In estimating a VAT's revenue yield, economists and public officials use the operating assumption that a VAT would be fully shifted to final consumers in the form of higher prices of goods. A VAT (or any other major tax increase) would have a contractionary effect on the economy unless offset by other economic policies. Consequently, a revenue estimate is generally made under the assumption that the Federal Reserve would use an expansionary monetary policy to neutralize the contractionary effects of a VAT. Also, a revenue estimate does not take into account the possible shifts in consumption patterns that might be expected if some items are taxed and others are excluded from taxation.

The potential revenue per 1% rate from a VAT would vary with the comprehensiveness of the tax base. A broad-based VAT would have limited exclusions, while a narrow-based VAT would have numerous exclusions. Obviously, the broader the tax base, the lower the tax rate necessary to raise a given amount of revenue.

Furthermore, the broader the VAT base, the more efficient it is. The exclusion of goods from taxation changes their prices relative to taxed goods. Changes in relative prices cause economic distortions. Consumers tend to substitute lower-priced goods for higher-priced goods.

There are three primary justifications for excluding specific items from taxation under a VAT.[13] First, the VAT would be difficult to collect because sellers of some types of goods and services could easily avoid reporting their sales. For example, VAT would be difficult to collect on expenditures for domestic services and expenditures abroad by U.S. residents. Second, some goods are excluded on equity grounds, since these goods claim disproportionately large percentages of the incomes of lower-income families. (Data on spending patterns do not, however, suggest that exclusions can have a very powerful effect on the distribution of a VAT.)[14] Third, some goods may be excluded because they are merit goods, that is "goods the provision of which society (as distinct from the preferences of the individual consumer) wishes to encourage."[15] Some items may be justified for exclusion for more than one reason.

William G. Gale of the Brookings Institution and C. Eugene Steuerle of the Urban Institute estimate that each percentage point of a VAT with only a few exclusions could generate net revenue equivalent to 0.4% of gross domestic product (GDP).[16] For calendar year 2005, U.S. gross domestic product was $12.5 trillion.[17] For calendar year 2005, each

1.0% rate for a VAT could have raised net revenue of approximately $50 billion with a broad base. Thus, for 2005, according to the Gale/Steuerle estimate, a U.S. VAT of 5% would have generated $250 billion in revenue. In comparison, for FY2005, the individual income tax yielded $927 billion.[18]

The VAT's high revenue yield at a low tax rate not only makes it a possible source revenue for tax reform but also has generated concerns among some that VAT revenues may finance a larger public sector. The issue of VAT and the size of government is examined in a later section of this report.

INTERNATIONAL COMPARISON OF COMPOSITION OF TAXES

One argument frequently made for a U.S. VAT is the relatively heavy reliance on consumption taxes by other developed countries. For 2005, for taxes on general consumption (e.g., VATs and sales taxes), the United States (federal, state, and local governments) had a lower reliance (8.0%) of total tax revenues than any other OECD nation.[19] Also for 2005, the United States' (federal, state, and local governments) general consumption taxes as a percentage of gross domestic product (2.2%) were lower than any other nation in the OECD.[20]

This lower reliance on consumption taxes may result from all other developed nations having a VAT at the national level. A VAT is a requirement for membership in the European Union (EU).[21] Sweden, Norway, Iceland, and Switzerland had retail sales taxes at the national level but eventually switched to a VAT.[22] According to the OECD:

> The spread of Value Added Tax (also called Goods and Services Tax — GST) has been the most important development in taxation over the last half-century. Limited to less than 10 countries in the late 1960s it has now been implemented by about 136 countries; and in these countries (including OECD member countries) it typically accounts for one-fifth of total tax revenue. The recognized capacity of VAT to raise revenue in a neutral and transparent manner drew all OECD member countries (except the United States) to adopt this broad based consumption tax.[23]

Policy insights can be obtained by examining the experiences of other nations; however, just because other nations exhibit a specific tax policy does not necessarily mean that it is appropriate for the United States to adopt this policy. Economic analysis of optimal taxation suggests that those choices depend on issues of efficiency, equity, and administrative and compliance costs, and should be made in the context of the overall tax and spending structure. These considerations may vary from one country to another.

EQUITY

A major topic concerning any proposed tax or tax change is the distribution or equity of the tax among households. There are two types of equity: vertical and horizontal. Vertical equity concerns the tax treatment of households with different abilities-to-pay. Horizontal equity concerns the degree to which households with the same ability-to-pay are taxed equally. Both vertical and horizontal equity may be affected by the measure of ability-to-pay and the tax period.

Ability-to-Pay

The most common measure of ability-to-pay is income.[24] Proponents of income as a measure of ability-to-pay argue that saving yields utility by providing households with greater economic security. Federal data are more readily available on different measures of income than different levels of consumption. For example, the federal government reports levels of disposable income, which equals consumption plus saving. Thus, tax economists can more easily calculate tax incidence if income instead of consumption is the measure of ability-to-pay.

Some arguments for the consumption tax base suggest that personal consumption is the best measure of ability-to-pay because consumption is the actual taking of scarce resources from the economic system. Some economists argue that consumption may be a better proxy for permanent income than is current income (see discussion below).

Time Period

Tax incidence usually is measured by using a one-year period. Data on consumption and income are readily available in one-year increments and the concept of a one-year period is easily understood. But many economists believe tax incidence is more accurately determined by measuring consumption and income over a household's lifetime. Lifetime income and consumption are affected by the life cycle concept and transitional components of income. According to this life cycle concept, a household makes current consumption decisions based on its expected future flow of income, averaging its consumption over its lifetime.

For example, a common life cycle is low income in the household's early years, high income in the household's middle years, and low income in the household's retirement years. A young household may save a small percentage of its income in order to acquire consumer durables. In its middle years, this household may save a high percentage of its income while its income is highest. Finally, during its retirement years, this household may save a small percentage of its income in order to maintain its consumption level. Thus, annual consumption tends to be more stable than annual income over the household's life cycle.

Although many economists prefer the concept of lifetime income, federal data are not collected on a lifetime basis. Consequently, economists have developed life-cycle models in an attempt to measure equity, but the distributional results from these models are subject to widespread debate.

Vertical Equity[25]

If disposable income over a one-year period is the measure of ability-to-pay, then a VAT would be viewed as extremely regressive; that is, the percentage of disposable income paid in VAT would decrease rapidly as disposable income increases. In most discussions of tax policy, both a one-year period and annual disposable income (or some other annual income measure) are used; consequently, the VAT is viewed as being extremely regressive. For example, CBO calculated the annual incidence of a 3.5% broad-based VAT for 1992. CBO found that all families would have paid 2.2% of their income in VAT. The burden on family income was 4.8% on the lowest quintile, 3.2% on the second quintile, 2.8% on the middle quintile, 2.3% on the fourth quintile, and 1.5% on the highest quintile.[26]

If disposable income over a lifetime is the measure of ability-to-pay, a VAT would be mildly regressive. For lower- and middle-income households, it appears that nearly all savings are eventually consumed.[27] Thus, it may be that for the vast majority of households, lifetime consumption and lifetime income are approximately equal. High-income households tend to have net savings over their lifetimes; consequently, they would pay a lower proportion of their disposable incomes in VAT than would lower-income groups. But these highly stylized life-cycle models are controversial.[28]

If consumption is used as a measure of ability-to-pay, a single-rate VAT with a broad base would be approximately proportional regardless of the time period. In other words, the percentage of consumption paid in VAT by households would be approximately constant as the level of household consumption rises.

Another equity issue concerns the burden of a VAT on different age groups. If older individuals on the average consume more out of savings than younger individuals, then a VAT would fall more heavily on the old than the young. Conversely, an increase in the personal income tax would fall more heavily on the young than the old.

Policy Options to Alleviate Regressivity

Some supporters of progressive taxation oppose the VAT primarily because they believe that it is regressive. No mechanism is likely to introduce progressivity at higher income levels. But critics are especially concerned about the absolute burden of a VAT on low-income households. The degree of regressivity on lower-income households, however, can be reduced by government policy. Three often-mentioned policies are exclusions and multiple rates, income tax credits, and earmarking of some revenues for increased social spending (including indexed transfer payments).

Exclusions and Multiple Rates

The incidence of the VAT depends on its tax base; therefore, the regressivity of the VAT can be reduced or eliminated by excluding (zero-rating or exempting) those goods that account for a disproportionately high percentage of the incomes of lower-income households. The exclusion of many necessities on equity grounds from retail sales taxes has been politically popular at the state level. All members of the European Union (EU) exclude some goods from VAT on equity grounds. Also, most EU nations have multiple tax rates on equity grounds. Reduced rates are applied to necessities and premium rates are levied on luxuries.

Despite the existing policies in the EU, most tax economists oppose exclusions and multiple rates to reduce regressivity for three reasons. First, the administrative costs, compliance costs, and neutrality costs are substantial.[29] If a VAT is to raise a given amount of revenue, then revenue lost from excluding goods must be offset by higher VAT rates. These higher rates increase the distortion in relative prices, and consequently, reduce the neutrality of the tax system. Second, the possible reduction in regressivity from exclusion and multiple rates is declining because consumption patterns for different income levels are becoming more similar.[30] Third, for a one-year time period, the reduction in regressivity is limited, particularly for low-income households. Money saved for exclusions is largely offset by higher tax rates (needed for revenue neutrality) on taxed goods.[31]

Tax Credits

The federal government could allow either a flat tax credit or a credit that diminishes as income rises, in order to overcome the regressivity of a VAT. This credit method could be operated in two ways. First, an individual could apply the credit against his federal income tax liability, thus lowering his liability on a dollar-for-dollar basis. If the tax credit exceeded the individual's tax liability, he could apply for a refund of the excess credit. A taxpayer already due a tax refund could increase the size of his refund by the amount of the tax credit. A household not subject to income taxation could apply for a tax refund equal to the credit. An income tax credit that declines as income increases could reduce regressivity more sharply than a flat income tax credit.

Second, a stand-alone credit system could be established which would not require an eligible household to file an income tax return in order to obtain a refund for VAT paid. An eligible household would have to submit a simple form in order to receive a refund. A stand-alone credit system may be more effective than the income tax credit in encouraging low-income households to file for a refund, but administrative and compliance costs would be higher.

As stated previously, the President's Advisory Panel on Federal Tax Reform examined a proposal for a partial replacement VAT. The Panel believed that compared to current law "it would be possible to develop an approximately distributionally neutral tax credit and rate structure."[32]

But a federal credit system would incur some administrative costs, which would increase the total administrative costs of a VAT. Furthermore, households incur implicit taxes if their credits are phased out (or income tested transfers reduced).

At the federal level, studies have concluded that the refundable earned-income tax credit (EITC) has had "a significant positive impact on participation in the labor force."[33] But compliance with EITC provisions has been an ongoing issue.[34]

Earmarking of VAT Revenues

A third option to reduce or eliminate regressivity is to earmark some of the revenue from a VAT to finance an increase in income tested transfers. Aaron estimated that an increase in benefits of approximately $5 billion for a VAT yielding $100 billion could fully protect low-income families from paying the VAT.[35]

> For example, a 10 percent increase in food stamp entitlements would approximately offset the effect on households eligible for the full food stamp allotment of a VAT that raised $100 billion in revenue. This estimate is based on the fact that $100 billion will be approximately three percent of consumption in 1989 and that food is estimated to absorb about 30 percent of the budget in estimates of poverty thresholds.[36]

Many households with low taxable incomes do not currently receive transfers and would not be protected by Aaron's proposal.

Horizontal Equity

If disposable income is the measure of ability-to-pay, the horizontal equity of a VAT would depend on the time period. For a one-year period, a VAT would be very inequitable because households with the same level of disposable income would have widely differing levels of consumption and, consequently, payments of VAT.

For a lifetime period, the VAT would have a high degree of horizontal equity. For low- and middle-income households, almost all income is consumed over these households' lifetimes; consequently, households with the same lifetime incomes would have the same levels of consumption and the same VAT payments.[37] Over their lifetimes, high-income households with equal incomes differ in their levels of consumption and, consequently, VAT payments. For example, assume that two households have $10 million in lifetime income, but the first household spends $4.5 million on consumption and the second household spends $9 million on consumption. The second household would pay twice as much in VAT as the first household. Thus, for a lifetime period, the VAT is not horizontally equitable for high-income households.

NEUTRALITY

In public finance, the more *neutral* is a tax, the less the tax affects private economic decisions and, consequently, the more efficient is the operation of the economy. Conceptually, a VAT on all consumption expenditures, with a single rate that is constant over time, would be relatively neutral compared to other major revenue sources.

For households, two out of three major decisions would not be altered by this hypothetical VAT. First, this VAT would not alter choices among goods because all would be taxed at the same rate. Thus, *relative* prices would not change. In contrast, other taxes, such as excise taxes, which change relative prices, would distort household consumer choices by encouraging the substitution of untaxed goods for taxed goods. But a hypothetical income tax on all income would be neutral in this respect.

Second, a VAT does not affect the relative prices of present and future consumption. In contrast, the individual income tax affects the relative prices of present and future consumption because the income tax is levied on income which is saved, and then the returns on saving are taxed.

A household's work-leisure decision, however, would be affected by a VAT or any other tax on either consumption or income.[38] Since leisure would not be taxed, any tax increase would fall on the returns to work.

A VAT would have conflicting effects on the number of hours worked by each household. A household would have an incentive to substitute leisure for work because of the relative rise in the value of leisure to work (substitution effect). Conversely, a household would have an incentive to increase its hours worked in an attempt to maintain its current living standards (income effect). Thus, a VAT could decrease, increase, or not change a household's hours worked.

For a firm, the VAT would not affect decisions concerning method of financing (debt or equity), choice among inputs (unless some suppliers are exempt or zero-rated), type of business organization (corporation, partnership, or sole proprietorship), or goods to produce. Other types of taxes may affect one or more of these types of decisions.

But a VAT cannot be levied on all consumer goods; consequently, prices of taxed goods will rise relative to untaxed goods. Furthermore, most nations with VATs have more than one rate.[39] Multiple VAT rates alter relative prices of taxed goods. Finally, VAT rates in most nations have tended to rise over time. Despite these deviations from a pure form of VAT, a broad-based VAT is relatively neutral compared to most other taxes. This neutrality is greater if the tax rate is relatively low. But the relative neutrality of a VAT compared to an increase in the personal income tax is uncertain.[40]

INFLATION

If the Federal Reserve implemented an expansionary monetary policy to offset the contractionary effects of a VAT then there would be a one-time increase in the price level. For example, an expansionary monetary policy to accommodate a 5% VAT on 60% of consumer outlays might directly cause an estimated one-time increase in consumer prices of approximately 3%. There would also be some secondary price effects. Some goods would rise in price because their factors of production, especially labor, are linked to price indexes. Yet, if the Federal Reserve disregarded these secondary price increases in formulating monetary policy, these secondary price increases would tend to be offset by price reductions in other sectors of the economy.

An examination of VATs in the OECD has found only an initial effect of a VAT on the price level. But it is difficult to empirically isolate the effect of a VAT from other possible causes of a change in the price level.

It has been suggested that the federal government exclude the VAT from price indexes. Hence, existing indexing would not have an inflationary effect.[41] But such an approach might prove unpopular and it might be contested in court.

In summary, the proper monetary accommodation for a VAT would probably cause a one-time increase in the price level but not affect the subsequent rate of inflation (i.e., cause continual increases in the general price level).

BALANCE-OF-TRADE

Currently, all nations with VATs zero-rate exports and impose their VATs on imports. This procedure for taxing trade flows is referred to as the *destination principle* because a commodity is taxed at the location of consumption rather than production. An alternative would be to apply the *origin principle* by having all nations levy their VATs on exports but not imports. All experts on the VAT recommend that nations adopting a VAT use the destination principle in order to be consistent with existing practices of other countries.

The destination principle creates a level playing field because imported commodities rise in price by the percentage of the VAT, but exported commodities do not increase in price. For a particular nation, the VAT rate on domestically produced and imported products would be the same. The VAT rate on a particular good would still vary among nations.

A simple example demonstrates this concept of a level playing field. Assume nation A has a 10% VAT and nation B has a 20% VAT. Exports from nation A to nation B would not be taxed by nation A. But nation B would levy a 20% VAT on imports from nation A. Thus, consumers in nation B would pay a 20% VAT regardless of whether their purchased goods were domestically produced or imported. Furthermore, exports from nation B to nation A would not be taxed by nation B. Nation A would levy a 10% VAT on imports. Hence, consumers in nation A would pay a 10% VAT on both domestically produced and imported commodities.

In 1962, the rules applicable to taxation were included in the General Agreement on Tariffs and Trade (GATT). Under these GATT rules, indirect taxes were rebatable on exports but direct taxes were not rebatable. Taxes which are not shifted but borne by the economic entity on which they are levied are classified as direct taxes. From 1962 through 1972, a fixed exchange rate system prevailed and the United States ran deficits in its balance-of-payments. U.S. officials complained that the GATT rules favored nations with VATs because their exports were zero-rated. In contrast, corporate income taxes were not rebated on exports.

In early 1973, the United States and its major trading partners formally shifted to a flexible exchange rate system. Under this system, the supply and demand for different currencies determine their relative value. If a country has a deficit in its balance-of-trade, this deficit must be financed by a net importation of foreign capital. But net capital inflows cannot continue indefinitely. Thus, over time, this country's currency will tend to decline in value relative to the currencies of other nations. Consequently, this country's balance-of-trade deficit will eventually decline as its exports rise and imports fall. Hence, economic theory indicated that a VAT offers no advantage over other major taxes in reducing a deficit in the balance-of-trade. Thus, U.S. officials ended their complaints about the effects of GATT tax rules on international trade.

Since early 1973 there have been periods when exchange rates have been "managed" by mutual agreement among governments. Central banks have coordinated purchases and sales of different currencies in order to stabilize their relative values to promote international economic stability.

Even if there were a fixed exchange rate, a U.S. VAT would have slight impact on the balance-of-trade because the proposed VAT rate of 5% or less is a low tax rate. During the last 25 years the value of the dollar has fallen relative to an index of major currencies, yet a serious U.S. balance-of-trade deficit persists. In summary, a U.S. VAT offers no major advantage over other major tax increases in reducing the U.S. balance-of-trade deficit.

Any large U.S. tax increase, which reduces the federal deficit, could reduce the U.S. balance-of-trade deficit. The U.S. Treasury would reduce its borrowing on financial markets, interest rates would decline, and foreign capital would flow out of the United States. This capital outflow would reduce the demand for dollars relative to other currencies. This decline in the value of the dollar would raise exports, reduce imports, and, consequently, reduce the U.S. balance-of-trade deficit.

NATIONAL SAVING

National saving consists of government saving, business saving, and personal saving.[42] A VAT or any other tax that reduces the budget deficit would be expected to reduce government dissaving, and, consequently, raise national saving.

A second issue concerns the effect on the personal savings rate of levying a VAT compared to increasing income taxes. A VAT would tax savings when they are spent on consumption, allowing savings to compound at a pre-tax rate. But an income tax is levied on all income at the time it is earned, regardless of whether the income is consumed or saved. The income tax is also levied on the earnings from income saved. Consequently, some proponents of the VAT have argued that choosing a VAT, rather than an income tax, to raise revenue would increase the return from saving and, consequently, raise the savings rate.

The rate of return on savings, however, has never been shown to have a significant effect on the savings rate because of two conflicting effects. First, each dollar saved today results in the possibility of a higher amount of consumption in the future. This relative increase in the return from saving causes a household to want to substitute saving for consumption out of current income (substitution effect).

But a higher rate of return on savings raises a household's income; consequently, the household has to save less to accumulate some target amount of savings in the future (income effect). Thus, this income effect encourages households to have higher current consumption and lower current saving.

A CRS study compared the long-run effects on the capital stock and consumption of a $60 billion VAT and a $60 billion increase in individual income taxes. This study's results suggest that selecting a VAT instead of an increase in individual income taxes would raise the capital stock by less than 2% and consumption by only a quarter to a third of a percent after 50 years.[43]

An empirical study by the Congressional Budget Office analyzed the economic effects of replacing a quarter of the current income tax with a 6% VAT on all consumption. CBO estimated that this tax substitution would, in the long-run, increase the saving rate by 0.5%, raise the capital stock by 7.9%, increase output by 1.5%, and raise consumption by 1.2%.[44] These CBO findings of only slight economic effects in the long-run are consistent with the estimates of the CRS study.[45]

ADMINISTRATIVE COSTS

The value-added tax would require the expansion of the Internal Revenue Service. But the high revenue yield from a VAT could cause administrative costs to be low measured as a percentage of revenue yield. The administrative expense per dollar of VAT collected would vary with the degree of complexity of the VAT, the amount of revenue raised, the national attitude towards tax compliance, and the level of the small business exemption.

For tax year 1995, the Government Accountability Office (GAO) estimated the cost of administering a U.S. VAT at $1.221 billion if the VAT had a single rate, a broad base, and an exemption for businesses with gross receipts of less than $100,000.[46] For tax year 1995, Professor Sijbren Cnossen estimated that the overall administrative cost of a hypothetical single rate U.S. VAT at $1billion.[47] He assumed that "the administration of the VAT would be fully integrated with the administration of the federal income taxes."[48] The OECD found that evidence suggests "a lower cost per dollar on revenue collected for VAT than for income tax."[49]

COMPLIANCE

Although considerable research has been conducted over the past 15 years on income tax compliance, research on VAT compliance has been limited.[50] For tax year 1995, Professor Sijbren Cnossen estimates the compliance costs of a single rate U.S. VAT would equal approximately $5 billion.[51] He emphasizes that compliance costs "can be reduced by broadening the base of the VAT, imposing a single rate, and increasing the threshold for registration."[52] Agha and Haughton summarized estimates of VAT evasion for five European countries.[53] These five countries and their percentage of revenue lost through evasion were Belgium (8%), France (3%), Italy (40%), Netherlands (6%), and United Kingdom (2%-4%).[54] In comparison to other broad-based consumption taxes such as the retail sales tax, a VAT has produced relatively good compliance for four reasons.

First, a VAT collected using the credit-invoice method offers the opportunity to cross-check returns and invoices. For example, VAT shown on a sales invoice of a wholesaler will appear on the purchase invoice of a retailer. A tax auditor can examine both invoices to cross-check the accuracy of the tax returns of both the wholesaler and the retailer.

Second, each firm has an incentive not to allow suppliers to understate VAT on their sales invoices. A firm is able to credit VAT paid on inputs against VAT collected on sales; consequently, a firm's net VAT liability will increase if VAT shown on its purchase invoices was understated by suppliers.

Third, tax auditors can compare information about a VAT with information about business income taxation, which will increase compliance with both types of taxes. For example, the sales revenue figure reported on business income tax forms may be checked for consistency with gross VAT collected as shown on VAT forms. Also, a check of cash receipts during a VAT audit may identify the under reporting of sales. Firms may attempt not only to evade the VAT but also to evade the business income tax.[55]

Fourth, some firms legally required to remit VAT may not register. But these firms receive no credit for VAT paid on inputs. Hence, these firms are only partially able to evade the VAT because of the compliance with the VAT by suppliers.

Although compliance with a VAT is higher than other broad-based consumption taxes, the level of noncompliance is significant. As previously discussed, some firms legally required to remit VAT may not register.

Furthermore, firms may evade VAT by altering or omitting information as indicated in the following 10 major types of evasion. First, a registered firm may not record resales of goods purchased from unregistered suppliers. Second, a seller of both exempt and taxable goods may divert purchased inputs on which VAT is claimed against taxed sales to help produce and sell exempt goods. Third, a firm may claim credit for purchases that are not creditable. For example, a firm's owner may claim credit for VAT paid on an automobile but then use it for nonbusiness purposes. Fourth, a firm may illegally import goods, charge VAT on their sale, but not report this VAT. Fifth, a firm may simply under-report sales, which is the most common type of evasion. Retailers are the most frequent users of this type of evasion. Sixth, a firm may collect VAT on sales and then disappear. This type of evasion is particularly common to small firms in the construction industry. Seventh, in those nations with multiple rates, a firm may illegally reclassify goods into categories with lower tax rates. Eighth, the owners of some small firms, particularly retailers, may consume part of their firms' production but not record their consumption. Ninth, a firm may submit completely false export claims in order to obtain illegal VAT refunds. And tenth, two firms may barter goods in order to evade the VAT.[56]

INTERGOVERNMENTAL RELATIONS

For the United States, a federal VAT raises two primary intergovernmental issues: the federal encroachment of the state sales tax and the joint collection of a VAT.[57]

Encroachment on a State Tax Source

It has been claimed that broad-based consumption taxation has traditionally been a state source of revenue while income taxation has been a federal revenue source; consequently, a federal VAT would encroach on a primary source of tax revenue for the states.[58]

Most states, however, adopted their individual income taxes before they adopted their general sales taxes. Thirty-nine states levy both individual income taxes and general sales taxes. Twenty-three of these states adopted their individual income taxes in an earlier year then they adopted their general sales taxes. Three states adopted both taxes in the same year. Thirteen states adopted their general sales taxes in an earlier year than they adopted their individual income taxes.[59]

No constitutional restriction prevents the federal government from levying a VAT. Precedents exist for the federal government to levy a new tax that many states already levy. For example, the federal government levied the personal income tax after many states had already imposed this tax. Also, both the federal government and the states impose many of the same excise taxes.

The federal government relies primarily on income taxes, but taxation of income by states has risen steadily over the years.[60] For FY2003, 33.3% of state tax collections consisted of individual income taxes and 5.2% consisted of corporation income taxes.[61] Thus, total state taxes on income accounted for 38.5% of all state taxes collected. In comparison, for FY2003, general sales taxes accounted for 33.8% of state taxes collected.[62] Hence, it can be argued that the states have encroached on the primary source of revenue of the federal government.

States could continue to levy their retail sales taxes while the federal government levies a VAT. In Canada, the federal government levies a VAT, and the provinces continue to collect their retail sales taxes.

Joint Collection

States could piggy-back on a federal VAT. To do this, states would have to replace their retail sales taxes with a VAT and adopt the federal tax base. Because a federal VAT would probably have a broader base than any state sales tax, more revenue would be yielded for each 1% levied. Also, the VAT would eliminate duplication of administrative effort, permit the taxation of interstate mail order sales, permit the taxation on Internet sales, and lower total compliance costs of firms.

But, states may decline the opportunity for joint collection because of their desire to maintain greater fiscal independence from the federal government. In 1972, federal legislation permitted states to adopt the federal individual income tax base and have the federal government collect its state income tax, without cost to the states.[63] No state delegated collection of its income tax to the federal government. The law was repealed in 1990.[64]

In Canada, differences in tax bases for retail sales taxes in the provinces and the federal VAT have resulted in unexpectedly high administrative and compliance costs. Different tax bases have caused products to fall in four different tax categories: taxed by both political jurisdictions, taxed at the provincial level but not at the federal level, taxed at the federal level but not at the provincial level, and not taxed by either political jurisdiction. The federal government has tried to persuade the provinces to adopt the same tax base but they have refused.[65]

APPENDIX A. CREDIT-INVOICE, SUBTRACTION, AND ADDITION METHODS

This appendix provides numerical examples of the three methods of calculating a VAT: credit-invoice, subtraction, and addition methods. The tax rate for a VAT may be *price inclusive* (included in the sales price) or *price exclusive* (added to the sales price). Most developed nations levy their VAT rates on a price exclusive basis.

The *credit-invoice method* of calculating a VAT is demonstrated in Table A1. The rate for the value-added tax is assumed to be 10% on a price-exclusive basis. The product manufactured and sold is a widget. The production of widgets involves firms at four different stages of production: raw material producer, manufacturer, wholesaler, and retailer. The operating assumption is that the VAT is fully shifted forward to the next stage of production; consequently, the consumer pays the entire VAT.[66] The seller indicates the amount of VAT on each sales invoice.

At the first stage of production, the simplifying assumption is made that the raw material producer provides all of his own inputs. The raw material producer has sales of $200 plus VAT on sales of $20 (10% of $200). Sales plus VAT equal $220 ($200 + $20). Because the raw material producer purchased no inputs, he receives no credit for prior VAT paid. Hence, the raw material producer remits $20 to the government.

At the second stage of production, the manufacturer has sales of $500 plus VAT on sales of $50 (10% of $500), which is shown separately on the sales invoice. Sales plus VAT equal $550 ($500 + $50). The manufacturer purchased $200 in raw material plus $20 was paid in VAT as listed on the purchase invoice. The manufacturer credits the $20 paid in VAT on inputs against the $50 in VAT collected on sales and remits the difference of $30 to the government.

At the third stage of production, the wholesaler has sales of $750 and adds a VAT of $75 (10% of $750). Sales plus VAT equal $825 ($750 + $75). The wholesaler purchased inputs for $500 and paid an additional $50 in VAT. Consequently, the wholesaler credits $50 in VAT paid on inputs against $75 in VAT collected on sales and remits $25 in VAT to the government.

Finally, the retailer has sales of $1,000 and adds VAT of $100 (10% of $1,000). Sales plus VAT equal $1,100 ($1,000 + $100). The retailer purchased $750 in inputs and paid an additional $75 in VAT. The retailer credits the $75 in VAT paid on inputs against the $100 in VAT collected on sales and remits $25 to the government.

The VAT remitted by the four firms was $100. The consumer paid $100 in VAT on top of $1,000 in retail sales. The last line of figures in Table Al indicates the value added at each stage of production. The sum of all firms' value added is $1,000, which equals the sales price exclusive of the VAT.

Table A1. Credit-Invoice Method
(Data in dollars, price-exclusive VAT rate assumed at 10%)

Transaction	Stage of Production of Widgets								Total VAT Remitted
	Raw Material Producer[a]		Manu-facturer		Whole-saler		Retailer		
Sales (Excluding VAT)	$200		$500		$750		$1,000		
VAT on Sales		20		50		75		100	
Purchases of Inputs	0		200		500		750		
(Excluding VAT)	0		200		500		750		
VAT on Inputs	0		20		50		75		
Credit, VAT on Inputs		-0		-20		-50		-75	
VAT to be Remitted		20		30		25		25	100
Value Added	200		300		250		250		

a. As a simplification, the raw material producer is assumed to provide all of his inputs.

The subtraction method is demonstrated in Table A2. In order to simplify a comparison with figures in Table Al, a tax inclusive VAT rate of 9.091% is assumed. This tax inclusive rate is equivalent to a tax exclusive rate of 10%.

The raw material producer has sales including VAT of $220. Because he has no purchases of inputs, his VAT base (sales including VAT less purchases of inputs) is $220. His VAT to be remitted is $20 (9.091% of $220).

The manufacturer has sales including VAT of $550 and purchases including VAT of $220. His VAT base is $330 ($550 less $220). His VAT to be remitted is $30 (9.091% of $330).

The wholesaler has sales including VAT of $825 and purchases including VAT of $550. His VAT base is $275 ($825 less $550). His VAT to be remitted is $25 (9.091% of $275).

Lastly, the retailer has sales including VAT of $1,100, purchases including VAT of $825, and his VAT base is $275 ($1,100 less $825). He remits VAT of $25 (9.091% of $275). The total VAT remitted to the government by all four firms is $100 ($20 + $30 + $25 + $25). This $100 in VAT equals 9.091% of $1,100.

Table A2. Subtraction Method
(Data in dollars, price-inclusive VAT rate assumed at 9.091%)

Transaction	Stage of Production of Widgets								
	Raw Material Producer[a]		Manu-facturer		Whole-saler		Retailer		Total VAT Remitted
Sales (Including VAT)	$220		$550		$825		$1,100		
Purchases	0		200		500		750		
(Including VAT)	0		220		550		825		
VAT Base	220		330		275		275		
VAT to Be Remitted		20		30		25		25	100

a. As a simplification, the raw material producer is assumed to provide all of his inputs.

The *addition method* is shown in Table A3. The raw material producer calculates its value added by adding all payments for factors of production which the firm owned and applied to the production process. Thus, the raw material producer had value added of $200 (wages of $100, rent of $50, interest of $30, and profit of $20). Next, the raw material producer calculates its VAT by multiplying its value added by the tax rate. Thus, the raw material producer must remit $20 ($200 x 0.1) to the government. This procedure applies to all other stages of production and total VAT remitted is $100.

Table A3. Addition Method
(Data in U.S. dollars, VAT rate assumed at 10%)

Return on Factors of VAT Production Remitted	Raw Material Producer[a]	Manufacturer	Wholesaler	Retailer	Total
Wages	$100	$150	$110	$80	
Rent	50	100	90	115	
Interest	30	25	35	30	
Profit	20	25	15	25	
Value added	200	300	250	250	
Value-added	20	30	25	25	100
Tax					

a. As a simplification, the raw material producer is assumed to provide all of his inputs.

APPENDIX B. ECONOMIC EFFECTS OF A SPECIAL VAT TREATMENT

Table B1. Economic Effects of a Special VAT Treatment

Special VAT Treatment	Break in Chain of VAT Credits	Price of Commodity Plus VAT	Total VAT Remitted
Exempt Retailer	No	Decline Equal to a Fraction of Initial VAT	Decline
Zero-rated Retailer	No	Decline Equal to Eliminated VAT	Decline (VAT Eliminated)
Exempt Manufacturer	Yes	Rise	Rise
Zero-rated Manufacturer	Yes	No Change	No Change

APPENDIX C. GENERAL CONSUMPTION TAXES IN OECD COUNTRIES

Table C1. Data on General Consumption Taxes in OECD
(All levels of government)

Country	Total tax revenue as a % of GDP[a] at market prices (2005)	General consumption taxes as a % of GDP (2005)	General consumption taxes as a % of total tax revenues (2005)
Australia	30.9%	4.1%	13.4%
Austria	42.1	7.9	18.9
Belgium	45.4	7.3	16.1
Canada	33.4	5.0	15.0
Czech Republic	37.8	7.2	19.2
Denmark	50.3	10.0	19.9
Finland	44.0	8.7	19.8
France	44.1	7.6	17.1
Germany	34.8	6.3	18.0
Greece	27.3	6.0	22.2
Hungary	37.2	10.5	28.1
Iceland	41.4	11.5	27.7
Ireland	30.6	7.7	25.1
Italy	41.0	6.0	14.6
Japan	27.4	2.6	9.5

Table C1. (Continued).

Country	Total tax revenue as a % of GDP[a] at market prices (2005)	General consumption taxes as a % of GDP (2005)	General consumption taxes as a % of total tax revenues (2005)
Korea	25.5	4.5	17.5
Luxembourg	38.6	6.2	16.1
Mexico	19.9	3.8	19.1
Netherlands	39.1	7.6	19.5
New Zealand	37.8	9.0	23.8
Norway	43.7	7.9	18.1
Poland	34.3	7.7	22.5
Portugal	34.8	8.3	23.8
Slovak Republic	31.1	7.9	25.1
Spain	35.8	6.2	17.5
Sweden	50.7	9.4	18.5
Switzerland	29.7	4.0	13.4
Turkey	32.3	7.1	21.8
United Kingdom	36.5	6.8	18.6
United States	27.3	2.2	8.0

Source: Adapted by CRS from OECD, *Revenue Statistics 1965-2006*, Paris, 2007.

a. GDP is an abbreviation for gross domestic product, which is a measure of total domestic output of goods and services.

APPENDIX D. VAT RATES BY COUNTRY

Table D1. Value-Added Tax Rates by Country

EU Countries

Country	Standard Rate	Reduced Rate
Austria	20%	12% or 10%
Belgium	21%	12% or 6%
Bulgaria	20%	
Cyprus	15%	5%
Czech Republic	19%	5%
Denmark	25%	
Estonia	18%	5%
Finland	22%	17% or 8%
France	19.6%	5.5% or 2.1%
Germany	19%	7%
Greece	19%	9% or 4.5% (reduced by 30% to 13%, 6% and 3% on islands
Hungary	20%	5%

Country	Standard Rate	Reduced Rate
Ireland	21%	13.5% or 4.8%
Italy	20%	10%, 6%, or 4%
Latvia	18%	5%
Lithuania	18%	9% or 5%
Luxembourg	15%	12%, 9%, 6%, or 3%
Malta	18%	5%
Netherlands	19%	6%
Poland	22%	7% or 3%
Portugal	21%	15% or 5%
Romania	19%	9%
Slovakia	19%	10%
Slovenia	20%	8.5%
Spain	16%	7% or 4%
Canary Islands	5%	2%
Sweden	25%	12% or 6%
United Kingdom	17.5%	5%

Non-EU Countries

Country	Standard Rate	Reduced Rate
Argentina	21%	10.5%
Australia	10%	
Bosnia and Herzegovina	17%	
Canada	6% GST (5% effective 1 Jan. 2008) or 14% HST[a]	4.5%[b]
Chile	19%	
Columbia	16%	
People's Republic of China[c]	17%	6% or 3%
Croatia	22%	10%
Dominican Republic	16%	12%
Ecuador	12%	
Egypt	10%	
El Salvador	13%	
Georgia	18%	
Guatemala	12%	
Guyana	16%	14%
Iceland	24.5%	7%[d]
India[e]	12.5%	4% or 1%
Indonesia	10%	5%
Israel[f]	15.5%[g]	
Japan	5%	

(Continued).

Country	Standard Rate	Reduced Rate
South Korea	10%	
Jersey[h]	3%	
Jordan	16%	
Kazakhstan	14%	
Kosovo	15%	
Lebanon	10%	
Moldova	20%	5%
Republic of Macedonia	18%	5%
Malaysia	5%	
Mexico	15%	
Montenegro	17%	
New Zealand	12.5%	
Norway	25%	14% or 8%
Nepal	13%	
Pakistan	7.5%	1%
Panama	5%	
Paraguay	10%	5%
Peru	19%	
Philippines	12%	
Romania	19%	9%
Russia	18%	10%
Serbia	18%	8%
Singapore	7%	
South Africa	14%	
Sri Lanka	15%	
Switzerland	7.6%	3.6% or 2.4%
Thailand	7%	
Trinidad or Tobago	15%	
Turkey	18%	8% or 1%
Ukraine	20%	
Uruguay	22%	10%
Vietnam	10%	5%
Venezuela	9%	8%

Source: Adapted by CRS from Wikipedia, the free encyclopedia available at [http://en.wikipedia.org/wiki/VAT].

a HST is a combined federal/provincial VAT collected in some provinces. In the rest of Canada, the GST is a 6% federal VAT, and if there is a Provincial Sales Tax (PST) it is a separate non-VAT tax.

b No real "reduced rate," but rebates generally available for new housing effectively reduce the tax to 4.5%.

End Notes

c These taxes do not apply in Hong Kong and Macau, which are financially independent as special administrative regions.

d The reduced rate was 14% until March 1, 2007, when it was lowered to 7%. The reduced rate applies to heating costs, printed matter, restaurant bills, hotel stays, and most food.

e VAT is not implemented in 2 of India's 28 states.

f Except Eilat, where VAT is not raised.

g The VAT in Israel is in the process of being gradually reduced. It was reduced from 18% to 17% on March 2004, to 16.5% on September 2005, and was set to its current rate on July 1, 2006. There are plans to further reduce it in the near future, but they depend on political changes in the Israeli parliament.

h The value-added tax levied by the States of Jersey is effective January 1, 2008.

End Notes

[1] The President's Advisory Panel on Federal Tax Reform, *Simple, Fair, & Pro-Growth: Proposals to Fix America's Tax System* (Washington: U.S. Department of the Treasury, Nov. 1, 2005), pp. 191-192. This report is available at [http://www.taxreformpanel.gov]. For an analysis of the Panel's proposals, see CRS Report RL33545, *The Advisory Panel's Tax Reform Proposals*, by Jane G. Gravelle.

[2] For an overview of fundamental tax reform proposals, see CRS Report RL33443, *Flat Tax Proposals and Fundamental Tax Reform: An Overview*, by James M. Bickley.

[3] The combined individual and business taxes proposed by the typical flat tax can be viewed as a modified value-added tax (VAT). The individual wage tax would be imposed on wages (and salaries) and pension receipts. Part or all of an individual's wage and pension income would be tax-free, depending on marital status and number of dependents. The business tax would be a modified subtraction-method VAT with wages (and salaries) and pension contributions subtracted from the VAT base, in contrast to the usual VAT practice. For a comprehensive analysis of the flat tax, see CRS Report 98-529, *Flat Tax: An Overview of the Hall-Rabushka Proposal*, by James M. Bickley.

[4] For example, see Committee for Economic Development, *A New Tax Framework: A Blueprint for Averting a Fiscal Crisis* (Washington, 2005), 45 p.

[5] The revenue for a VAT would vary depending on the tax base. For a discussion of this issue, see CRS Report RS22720, *Taxable Base of the Value-Added Tax*, by Maxim Shvedov.

[6] CRS figure derived from VAT revenue estimates in the following source: William G. Gale and C. Eugene Steuerle, "Tax Policy Solution," in Alice M. Rivlin and Isabel Sawhill, eds., *Restoring Fiscal Sanity — 2005* (Washington: Brookings Institution Press, 2005), p. 113.

[7] These factors of production have specific meanings to an economist. Labor consists of all employees hired by the firm. Land consists of all natural resources including raw land, water, and mineral wealth. Capital is anything used in the production process that has been made by man. The entrepreneur is the decision maker who operates the firm.

[8] Numerical examples with explanations of these three methods of calculating VAT are shown in Appendix A.

[9] An exception is the final retail stage where policymakers have the option of including or excluding the VAT from the retail sales slip.

[10] For a comprehensive explanation and analysis of methods to calculate VAT, see *Value-Added Tax: Methods of Calculation*, by James M. Bickley, a CRS general distribution memorandum available from the author.

[12] John F. Due, Some Unresolved Issues in Design and Implementation of Value-Added Taxes, *National Tax Journal*, vol. 43, no. 4, Dec. 1990, p. 385.

[13] This classification of justifications for exclusion from VAT taxation was derived from the following source: Alan A. Tait, *Value-Added Tax: International Practice and Problems* (Washington, International Monetary Fund, 1988), p. 56.

[14] U.S. Congressional Budget Office, *Effects of Adopting a Value-Added Tax* (Washington, U.S. Govt. Print. Off., Feb. 1992), pp. 22-26.

[15] Richard A. Musgrave and Peggy B. Musgrave, *Public Finance in Theory and Practice*. 4th ed. (New York: McGraw-Hill, 1984), p. 78.

[16] William G. Gale and C. Eugene Steuerle, p. 113.

[17] Bureau of Economic Analysis, U.S. Department of Commerce, [http://www.bea.gov/bea/dn/dpga.txt].

[18] U.S. Executive Office of the President, Office of Management and Budget, *Historical Tables, Budget of the United States Government, Fiscal Year 2007* (Washington: GPO, 2006), p. 30.

[19] OECD, *Revenue Statistics: 1965-2006* (Paris: OECD Publishing, 2007), p. 89. For data by country, see table C1 in appendix C.

[20] Ibid. For data by country, see table C1 in Appendix C.

[21] Sijbren Cnossen, "VAT and RST: A Comparison," *Canadian Tax Journal*, vol. 35, no. 3, May/June 1987, p. 583.

[22] Cnossen, *VAT and RST: A Comparison*, p. 585 and OECD, *Consumption Tax Trends* (OECD, March 2005), p. 11.

[23] OECD, *International VAT/GST Guidelines* (OECD, Feb. 2006), p. 1. Available at [http://www.oecd.org].

[24] For an overview of the incidence of the VAT using income as a measure of ability-to-pay, see U.S. Congressional Budget Office, *Effects of Adopting a Value-Added Tax* (Washington: Feb. 1992), pp. 31-47.

[25] For a comprehensive analysis of the vertical equity of a VAT, see Erik Caspersen and Gilbert Metcalf, "Is a Value-Added Tax Progressive? Annual Versus Lifetime Incidence Measures," *National Tax Journal*, vol. 47, no. 4, Dec. 1994, pp. 731-746; and U.S. Congressional Budget Office, *Effects of Adopting a Value-Added Tax*, pp. 31-47.

[26] U.S. Congressional Budget Office, *Effects of Adopting a Value-Added Tax*, p. 35.

[27] Franco Modigliani, a Nobel Laureate in economics, estimated that at least 80% of all savings by households are eventually spent on consumption. See Franco Modigliani, "The Role of Intergenerational Transfer and Life Cycle Saving in the Accumulation of Wealth," *Journal of Economic Perspectives*, vol. 2, no. 2, spring 1988, pp. 15-23.

[28] For examples of life-cycle models, see Don Fullerton and Diane Lim Rogers, "Lifetime Effects of Fundamental Tax Reform," in *Economic Effects of Fundamental Tax Reform*, Henry J. Aaron and William G. Gale, eds. (Washington: Brookings Institution Press, 1996), pp 321-352; and David Altig, Alan J. Auerbach, Laurence J. Kotlikoff, Kent A. Smetters, and Jan Walliser, "Stimulating Fundamental Tax Reform in the United States," *The American Economic Review*, vol. 91, no. 3, June 2001, pp. 574-595.

[29] For an examination of increased administrative and compliance costs resulting from exclusions and multiple rates, see Liam Ebrill, Michael Keen, Jean-Paul Bodin, and Victoria Summers, *The Modern VAT* (Washington, D.C.: International Monetary Fund, 2001), pp.78-79.

[30] Alan A. Tait, *Value-Added Tax: International Practice and Problems* (Washington, D.C.: International Monetary Fund, 1988), p. 218.

[31] Edith Brashares, Janet Furman Speyrer, and George N. Carlson, "Distributional Aspects of a Federal Value-Added Tax," *National Tax Journal*, vol. 41, no. 2, June 1988, p. 165.

[32] The President's Advisory Panel on Federal Tax Reform, *Simple, Fair, & Pro-Growth*, p. 194.

[33] CRS Report RL31768, *The Earned Income Tax Credit (EITC): An Overview*, by Christine Scott, pp. 14-15.

[34] Ibid., pp 16-17.

[35] Henry J. Aaron, "The Political Economy of a Value-Added Tax in the United States," *Tax Notes*, vol. 38, no. 10, March 7, 1988, p. 1,113.

[36] Ibid.

[37] Henry J. Aaron, "The Value-Added Tax: Sorting Through the Practical and Political Problems," *The Brookings Review*, summer 1988, p. 13.

[38] In economics, leisure is any time spent not working.

[39] For a list of standard and reduced VAT rates for selective countries, see Appendix D.

[40] See U.S. Congressional Budget Office, *Effects of Adopting a Value-Added Tax*, pp. 56-60; and Jane G. Gravelle, "Income, Consumption, and Wage Taxation in a Life-Cycle Model: Separating Efficiency from Redistribution," *American Economic Review*, vol. 81, no. 4, Sept. 1991, pp. 985-995.

[41] Aaron, "The Political Economy of a Value-Added Tax in the United States," p. 1,113.

[42] For an explanation of the components of national saving, see CRS Report RL30873, *Saving in the United States: How Has It Changed and Why Is It Important?*, by Brian W. Cashell and Gail Makinen.

[43] CRS Report 88-697 S, *Economic Effects of a Value-Added Tax on Capital Formation*, by Jane G. Gravelle, p. 2. (Archived report available on request).

[44] CBO, *Effects of Adopting a Value-Added Tax*, pp. 52-53.

[45] For a comprehensive analysis of the issue, see CRS Report RS22367, *Federal Tax Reform and Its Potential Effects on Savings*, by Gregg A. Esenwein and CRS Report RL30351, *Consumption Taxes and the Level and Composition of Savings*, by Steven Maguire.

[46] U.S. General Accounting Office, *Value-Added Tax: Administrative Costs Vary with Complexity and Number of Businesses*, Washington, May 1993, p. 63.

[47] Sijbren Cnossen, "Administrative and Compliance Costs of the VAT: A Review of the Evidence," *Tax Notes*, vol. 62, no. 12, June 20, 1994, p. 1,610.

[48] Ibid.

[49] Organization for Economic Co-Operation and Development, *Taxing Consumption* (Paris: OECD, 1988), p. 203.

[50] For a current examination of VAT compliance from the approach of behavior economics, see Paul Webley, Caroline Adams, and Henk Elffers, "Value Added Tax Compliance," in *Behavioral Public Finance*, eds. Edward J. McCaffery and Joel Slemrod (New York: Russell Sage Foundation, 2006), pp. 175-205.

[51] Sijbren Cnossen, "Administrative and Compliance Costs of the VAT: A Review of the Evidence," p. 1,609.

[52] Ibid., p. 1,615.

[53] Ali Agha and Jonathan Haughton, "Designing VAT Systems: Some Efficiency Considerations," *Review of Economics and Statistics*, vol. 78, no. 2, May 1996, pp. 304-305.

[54] Ibid., p. 305.

[55] Organization of Economic Co-Operation and Development, *Taxing Consumption*, pp. 199-200.

[56] For a detailed discussion of these 10 types of evasion, see Alan A. Tait, *Value-Added Tax: International Practice and Problems* (Washington: International Monetary Fund, 1988), pp. 308-314.

[57] For an overview of state tax officials' concerns related to the enactment of a broad-based federal consumption tax, see U.S. General Accounting Office, *State Tax Officials Have Concerns About a Federal Consumption Tax*, Washington, March 1990, 77 p.

[58] For an examination of this issue, see Robert P. Strauss, "Administrative and Revenue [59] For data on the dates of adoption of major state taxes by state, see Tax Foundation, *Facts and Figures on Government Finance*, 38th Edition (Washington: Tax Foundation, 2004), p. 215.

[60] For historical data on state tax collection by source, see Tax Foundation, *Facts & Figures on Government Finance*, 38th Edition (Washington: Tax Foundation, 2004), pp. 188-189. Historical data on federal receipts by source is available from the following source: Office of Management and Budget, *Budget of the U.S. Government, Historical Tables, Fiscal Year 2008* (Washington: GPO, 2007), pp. 29-34.

[61] Tax Foundation, *Facts & Figures on Government Finance*, p. 189.

[62] Current data on sales tax rates by state are available at [http://www.taxfoundation.org/ taxdata/show/245.html].

[63] The Federal-State Tax Collection Act was enacted as Title II of the legislation that created the federal revenue sharing program. U.S. Congress, Joint Committee on Internal Revenue Taxation. *State and Local Fiscal Assistance Act and the Federal-State Tax Collection Act of 1972, H.R. 14370, 92d Congress, Public Law 92-512*, JCS-1-73, Feb. 12, 1973, Washington, GPO, 1973, pp. 51-72.

[64] Provisions of the Federal-State Tax Collection Act of 1972 (subchapter 64(E), sec. 6361 through 6365 of the Internal Revenue Code) were repealed by the Omnibus Budget Reconciliation Act of 1990, P.L. 101-508, sec. 11801(a)(45).

[65] Michael Rushton, A Value-Added Tax for the United States: Lessons from Canadian Experience, *National Tax Association — Proceedings of the Eighty-Sixth Annual Conference*, 1993, p. 98.

INDEX

A

accounting, 29, 62, 63, 71, 74, 75, 82, 83, 99, 113, 133, 137, 138

aggregate demand, 108

assets, 62, 68, 92, 104, 107, 109, 128, 134, 135, 136, 140, 141

audit, 17, 40, 54, 61, 62, 72, 73, 76, 79, 86, 87, 88, 156

audits, 55, 59, 62, 71, 73, 76, 80

average costs, 62

B

banks, 14, 68, 91, 92, 111, 133, 154

barter, 17, 157

BEA, 46, 48, 49

benefits, 11, 20, 42, 63, 86, 102, 108, 113, 114, 131, 132, 133, 151

beverages, 48, 65, 88, 89

Bipartisan Policy Center, vii, 1, 2, 3, 33

bonds, 110, 112, 123, 131, 132

bonuses, 141

borrowers, 68, 111

budget deficit, vii, 1, 2, 15, 155

Bureau of Labor Statistics, 101, 119

Bureau of National Affairs, 142

Business Activity Statement (BAS), 82

business cycle, 108, 116

businesses, 6, 16, 19, 28, 29, 39, 52, 53, 54, 55, 56, 59, 61, 62, 63, 64, 65, 67, 69, 71, 72, 73, 74, 75, 76, 78, 79, 80, 81, 82, 83, 84, 85, 86, 89, 91, 93, 96, 98, 102, 109, 111, 113, 116, 121, 132, 134, 135, 137, 138, 145, 155

buyer(s), 4, 39, 40, 61, 93, 111, 144

C

CAD, 26

capital accumulation, 107

capital flows, 107, 115, 116, 123, 130

capital gains, 53, 113, 135

capital goods, 125, 128

capital inflow, 14, 130, 154

capital input, 38, 100, 144

capital intensive, 131

capital markets, 110

capital outflow, 15, 130, 154

cash, 5, 17, 39, 49, 61, 63, 112, 134, 135, 136, 137, 145, 156

cash flow, 5, 63, 112, 135, 136, 145

charitable organizations, 66, 67, 98, 109, 110, 116

charities, 89, 90

commercial, 6, 29, 55, 64, 67, 69, 89

commodity, 14, 89, 146, 153

commodity futures, 89

compensation, 59, 112, 133

competition, 66, 67

competitive advantage, 146

complications, 53, 113

composition, 4, 130, 131

computer, 76, 77, 83, 93

computer software, 83

computer systems, 76

Congress, 2, 36, 38, 43, 44, 97, 98, 101, 110, 111, 115, 118, 121, 126, 141, 167

Congressional Budget Office (CBO), 2, 10, 16, 33, 34, 35, 43, 49, 53, 95, 120, 121, 150, 155, 165, 166

constituents, 81

consumer choice, 12, 105, 152

consumer goods, 13, 153

consumer price index, 101

consumption patterns, 7, 11, 147, 151

consumption tax, vii, viii, ix, 1, 2, 4, 7, 8, 9, 16, 17, 18, 19, 36, 37, 38, 40, 42, 43, 45, 46, 49, 51, 52, 53, 54, 55, 56, 58, 77, 78, 80, 81, 84, 86, 87, 90, 96, 97, 98, 99, 101, 104, 105, 106, 107, 113, 114, 115, 117, 118, 119, 123, 124, 125, 126, 127, 128, 129, 130, 131, 133, 134, 135, 136, 140, 141, 142, 143, 144, 148, 149, 156, 157, 161, 162, 167
conversion rate, 64
cost, vii, 4, 5, 10, 16, 19, 37, 38, 39, 40, 49, 53, 62, 68, 71, 78, 79, 86, 92, 100, 102, 104, 124, 129, 130, 131, 133, 135, 136, 138, 142, 145, 155, 158
CPI, 119
creditors, 137
criminal activity, 138
currency, 14, 64, 73, 91, 96, 154

D

Debt Reduction Task Force, vii, 1, 2, 3, 33
debts, 91
deduction, 39, 85, 102, 106, 107, 110, 111, 112, 120, 128, 132, 137, 141, 144
deficit, 2, 14, 15, 154
dental care, 88, 89
deposit accounts, 91
deposits, 68, 90, 91
depreciation, 53, 62, 96, 102, 109, 113, 129, 133, 135, 136, 137, 138
developed countries, vii, 7, 37, 43, 148
developed nations, ix, 1, 4, 8, 20, 39, 42, 98, 111, 114, 115, 117, 125, 143, 148, 158
differential rates, 141
differential treatment, 18
direct taxes, 14, 154
disposable income, 9, 10, 12, 140, 149, 150, 152
dissaving, 15, 105, 129, 155
distortions, 18, 41, 66, 92, 106, 127, 147
distribution, 7, 9, 19, 43, 53, 54, 82, 86, 87, 95, 124, 140, 146, 147, 148, 165
domestic resources, 131
donations, 110

E

earnings, 15, 131, 155
economic activity, 54, 77, 87, 94
economic efficiency, viii, 41, 59, 98, 109, 113, 114, 116, 123, 124, 126, 127, 128
economic growth, 47, 101, 103, 139
economic performance, 86
economic resources, 131
economic theory, 14, 105, 106, 115, 116, 154

economic welfare, 131
economics, 35, 106, 166, 167
economies of scale, 62
education, 3, 6, 18, 48, 56, 62, 66, 67, 71, 81, 82, 83, 84, 88, 89
education expenditures, 3
educational institutions, 83
empirical studies, 20, 106
employee compensation, 94
employees, 33, 82, 102, 112, 114, 118, 121, 132, 165
energy, 3, 80, 89
environmental protection, 67
equipment, vii, 37, 38, 89, 100, 102, 107, 109, 135, 141, 144
equities, 104, 116
equity, 1, 4, 6, 7, 8, 9, 10, 13, 59, 86, 98, 99, 103, 104, 105, 113, 114, 116, 119, 133, 135, 142, 147, 148, 149, 150, 153
European Union (EU), 8, 10, 11, 42, 61, 63, 66, 76, 91, 93, 148, 150, 162, 163
exchange rate, 2, 14, 107, 143, 154
exclusion, ix, 1, 7, 10, 11, 34, 41, 106, 128, 143, 147, 150, 151, 165
exercise, 99
expenditures, viii, 1, 3, 7, 12, 45, 46, 47, 49, 58, 63, 105, 136, 143, 144, 147, 152
exports, 14, 15, 25, 47, 60, 93, 96, 107, 115, 129, 130, 131, 153, 154

F

federal government, 9, 11, 13, 18, 19, 37, 40, 49, 55, 77, 78, 79, 80, 90, 113, 114, 132, 149, 151, 153, 157, 158
financial, 6, 15, 41, 48, 60, 65, 68, 79, 83, 88, 89, 90, 91, 92, 98, 109, 110, 111, 116, 126, 132, 133, 135, 136, 137, 154
financial capital, 110
financial institutions, 111, 132
financial intermediaries, 111
financial markets, 15, 154
financial sector, 48, 133
firearms, 59
firm size, 17
food, viii, 11, 45, 47, 55, 65, 67, 71, 72, 88, 89, 151, 165
forecasting, 108, 116
foreign firms, 130
foreign investment, 2, 13
formation, 107
formula, 7
fraud, 55, 61, 76, 87, 93, 94, 96

Index

171

fringe benefits, 102, 104, 108, 114, 121, 123, 132, 133

full employment, 134

fundamental tax reform discussions, viii, 45, 46

funding, viii, 45, 46, 90

funds, 55, 61, 90, 91, 107, 110, 111, 112

G

gambling, 89

GAO, viii, 16, 18, 19, 34, 42, 44, 51, 52, 57, 60, 61, 64, 65, 66, 68, 69, 78, 83, 86, 95, 96, 155

GATT, 14, 15, 115, 154

GDP, 22, 23, 59, 94, 105, 147, 161, 162

General Accounting Office, 35, 36, 167

General Agreement on Tariffs and Trade, 14, 115, 154

General Motors, 109

global taxation, 87

GNP, 107

goods and services, viii, 6, 7, 8, 23, 25, 37, 38, 40, 41, 44, 46, 51, 53, 55, 56, 58, 59, 60, 64, 65, 66, 67, 70, 71, 72, 75, 88, 89, 90, 93, 99, 106, 107, 129, 130, 133, 147, 162

government policy, 10, 150

government spending, 42, 115, 117, 125, 130, 139

governments, 8, 14, 19, 52, 55, 60, 66, 67, 77, 148, 154

grants, 83

greed, 79, 80

gross domestic product (GDP), 8, 22, 23, 59, 94, 105, 115, 117, 147, 148, 161, 162

gross national product, 95, 107

growth, 19, 20, 47, 107, 112, 116, 123, 131, 139

growth rate, 107, 123, 131

H

health, vii, viii, 2, 6, 12, 33, 37, 38, 43, 45, 46, 55, 60, 65, 66, 67, 68, 88, 98, 109, 112, 115, 116, 123, 131, 132

health care, vii, 12, 37, 38, 46, 55, 60, 65, 66, 67, 88, 98, 109, 112, 115, 116, 123, 131

health care sector, 123, 131

health care system, 46

health insurance, viii, 2, 12, 33, 43, 45, 46, 88, 132

health services, 6

higher education, 47

historical data, 36, 167

home ownership, 110

homeowners, 46, 68, 110, 111

horizontal equity, 9, 12, 104, 149, 152

House, 3, 53, 118, 119

housing, viii, 3, 45, 46, 47, 48, 49, 68, 89, 93, 98, 104, 106, 109, 110, 111, 116, 123, 131, 132, 133, 141, 164

I

IMF, 8, 18

imported products, 14, 15, 115, 154

imports, 14, 15, 61, 62, 75, 76, 81, 93, 94, 96, 107, 129, 130, 131, 153, 154

incidence, 9, 10, 34, 103, 104, 105, 116, 119, 149, 150, 166

income distribution, 142

income tax, iv, vii, viii, ix, 1, 2, 10, 11, 12, 13, 14, 15, 16, 17, 18, 19, 37, 38, 43, 49, 53, 55, 58, 59, 61, 62, 63, 67, 70, 76, 84, 85, 86, 96, 97, 98, 99, 100, 101, 102, 103, 104, 105, 106, 107, 108, 109, 110, 112, 113, 114, 115, 116, 117, 118, 119, 123, 124, 125, 126, 127, 128, 129, 130, 131, 132, 134, 135, 136, 137, 138, 139, 140, 141, 143, 148, 150, 151, 152, 153, 154, 155, 156, 157, 158

income tax system, vii, viii, ix, 2, 37, 38, 53, 67, 84, 85, 86, 97, 98, 101, 105, 106, 107, 108, 113, 114, 115, 116, 117, 119, 123, 124, 126, 138, 143

indexing, 13, 153

individual taxpayers, 114, 124, 137

individuals, 10, 28, 53, 59, 62, 67, 93, 101, 102, 104, 106, 112, 113, 114, 124, 125, 127, 128, 132, 133, 134, 135, 137, 140, 141, 142, 150

Indonesia, 31, 163

industrialized countries, 56

industries, 28, 83, 98, 108, 110, 116, 126, 129, 132

industry, 17, 28, 56, 73, 82, 83, 84, 109, 111, 131, 145, 146, 157

inflation, 2, 4, 13, 102, 112, 119, 132, 134, 136, 143, 153

institutions, 2, 54, 87, 88, 111, 132

intangible services, 75

interagency committees, 81

interest groups, 114

interest rates, 15, 90, 98, 103, 108, 110, 111, 112, 116, 120, 130, 154

Internal Revenue Service, 16, 53, 114, 120, 121, 136, 142, 155

International Monetary Fund, 8, 17, 34, 42, 44, 54, 81, 87, 165, 166, 167

international trade, 14, 98, 103, 129, 154

intervention, 62

investment, 6, 7, 47, 68, 89, 90, 91, 96, 99, 101, 106, 107, 109, 110, 113, 116, 123, 127, 130, 131, 132, 133, 135, 142

investment incentive, 142

172 Index

investments, 46, 96, 109, 111, 112, 131, 132, 133, 135

itemized deductions, 131, 139

L

labor force, 11, 151

legislation, 18, 19, 36, 38, 44, 81, 82, 85, 118, 124, 158, 167

leisure, 1, 13, 35, 105, 106, 107, 126, 127, 143, 152, 166

life cycle, 9, 129, 149

lifetime, 9, 10, 12, 103, 104, 140, 149, 150, 152

loans, 90, 111, 135

lobbying, 114

local authorities, 89

local government, 8, 58, 66, 98, 109, 112, 116, 132, 148

Long-term fiscal problems, vii, 1, 2

low risk, 107

M

major decisions, 12, 105, 152

market economy, 95

market share, 131

marketing, 75

married couples, 141

medical, 47, 64, 65, 88, 89, 112, 132

medical care, 47, 64, 88, 89, 112, 132

Medicare, viii, 45, 46, 59, 124

medicine, 88, 89

merit goods, 7, 147

metals, 88

methodology, 49, 54

Missing Trader Intra-Community (MTIC), 76

monetary expansion, 134

monetary policy, 2, 7, 13, 143, 147, 153

money supply, 104

multinational corporations, 114

museums, 67, 89

N

National Commission on Fiscal Responsibility and Reform, vii, 1, 3, 33

national consumption data, 76

national debt, vii, 1, 2

national health care., vii, 37, 38

national health insurance, viii, 2, 33, 43, 45, 46

national origin, 15

national sales tax (NST), vii, 37, 38, 39, 40, 41, 42, 43, 49, 124, 125, 137, 138

natural gas, 80

natural resources, 33, 118, 165

net investment, 108, 135

neutral, 1, 8, 12, 13, 43, 104, 105, 106, 107, 126, 139, 141, 143, 148, 151, 152, 153

nonprofit organizations, 64, 67, 69, 90, 102

nursing home, 64

O

Office of Management and Budget (OMB), 2, 36, 166, 167

Organization for Economic Cooperation and Development, 4, 39, 43, 53, 87, 94

outreach, 56, 82, 84

overlap, 59, 98, 137

ownership, 6, 110, 135

P

Parliament, 78

payroll, 3, 61, 85, 139

penalties, 141

platinum, 64

playing, 14, 154

policy, vii, viii, 2, 8, 13, 19, 38, 40, 43, 45, 46, 47, 48, 81, 82, 86, 92, 98, 103, 117, 120, 126, 130, 143, 148, 153

policy issues, 98, 103, 117

policy options, viii, 45, 46

policymakers, 34, 38, 40, 42, 43, 108, 116, 165

postal service, 67, 89

poverty, 12, 151

preferential treatment, 55

present value, 68, 131

President, viii, 3, 20, 36, 43, 95, 123, 124, 126, 141, 142, 151, 165, 166

President Obama, 3

price effect, 13, 142, 153

price index, 13, 153

private firms, 67

private practice, 87

professionals, 2, 62, 69, 83, 87

profit, 93, 123, 131, 132, 134, 138, 160

profit margin, 134, 138

progressive tax, 10, 104, 150

property taxes, 58, 102, 132

PST, 164

public administration, 95

public finance, 12, 105, 152

public officials, 6, 147
public policy, 19
public sector, 6, 19, 20, 36, 42, 65, 66, 67, 89, 115, 117, 148
public service, 6, 19
purchasing power, 64, 104, 135, 136, 142
purchasing power parity, 64

R

rate of return, 15, 105, 128, 155
real estate, 6, 46, 60, 65, 69, 90, 93, 95, 102, 131, 135
real income, 107
real property, 93
real terms, 139
recession, vii, 1, 2, 108
recommendations, iv, viii, 3, 51, 54, 87
recovery, 3, 73, 102, 136
Reform, vii, viii, 1, 3, 20, 33, 35, 36, 37, 38, 43, 53, 95, 96, 98, 107, 110, 118, 119, 120, 121, 123, 124, 126, 128, 132, 137, 141, 142, 151, 165, 166
regression, ix, 1, 143
regulations, 136, 137
relative prices, 1, 11, 12, 13, 105, 130, 143, 147, 150, 152, 153
replacement taxes, vii, 37, 38
requirements, 5, 28, 52, 54, 55, 56, 59, 62, 63, 72, 79, 82, 83, 86, 127, 139, 145
resale, 125
resource allocation, 128, 131
resources, 52, 54, 62, 71, 73, 76, 80, 84, 99, 101, 125, 126, 130, 131
retail sales taxes (RST), 8, 10, 19, 34, 41, 42, 43, 44, 53, 56, 57, 58, 61, 72, 78, 79, 80, 99, 100, 138, 148, 150, 157, 158, 166
retirement, 9, 99, 100, 129, 149
revenue, viii, ix, 1, 2, 3, 4, 6, 7, 8, 11, 12, 15, 16, 17, 18, 19, 22, 33, 36, 37, 40, 41, 43, 45, 46, 48, 49, 52, 53, 54, 55, 56, 58, 59, 60, 61, 62, 63, 65, 70, 71, 72, 74, 75, 76, 77, 79, 80, 86, 87, 92, 96, 98, 99, 102, 103, 104, 105, 106, 108, 109, 113, 114, 116, 123, 124, 125, 127, 139, 140, 143, 144, 146, 147, 148, 150, 151, 152, 155, 156, 157, 158, 161, 162, 165, 167
risk, 55, 63, 71, 72, 73, 76, 86, 111
risk assessment, 73
risks, 52, 54, 55, 60, 61, 62, 63, 72, 73, 76, 86, 87
rules, 14, 15, 28, 62, 66, 69, 71, 78, 90, 91, 109, 127, 128, 129, 130, 132, 135, 154

S

sales activities, 72
Saudi Arabia, 8
savings, 10, 15, 35, 68, 91, 99, 100, 105, 106, 107, 111, 112, 116, 123, 125, 126, 127, 128, 129, 130, 133, 139, 140, 141, 150, 155, 166
savings account, 100
savings rate, 15, 35, 105, 106, 107, 123, 125, 128, 155
scarce resources, 9, 149
securities, 91, 110, 112
security, 9, 89, 149
Senate, 2, 3
services, iv, 4, 6, 7, 28, 40, 41, 46, 48, 52, 53, 54, 55, 56, 59, 60, 62, 64, 65, 66, 67, 68, 69, 70, 71, 72, 75, 79, 80, 82, 83, 88, 89, 90, 91, 92, 95, 98, 109, 111, 112, 116, 129, 147
shortfall, 139
Sixth Council Directive, 91
small businesses, 29, 52, 56, 60, 63, 72, 74, 83, 84, 120
small firms, 17, 157
social benefits, 115
social policy, 43, 67
social programs, viii, 45, 46
Social Security, viii, 10, 45, 46, 59, 102, 124
SOI, 142
sole proprietor, 2, 13, 105, 153
specific tax, 8, 43, 148
spending, ix, 1, 2, 3, 7, 8, 10, 19, 20, 46, 101, 112, 139, 143, 147, 148, 150
spillover effects, 110
stability, 14, 108, 154
standard of living, 106, 107
state, 2, 8, 10, 18, 19, 20, 36, 38, 41, 42, 46, 58, 59, 77, 83, 87, 98, 102, 107, 109, 111, 112, 113, 116, 123, 131, 132, 144, 148, 150, 157, 158, 167
state sales taxes, 38, 41, 46, 77
states, 18, 19, 41, 44, 77, 82, 91, 112, 113, 121, 126, 132, 138, 157, 158, 165
statistics, 87
stimulus, 129
stock price, 136
stockholders, 137
structure, viii, 8, 19, 55, 81, 97, 99, 100, 110, 123, 124, 130, 131, 132, 138, 140, 141, 148, 151
subsidy, 15, 112
substitution, 12, 13, 15, 16, 105, 106, 128, 152, 155
substitution effect, 13, 15, 106, 128, 152, 155
subtraction, vii, 4, 5, 15, 20, 33, 34, 37, 39, 43, 96, 97, 100, 102, 115, 116, 117, 118, 125, 132, 138, 141, 144, 145, 158, 159, 165

T

target, 15, 56, 82, 106, 155
tax base, 4, 9, 10, 19, 33, 39, 40, 41, 43, 46, 55, 60, 63, 64, 65, 70, 71, 79, 87, 97, 98, 99, 100, 101, 102, 113, 114, 115, 116, 117, 118, 123, 124, 125, 127, 131, 132, 138, 139, 140, 141, 147, 149, 150, 158, 165
tax collection, 19, 36, 40, 62, 157, 167
tax cuts, 106, 123, 128, 139, 140
tax data, 85, 87
tax deduction, 110, 111, 123, 139
tax evasion, 136, 138
tax incentive, 129
tax incidence, 9, 149
tax increase, 2, 3, 7, 13, 15, 20, 105, 106, 144, 147, 152, 154
tax policy, 10, 81, 129, 130, 131, 150
tax rates, viii, 5, 11, 17, 39, 41, 44, 51, 52, 53, 64, 104, 105, 114, 125, 127, 133, 136, 138, 139, 140, 145, 150, 151, 157, 167
tax reform(s), viii, 11, 41, 45, 46, 51, 53, 81, 86, 98, 110, 118, 120, 123, 124, 126, 127, 131, 134, 136, 137, 138, 139, 148, 165
tax system, viii, 11, 41, 43, 48, 51, 52, 53, 54, 55, 59, 61, 62, 63, 78, 80, 85, 86, 90, 97, 98, 101, 105, 106, 107, 108, 113, 114, 115, 116, 117, 124, 125, 126, 129, 131, 136, 137, 138, 141, 151
tax threshold, 141
taxable base, viii, 45, 46, 47, 48, 49
taxation, ix, 1, 5, 7, 8, 11, 14, 18, 19, 34, 38, 40, 41, 42, 53, 58, 60, 68, 84, 92, 100, 101, 102, 103, 106, 120, 123, 125, 140, 143, 147, 148, 151, 154, 157, 158, 165
taxpayers, 20, 28, 29, 47, 59, 62, 98, 101, 102, 103, 106, 110, 113, 114, 116, 128, 132, 136, 137, 138, 141
tax-reform debate, vii, 37, 38
technological change, 19
Title I, 36, 167
Title II, 36, 167
total revenue, 58
trade, 2, 4, 5, 14, 15, 59, 62, 63, 83, 93, 95, 107, 115, 116, 123, 124, 129, 130, 131, 143, 153, 154
trade benefits, 123
trade deficit, 14, 15, 107, 129, 130, 154
trade-off, 59, 63
trading partners, 14, 154

supplier, 28, 69, 83, 92
suppliers, 2, 13, 17, 28, 45, 83, 90, 141, 146, 153, 156
surplus, 94, 130

transactions, 39, 46, 47, 60, 61, 65, 68, 69, 76, 89, 90, 91, 92, 93, 96, 138, 144
transfer payments, 10, 67, 140, 150
transition period, 132
transport, 88, 89
Treasury, 53, 81, 83, 95, 104, 119, 139, 140, 142
treatment, vii, 9, 15, 37, 38, 66, 67, 71, 79, 100, 103, 106, 112, 127, 132, 133, 141, 144, 145, 148
triggers, 73

U

U.S. Department of Commerce, 49, 166
U.S. Department of the Treasury, 36, 142, 165
U.S. economy, 106, 131
U.S. tax reform, viii, 51
U.S. Treasury, 15, 104, 119, 154
Ukraine, 32, 164
United Kingdom, viii, 6, 16, 22, 23, 25, 28, 32, 42, 51, 54, 55, 62, 63, 65, 66, 67, 68, 69, 71, 74, 75, 76, 77, 87, 89, 93, 94, 156, 162, 163
United States, iv, v, ix, 1, 2, 4, 5, 8, 14, 15, 18, 23, 35, 39, 41, 42, 43, 46, 47, 51, 53, 58, 59, 61, 76, 86, 87, 94, 95, 98, 115, 117, 119, 125, 129, 130, 142, 143, 145, 148, 154, 157, 162, 166, 167
universities, 90

V

value-added tax (VAT), 1, iii, iv, vii, viii, ix, 1, 2, 3, 4, 5, 6, 7, 8, 10, 11, 12, 13, 14, 15, 16, 17, 18, 19, 20, 21, 22, 24, 25, 26, 28, 29, 30, 31, 32, 33, 34, 35, 36, 37, 38, 39, 40, 41, 42, 43, 44, 45, 46, 47, 48, 49, 51, 52, 53, 54, 55, 56, 57, 58, 60, 61, 62, 63, 64, 65, 66, 67, 68, 69, 70, 71, 72, 73, 74, 75, 76, 77, 78, 79, 80, 81, 82, 83, 84, 85, 86, 87, 89, 90, 91, 92, 93, 94, 96, 97, 99, 100, 101, 102, 107, 108, 115, 116, 118, 123, 124, 125, 128, 130, 132, 133, 134, 135, 137, 138, 141, 142, 143, 144, 145, 146, 147, 148, 149, 150, 151, 152, 153, 154, 155, 156, 157, 158, 159, 160, 161, 162, 164, 165, 166, 167
variations, 113, 126, 136
VAT receipts, 76
VAT tax gap, 76
VAT Theoretical Tax Liability (VTTL), 76, 96
vertical equity, 34, 166
vote, 3, 126
voters, 20

W

wages, 4, 33, 39, 53, 97, 99, 100, 101, 102, 103, 109, 110, 116, 124, 125, 127, 132, 134, 140, 145, 160, 165
Washington, 33, 34, 35, 36, 44, 49, 88, 95, 96, 118, 119, 120, 121, 141, 142, 165, 166, 167
welfare, ix, 1, 47, 89, 143
welfare spending, ix, 1, 143
workers, 128, 134
working hours, 127
workload, 56, 85

World Trade Organization (WTO), 15, 130

Y

yield, 2, 3, 5, 6, 8, 16, 19, 20, 40, 41, 48, 49, 108, 116, 144, 145, 147, 148, 155

Z

zero tax rate, 6, 146
zero-rated business, 6, 146